THE FIT ATHLETE

THE
FIT ATHLETE

R. J. SHEPHARD

OXFORD LONDON NEW YORK
OXFORD UNIVERSITY PRESS
1978

Oxford University Press, Walton Street, Oxford OX2 6DP

OXFORD LONDON GLASGOW
NEW YORK TORONTO MELBOURNE WELLINGTON
IBADAN NAIROBI DAR ES SALAAM LUSAKA CAPE TOWN
KUALA LUMPUR SINGAPORE JAKARTA HONG KONG TOKYO
DELHI BOMBAY CALCUTTA MADRAS KARACHI

ISBN 0 19 2175491

© R. J. Shephard 1978

All rights reserved. No part of this publication may be reproduced, stored in a retrieval system, or transmitted, in any form or by any means, electronic, mechanical, photocopying, recording or otherwise, without the prior permission of Oxford University Press

British Library Cataloguing in Publication Data

Shephard, R J
   The fit athlete.
     1. Athletes—Hygiene
   I. Title
     613.7'1   RA781   77-30347

ISBN 0-19-217549-1

Filmset by
Richard Clay (The Chaucer Press), Ltd., Bungay, Suffolk
and printed in Great Britain by
Fletcher & Son Ltd., Norwich

Contents

1	Introduction	1
2	The stage is set *Neolithic beginnings—The classical period—The Middle-Ages—The Renaissance and beyond*	5
3	The Olympic revival *The Olympic phenomenon—The role of government—The role of sports medicine—The development of athletic records*	12
4	Shape, strength, and skill *Body-build of the successful athlete—Biological ingredients of success—The role of skill—Developing a performance index*	31
5	Mind over matter *Personality and attitudes of coach and athlete—Perception of pain—Aggression—Intelligence and mental health—Group dynamics*	49
6	Choosing your parents *The inherited component of success—The environmental component—The role of training—Implications for athletic selection*	62
7	Preparing the athlete *Diet—Physiological preparation—Psychological preparation*	81
8	Doping the athlete *Definition of doping—Drugs and their dangers—Prevention of doping*	110
9	The athlete's environment *High altitude—Heat—Cold—Underwater*	124
10	Hazards of sports *Injuries—Disease—Death*	139

CONTENTS

11 **The female athlete** — 155
Vive la différence—Sports records for women—Sex determination and femininity—Performance and the menstrual cycle—Other medical considerations

12 **The adolescent athlete** — 167
Training in adolescence—Optimum age of competition—Physical dangers of activity in adolescence—Psychological effects of intense competition—Physical activity and development

13 **The ageing athlete** — 174
Health of the ageing athlete—The heart of the athlete—Rate of ageing of athletes—Longevity of athletes

14 **The handicapped athlete** — 183

15 **The athlete and society** — 189
Professionalism—Spectatorism—Sport and democracy—Emancipation—Nationalism and internationalism

Suggestions for further reading — 203

Index — 207

Illustrations

1	Olympia as it appeared about a century ago	6
2	A reconstruction of Olympia	7
3	Baron Pierre de Coubertin, the founder of the modern Olympic Games	13
4	The growth of the modern Olympic Games	17
5	A comparison between an early and a modern ski jumper	29
6	Changes in the stature of the British twelve-year-old boy, from 1833 to 1958	34
7	The rating of 'perceived exertion'	54
8	The use of twins to apportion the variability of data between environmental effects and inheritance, taking into account measurement errors	64
9	The relative importance of training and an exhaustive search of the population in the emergence of an athlete with an exceptional oxygen transporting power	68
10	A possible scheme for the selection of children with inherited athletic skills for advanced training	78
11	A regimen to boost the glycogen content of muscle fibres	87
12	Inter-convertibility of foodstuffs within the body	88
13	The types of training most needed by track athletes	
14	A one-year training plan for the competitive athlete	97

15	The time course for the learning of a complex athletic skill	101
16	The influence of arousal on the performance of the athlete	106
17	The oxygen-combining properties of the red cell pigment haemoglobin and the effect of altitude	125
18	Typical heat balance during a marathon race	131
19	Male and female chromosomes, together with normal and abnormal cell nuclei	161
20	The Canadian gymnast, Teresa McDonnell	164
21	Weight gain after the age of forty: a comparison between former athletes and non-athletes	175
22	The development of ST segmental depression in the chest electrocardiogram	178
23	Percentage survivors in the Finnish population at various ages: a comparison of skiers and sedentary members of the community	182
24	A fencing contest for the physically handicapped, with suitably modified rules	186
25	Spectator sports in the United States: attendance and expenditure	195

I
Introduction

I am convinced that anyone interested in winning Olympic Gold Medals must select his parents very carefully.

With this discouraging advice to the indifferent athlete, the noted Swedish exercise physiologist Dr. Per-Olof Astrand opened his contribution to a Toronto symposium on physical activity and cardio-vascular health. Is his viewpoint widely accepted in explanation of outstanding and ever-improving Olympic records? Must those of us who cannot cover a mile in less than eight or nine minutes assume we have been unlucky in the genetic lottery, or can we learn from the top athlete some secret of preparation that will bring us closer to a four-minute mile and its equivalent in other sports?

One thing the middle-aged business man lacks as he pants around the neighbourhood is the pressure of international competition. Major sport has moved far from the purity of its religious origins. The frivolity of the medieval village green and the idealism of the Olympic revivalist Baron de Coubertin have alike been discarded in favour of hard-nosed commercialism and political opportunism. In some nations, promising candidates for a given athletic event are snatched virtually from the cradle to receive all of the specialized nurture that well-paid trainers, scientists, and sports physicians can devise. Money is poured into elaborate facilities, and failure may even become a question for discussion with the secret police.

Watching the successes of Kip Keino and other Kenyan distance runners, we may wonder if we have made a bad choice not only in the matter of parentage, but also with respect to our place of birth. Recent athletic records apparently confirm the view of the scientist—if you are to compete in Mexico City, you should arrange to be born in the mountains, whereas if your contest is in Dakar you should spend your childhood in a steaming jungle. If by some unhappy chance your family has failed to make appropriate provision for your success, the next best thing (depending on the venue) seems to be to spend long months training at a mountain or a tropical resort.

Packed into a lift with seven-foot tall basketball players, a six-foot midget such as myself wonders also about the importance of an unusual body-build, whether inherited or acquired through a subsequent perversion of normal development. Can one improve upon athletic records by enlisting the skills of the anthropometrist to select appropriately shaped contestants—the freakishly tall for basketball, the lightly built distance runner, and the Herculean weight-lifter? And if selection is possible by a mere outward inspection of body form, may there not be an even greater scope for matching man and event by getting under the skin, asking the physiologist to make detailed measurements of heart, lung, and muscle function, and the tissue chemist to report on structure and function within the individual muscle cells?

Then there is the dimension of the mind. Dr. Robert Tait MacKenzie, a Canadian physical educator from the early part of the present century has given us many beautiful and expressive sculptures that speak of the agony and the ecstasy of the distance runner—faces racked by pain and gasping for air. Through such art, we can share something of the discomforts borne by the athlete, and appreciate the importance of the will to win. Determination to persist with a gruelling training schedule, an appropriate reaction to the many psychological pressures of international competition, and a capacity to ignore pain during an event are all ingredients of success.

Let us now suppose that the process of selection is complete. We have picked our potential athlete from athletic parents living in a region that is both tropical and mountainous. We have further deployed the combined skills of the anthropometrist, the physiologist, the biochemist, and the psychologist to reveal our potential élite performer, suggesting to him an appropriate mode of contest. What other measures could and should be taken to bring our candidate to a peak of condition?

While much has been written and said about the immediate preparation of the athlete, knowledge is limited. Coaches have cloaked their ignorance of physiology and psychology in a fierce dogmatism that has on occasion spurred their charges to outstanding results. Weird potions such as wheat-germ oil, queen-bee extract, and every conceivable vitamin preparation have been administered with tremendous enthusiasm, even when careful laboratory trials have shown that men receiving an innocuous substitute fare better. Some unscrupulous athletes and their promoters have gone further, doping themselves with potent drugs in an attempt to boost performance. Deaths have resulted, for example in the Tour de France and the Rome Olympics, and a substantial part of the medical effort at international games is currently directed at the protection of the athlete and his fellow contestants from such unfair and dangerous practices. Much has been accomplished, but problems remain in detecting the use of muscle-building anabolic steroids and the transfusion of stored blood to boost the performance of the endurance competitor.

Responsibility for the fit athlete does not end once he has reached peak condition. The team of advisers—physician, physiologist, psychologist, trainer, and coach—must sustain his performance in the face of an adverse environment, be it high altitude, an extreme of heat or cold, or the reactions of a hostile crowd. The sports doctor must be thoroughly familiar with all the risks of physical injury, disease, and death in the arena, and must know how such hazards can be minimized. He must understand the special problems of the female athlete and the adolescent. He must also be prepared to advise the athlete when the time comes for retirement. What sports can be pursued safely into middle-age, and what impact do they have upon health? Is the enlarged heart of the athlete a real and dangerous phenomenon? How does the rate of ageing of the ex-athlete compare with that of the average citizen? Is life-expectancy better or poorer than in a person who has always had a sedentary life style? Can sport safely be recommended to a person with physical disabilities?

Lastly, what should the relationship be between the fit athlete and the society in which he lives? Recent generations have conceived the athlete as a political weapon—a means for the emancipation of the working man, the liberation of womanhood, the development of black power, the winning of cold wars, and the preservation of cultural identity. The ordinary person no longer sees the top contestant as a healthy prototype of what he can and should become. Professionalism, whether admitted or covert, has relegated the common citizen to the status of a passive spectator in an ideological battle. Olympic budgets of over $1000 million patently deny the simple idealism of ancient Greece, and thoughtful people increasingly question the wisdom of vast expenditures on a few days of pageantry and excitement. International competition seems destined to a steady increase in the twenty-first century, as we become citizens of a global village. Unfortunately, present indications are that competition will become steadily less fun, as the high-spirited amateur is replaced by the scientifically chosen and government-sponsored candidate. The coming age of leisure may turn out to be a time of supreme boredom, as the less gifted individual abandons all thought of personal participation in sport.

These are some of the themes we shall explore in our study of the fit athlete. Hopefully, our exploration will allow us not only to watch the superb performer with new understanding, but will also stimulate us to a new pleasure in health-giving physical activity.

2
The stage is set

Neolithic beginnings

Greece is by no means the cradle of sport, as many have tacitly assumed. There is little direct evidence regarding the leisure pursuits of neolithic times; however, we can glimpse in isolated groups of North American Indians and Eskimos some picture of life 'before the coming of the white man', since remote tribes have apparently succeeded in preserving their traditional culture until quite recently.

Some of the earliest contact with the Indians of the Great Lakes—the Hurons and the Iroquois—were made by Jesuit missionaries from French Canada. In the early seventeenth century, Father Brebeuf gave a vivid description of how the village sorcerer would prescribe a 'game of crosse' for the healing of a sick member of the tribe. Although lacrosse was valued as a means of appeasing the anger of the gods and renewing health, it also provided an opportunity for settling boundary disputes and developing the stamina needed on the war path. Individual 'games' were held on a vast scale, several hundred participants ranging over a distance of five to ten miles, with play continuing for several days.

A rudimentary form of football has apparently been played by Eskimos of the northern coast of Alaska for many generations. Here, it is more difficult to be certain that the sport is truly indigenous; it could perhaps have been imported several centuries ago through the casual visit of a European whaling vessel. If so, it subsequently gained a deep religious significance, and a correctly played game of football became an important means of preparation for a successful whale hunt. If the ocean spirits enjoyed the game sufficiently to co-operate with the whaling, the returning Eskimos considered it appropriate to offer further thanks through a night of festivities, including blanket-tossing games and a drum dance.

In the Inca territory of Central America, archaeologists have found walled tennis courts dating back at least 2000 years. Ancient Egypt also had a strong interest in boxing, wrestling, and various ball-games, while China boasted its own indigenous ball games such as Kemari and Dakyu. At least one famous emperor (Ch'ang Ti, 36–32 B.C.) enjoyed participation in football to a degree that was considered unseemly by his subjects.

These few examples serve to show that sport was by no means a Greek invention. Despite the rigours of life at the dawn of history, men found time to enjoy a variety of sports. These were valued as a means of developing hunting skills, of preparing for war, and of placating the angry gods.

The classical period

The Greek interest in sports apparently dates back to the Bronze Age. Tumbling, bull-vaulting, boxing, wrestling,

FIG. 1. Olympia as it appeared about a century ago (illustration reproduced from *100 Jahre Deutsche Ausgrabung in Olympia*, by courtesy of Prestel-Verlag. Munich).

FIG. 2. A reconstruction of Olympia, as made by German archaeologists excavating the classical site of the Games (illustration reproduced from *100 Jahre Deutsche Ausgrabung in Olympia*, by courtesy of Prestel-Verlag, Munich).

archery, and distance running were all popular spectacles in the ancient Minoan civilization of Crete (3000–1200 B.C.). Building on this concept, many of the Greek city states began to organize major athletic festivals, the most famous being that held at Olympia, in honour of the God Zeus (Figs 1 and 2).

The simple purity of classical athleticism is well set-out in the eleventh Olympic Ode: 'Strength and beauty are the gifts of Zeus ... natural gifts imply the duty of developing them with God's help by cost and toil.' Such was the importance of the sacred festival that a 'Pax Olympica' guaranteed all participants safe-conduct, irrespective of immediate wars and ideological conflicts. Tradition has it that the first contest was held in 776 B.C., but some historians trace the games back much further into the mists of legend, linking the festival to either the Phaeacian games organized for Odysseus, or an elaborate funeral celebration arranged for the mythical hero Pelops.

Athletes performed naked. Legend has it that a runner tripped over his clothes and killed himself on the rocky ground; however, nudity was more likely a concession to the heat and humidity of the Greek mountain valleys. The Olympiad itself was strictly a male preserve, but the festival of Bera provided a separate contest for Greek maidens. Initially, all men of pure Hellenistic descent were eligible to compete at Olympia, and some of the contestants were formidable intellectuals. Thus Milo, an army commander-in-chief and a member of the learned society of Pythagoreans was reputed to have won at least six Olympiads and twenty-six other lesser crowns.

However, municipal pride led to the growth of professionalism, and, in time, all of the major Greek cities boasted at least one 'gymnasion' where professional competitors could prepare themselves for the games. The amateurs tended to look with scorn upon the professional products of the city-states; thus Plato, a talented wrestler, described the gymnasium athlete as 'but a sleepy thing and rather perilous to health ... We need a finer training for our champions ... with hard endurance training and exercise ...'

Although other sports were known in Minoa, tradition has it that the Olympiad began as a simple running match. The diaulos (a double-course running event) and the dolichos (or long race) were added in 724 B.C., and these events were later supplemented by the classical pentathlon. This last event comprised a triple jump, running, the throwing of a copper ingot (the fore-runner of our discus), the hurling of a javelin, and wrestling. A sequence of some 293 Olympiads was terminated around A.D. 400 by Theodosius the Great. Having embraced Christianity, the Roman Emperors objected strongly to the pagan overtones of the Greek festival. Theodosius issued an edict prohibiting the games, and reinforced this decree by burning the temple of Zeus in A.D. 408.

Even before the Christian era, the majority of Romans had little time for athletic festivals. Ennius (239–169 B.C.) wrote 'to strip naked among one's fellow citizens is the beginning of vice.' Later, we find Lucien complaining 'you will meet an army enlisted from the Greek gymnasium, listless because of their palaestrae course and hardly able to bear arms.' Sport became little more than the opiate of the plebeians. On the numerous public holidays, crowds of up to 400 000 would pack themselves into arenas such as the circus Maximus to watch events renowned mainly for their brutality—chariot-racing, gladiatorial combats, and fights with wild animals. Serious-minded patricians such as Seneca (4 B.C.–A.D. 65) saw athletics as something that interfered with military training. The practical nature of the Roman mind is well shown by his advice to the young man preparing himself for war—he should choose 'short and simple exercises that tire the body rapidly and so save time.'

The Middle-Ages

Although the Roman Emperors reacted against the paganism of the formal Olympic Games, some early Christian scholars saw asceticism and athleticism almost as interchangeable concepts. Thus Clemens of Alexandria (A.D. 150–215) strongly commended athletic pursuits as part of the proper education of Christian young men.

In the Middle-Ages, the Church retreated behind the walls of its monasteries, and the negative aspects of asceticism gained the upper hand. Fasting and contemplation were reinforced by a stern opposition to such body-building pursuits as athletics. Nevertheless, jousting and tournaments persisted among the knights, while the common people continued to enjoy such sports as football. Despite the strictures of the Church, popular games retained something of their dark pagan origins. The Good Friday football game at Wreyland, for example, was reputed to ensure a bumper potato crop. Even the local clergy occasionally yielded to the temptations of a spirited football match on the village green, and in 1584 the diocese of Oxford found it necessary to determine appropriate penalties for ministers and deacons convicted of playing the pernicious game.

The Renaissance and beyond

The reformation greatly changed the attitudes of Church and State towards sport. Theologians such as Martin Luther saw that a strong body could help the mind in its quest for piety, and spoke approvingly of the recreative and moral value of pursuits such as fencing and wrestling. Educational theorists such as Da Feltre in Italy, Comenius in Czechoslovakia, and Mulcaster in England also began to appreciate the contribution that sport could make to the learning process, both by improving the physical health of the pupils, and also by promoting the development of an integrated personality.

The English monarch Henry VIII was apparently himself a vigorous athlete, at least in his younger days. He layed down bowling alleys in the palace at Whitehall and tennis courts in the Hampton property 'donated' by Cardinal Wolsey, while enjoying wrestling matches with the King of France. The liberal attitude to sport continued through the Elizabethan era, and on a less flamboyant but more practical note James I promulgated his 'Declaration on Lawful Sport' (1618). This carefully preserved the rights of both Church and commoners. Subjects of the 'meaner sort' who laboured hard all the week were permitted to enjoy Sunday sports such as archery, leaping, vaulting, and dancing, but only 'after evening prayers ended'.

The Stuart kings soon found themselves in conflict with the sterner Puritan sects, and during the period of the Commonwealth it became fashionable to condemn not only Sunday sport, but any activity in which people were finding godless, bodily pleasure. Laughter from the common remained to tempt the young. John Bunyan (1628–88), the strongly moral author of *Pilgrim's Progress*, described with horror his many lapses from grace: 'I shook the sermon out of my mind, and to my old customs of sport and gaming I returned with great delight.'

The eighteenth century brought in its turn the age of reason, men such as Rousseau (1712–78) preaching a naturalism in education, with a strong emphasis on health and the unity of mind and body; games and sports were seen to have real therapeutic value, taking from man 'all the dangerous inclinations that spring from idleness'.

So to the nineteenth century, with Europe reeling before the armies of Napoleon. Friedrich Jahn, brooding amid the ruins of the German empire, sought to restore national morale through a system of outdoor gymnasia or *Turnverein*. The young turners became a guild, the *Turnerschaft*, pledged to the emancipation of their Fatherland. The heavy political overtones of the movement were regarded with disfavour by the authorities, and it was soon proscribed. Human ingenuity devised exercises that could be performed in a limited space, and the guild flourished behind closed doors, hatching a succession of plots against the monarchy. Civil war and defeat caused many of the turners to depart hurriedly for distant places, and a strong interest in gymnastics was thus carried to the United States and Canada. One of Jahn's pupils opened a Turnplatz near Regent's Park in London, but the combination of regimented gymnastics and heavy political discussion do not seem to have appealed to the British temperament.

Northern Europe also developed a strong interest in gymnastics during the nineteenth century. Here, the pioneers were Salzmann (1744–1811) and Ling (1776–1839); the latter moved from Lund to become principal of the world-renowned Royal Central Gymnastic Institute in Stockholm. The Swedish system was less politically oriented than German gymnastics; the four objectives of the Stockholm school were pedagogy, therapy, military preparation, and aesthetic development, with an emphasis on free exercises rather than apparatus work.

In Britain, sport continued in a socially stratified pattern. The upper classes enjoyed hunting, riding, and dancing, and the workers the boisterous games of the village green and industrial street. However, a new feature was the opening of 'public' schools such as Rugby for the developing upper middle-class. Here, sport was pursued with strong idealism; all pupils were indoctrinated in the precepts of fair play and gallant defeat. Barriers of class were perpetuated (pp. 189–90) in rigid distinctions between 'gentlemen' and 'players', but nevertheless interest in such games as rugby and association football, field hockey, lawn tennis, rowing, cycling, cricket, and track and field spread steadily through Victorian suburbia. Thus was set the stage for the Olympic revival of 1896.

3
The Olympic revival

The Olympic phenomenon

Stimulated by German successes in excavating the Olympic site, a wealthy Parisian, the Baron Pierre de Coubertin (1863–1937) conceived the yet more ambitious project of reviving the Games in all their pageantry (Fig. 3). Much can be learnt about the man and his ideas from his writings, as collected and translated into English by the Carl–Diem Institute of the German Sports High-School in Cologne. The Baron writes with nationalistic fervour 'Germany had brought to light what remained of Olympia. Why should not France succeed in restoring its splendours?'

Historians may dispute the novelty of the idea. Over the centuries, some Greek villages had continued to hold what were described as Olympic contests. Equally, the Parisian 'Directoire' had attempted to establish an Olympic celebration on the Champs de Mars at the end of the eighteenth century. However, the scope of de Coubertin's plans far outshadowed those of his predecessors. The germ of his idea was conceived when he was twenty-three, but at first he moved cautiously, fearing that such an ambitious project would arouse both hostility and scorn. After seven years of patient preparation, a Congress was called at Paris in the spring of 1893, under the auspices of the Council of French Athletic Sports Clubs, the organizers being the Baron, and his friends Mr. C. Herbert, secretary of the British Amateur Athletic Association, and Professor W. M. Sloane of Princeton University. The prime objective of the trio was cloaked in secrecy, the avowed reasons for the meeting being (1) the defence of amateur sport against the evils of lucre and professionalism, and (2) the clarification

FIG. 3. Baron Pierre de Coubertin (1863–1937), the founder of the modern Olympic Games (illustration reproduced by courtesy of *Universal Sports* and the International Olympic Committee).

of the rules governing amateur status, which were said to be full of compromises and contradictions, and respected more in letter than in spirit. Nevertheless, the Olympic project was piloted through the treacherous waters of the back-rooms, and a fourteen-member International Committee was charged with preparing a celebration every four years, visiting each 'large' capital of the world in turn.

The following June (1894), a further International Athletic Congress was held in Paris, with wider representation. Delegates attended from the Athletic Sports Union, the London Sports Club, the New York University Athletic Club, the Belgian Federation of Walking and Running Clubs, the Central Gymnastic Institute of Stockholm, the Swiss Lycée Montaigne, and the Royal School at Eger, Hungary. Again, much time was given to technicalities—the definition of an amateur, reasons for suspension, disqualification and requalification, the possibility of being a professional in one sport and an amateur in another, and the treatment of the athlete who received a work of art as a prize and promptly sold it to the highest bidder. Nevertheless, time was also found for a more detailed consideration of the Olympic project, and the athletic, moral, and international advantages that might stem from such a development.

In pressing for the re-establishment of the Games, de Coubertin was strongly influenced by the ideas of Victorian England—the 'muscular Christianity' of Kingsley, and the use of athletics in moral training, as preached by Dr. Arnold of Rugby School. His speeches continually stressed the search for physical beauty and health through a happy balance of mind and body, the healthy drunkenness of the blood nowhere so intense and exquisite as in bodily exercise, and the value of sport in promoting social democracy and international understanding.

From the outset, he envisaged the inclusion of all forms of competitive exercise 'widely used' in the modern world, although in order to keep the Games to a manageable size he proposed excluding certain 'regional sports' such as cricket, lacrosse, and baseball. Further, he stressed the need for individual nations to show responsibility in selecting worthy competitors, in order to avoid the tedium of an excessive number of heats.

Like Mayor Drapeau of Montreal, he was unable to envisage the possibility that the Games might make a financial loss: their celebration would entail only a minimal expenditure, 'about 150 000 francs, which would soon be more than recovered'. With an apparent disregard of accounting procedures worthy of his successors, de Coubertin set the ideal size of the Games at no more than 1200 individual participants and a further 200–500 team sportsmen. Spectators should not exceed 10 000. Larger numbers were aesthetically displeasing, particularly if they were non-sportsmen—they would create a need for ugly grandstands, enclosures, and barriers, with all the sordid transactions of the turnstile. The ideal arrangement would be to sell a limited number of seats at high prices to those who enjoyed conspicuous expenditure, and to distribute the remainder of tickets without charge in a tactful and intelligent manner. To judge the success of the Games on the count of spectators would be to court disaster—the time would soon come when the public would be sick of the sight of sport and would turn away from it.

The Baron accepted the Greek tradition that the Games were in a sense a religious rite, true religion being found not in the sacrifices made by the athlete at the altar of Zeus, but rather in spiritual preparedness, an inner feeling of devotion to an ideal greater than the athlete himself, as expressed in the Olympic Oath. 'Dishonour would not lie in defeat, but in failure to take part.'

The Games offered also a potential for the promotion of social peace and justice. 'On the grounds of what aristocratic privilege must there be a connection between bodily beauty, muscular strength, stamina, training, and the will to win on the one hand, and his genealogical table and the length of his purse on the other?' The Games could break down barriers not only between classes, but also between nations: 'Let us export rowers, runners, and fencers; there is the free-trade of the future.' Equally, differences between rival athletic factions could be resolved—the German could learn to appreciate the finer points of Swedish gymnastics, and the Englishman could come to enjoy American football.

The artist in the Baron insisted that the Games become a true festival, with its solemn ceremonies of oath and flags, and worthy opening and closing rites. The closing was an event which 'usually lacks dignity and into which banality for ever threatens to intrude'. Even the design of the grounds should make its contribution to the beauty of the spectacle. It was indeed the ceremony that distinguished the Olympic Games from a mere series of World Championships, making it a festival of youth, beauty, and strength, and uniting the present with the past and the future.

The first of the revived Games was held, naturally enough, in Athens in 1896. The scale was quite modest, a total of 285 competitors from 13 nations competing in 10 different classes of sport. The second Games (Paris, 1900) was much more successful, attracting 1066 athletes from 20 nations to contest 17 sports; on this occasion, 6 female competitors were seen. The third Games (St. Louis, 1904) was significant in establishing the event as world-wide, rather than European in scope.

At this juncture, de Coubertin's ideas became more expansive. Olympic Diplomas were established in 1905, well-known early recipients including President Theodore Roosevelt, Dr. Nansen, Dr. Wilfred Grenfell, and Count Zeppelin. The following year, there was a proposal that a festival of the arts—architecture, sculpture, music, writing, and painting, be associated with the Games, and in 1910 came the even more daring proposal of a permanent Olympic site, with an aesthetically pleasing design chosen by international competition; as yet, this last suggestion has not been realized. The London contest of 1908 was noteworthy for the greatly expanded range of sports, 26 in all. By 1912, the Games were of sufficient prominence to attract the attention of government, and the Stockholm festival was truly a state occasion, with sovereigns, governments, and public authorities doing their utmost to honour the Games.

Plans for 1916 were unfortunately interrupted by the First World War. The modern nations saw fit to discard the Greek concept of the Pax Olympica, with free passage of competing athletes through enemy territory. However, the International Olympic Committee was able to establish its head office in neutral Lausanne (1915), an arrangement that led some people to accuse the Baron, with little justice, of fleeing his country in time of war. The Lausanne headquarters was soon busy with plans to establish archives, a museum, and a restored version of the Greek gymnasium that would stimulate the interest of the common man more effectively than a simple quadrennial celebration.

As soon as hostilities had ceased, plans for a further contest were initiated. There was a brief threat that the YMCA would organize a rival 'Super-Olympiad', but this soon yielded to the caustic pen of the Baron. Despite all the difficulties of post-war reconstruction, Belgium made magnificent arrangements to act as host to the Games in a newly constructed stadium. Periodic

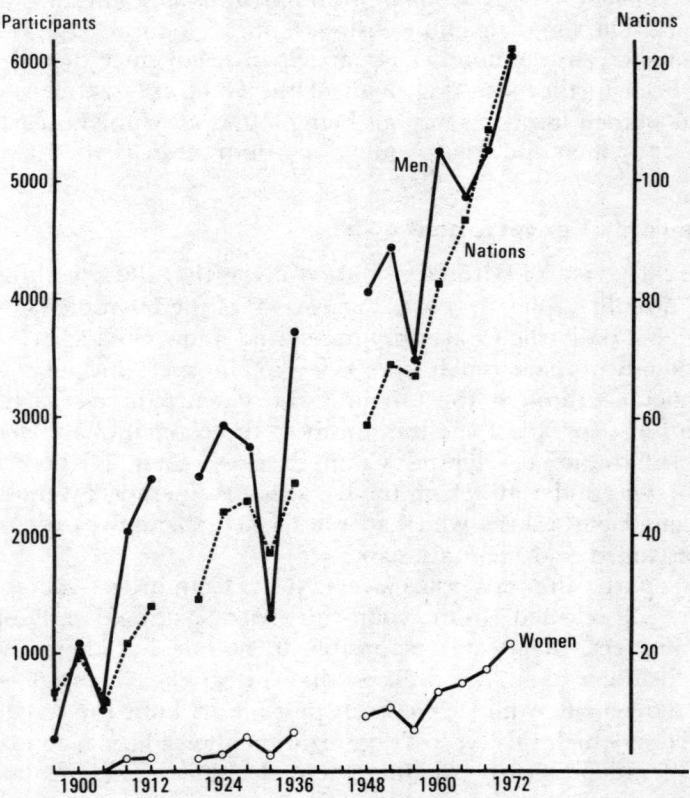

FIG. 4. The growth of the modern Olympic Games, measured in terms of the numbers of male and female participants and the number of nations represented. (At Montreal in 1976 there were 7777 men and 1111 women, representing 144 nations.)

rumblings of the Cassandras were heard thereafter. As de Coubertin wrote in 1931 'At every Olympiad I have heard it was going to be the last.' Nevertheless, there has been a steady growth in the number of athletes attending the Games (Fig. 4), with increasing representation from the under-developed nations of the 'Third World'.

The sombre shadow of totalitarianism gave to the Berlin Games (1936) a macabre splendour. Two further Olympiads were lost with the advent of the Second World War, but in 1948 an even greater body of athletes converged on London, 4030 men and 438 women from 59 nations contesting 138 events. The long travelling distances to Melbourne (1956) led to some dip in the number of participants, but since then there has been further steady growth of the Games: 6077 men and 1070 women from 122 nations being found at Munich in 1972, and 7777 men and 1111 women at Montreal in 1976.

The role of government

The early view of Baron de Coubertin was that the government had no role to play in sport. The revival of the Olympic Games was essentially the project of himself and a few close associates. Although he paid much lip service to the spreading of social democracy through the Olympic movement, there was little wish for a spread of egalitarianism to the council chambers of the International Olympic Committee. As early as 1908, the group was under attack on the basis that its members were self-recruited enthusiasts who had established themselves with an unrestricted and life-long mandate.

In part, the criticisms were just. Committee members were self-selected from countries with National Olympic Committees, and were responsible to no-one but themselves. On the other hand, it is unlikely that the rapid early progress of the movement would have been possible without the freedom of action which this type of organization allowed. As a committee of independently wealthy men, decisions could be taken with a patrician disdain for national passions and corporate interests alike. To the Baron, such a situation was far preferable to the control of a sporting group by a professional administrator or a politician—the latter would likely be a person with no particular knowledge of sport, seeking only to use the muscles of the athlete to advance his political fortunes. Despite these early attitudes, the first move towards the involvement of government seems to have come from the International Olympic Committee, through their decision to make the Stockholm festival a state occasion.

A further reason for turning to government was the sordid matter of finances; despite the optimistic predictions of the Baron, the Games obstinately refused to show a profit, and the provision of facilities that met the exacting requirements of the International Olympic Committee placed an ever greater burden on the host country. Equally, continued insistence on a rigid amateur status and rising travel costs led to the situation where almost all National Committees were compelled to ask subsidies of their state. The subsidies were often given tardily, and with demands on the observance of government regulations, and while they were usually inadequate from the viewpoint of the athletes they seemed outrageously profligate to other indignant taxpayers. Citizen protests have recently reached a climax with the rejection of the Olympic Winter Games by the city of Denver, Colorado, the rejection of the Pan American Games by Brazil, and the refusal of the Canadian Federal Government to offer other than indirect subsidies to the city of Montreal when it hosted the 1976 Olympic Games.

The organizers continue to argue the many indirect benefits of the Games—enhancement of national prestige, stimulation of national interest in sport, and the creation of outstanding physical facilities in the host city. However, it seems undeniable that in terms of the general population, more good would come from the spending of equivalent sums on less ambitiously designed local facilities; countries such as West Germany and Canada may have the wealth to build both massive stadia and local ice-rinks, but in less fortunate countries such as Mexico vast expenditures on a short-lived festival are hard to justify.

As early as 1920, the idea was mooted of reducing costs through the establishment of Olympic areas (such as Belgium, England, and France). Preliminary heats would be held within these areas, and only the top competitors would then have the expense of travel to the world competition. Other suggestions have been to restrict the number of individual competitions, to hold all team-sports at some other time, and to establish one or more permanent Olympic sites. To date, none of these money-saving ideas has found general acceptance, and the City of Montreal must still find ways of raising more than $200 million to cover its share of debts for the 1976 extravaganza.

Tied to these vast costs is the question of the interest of the general public in physical activity. All levels of Canadian government stated repeatedly that they were interested in helping the Games only if the event had a long-term effect on public participation in sports programmes. De Coubertin himself realized that the Olympic Committee had a responsibility to the proletariat, and pointed out that, if they did not exercise this authority, governments would take it from them. He accepted that the interest of the general population was not substantially augmented by the spectacle of the Games, particularly as this was occurring only once every four years. It was for this reason that he became interested in reviving the Greek gymnasium, seeing in the restoration of that institution a stimulus to regular physical activity on the part of the ordinary adult citizen. Projects would be developed in co-operation with municipal government, and could provide both a focus of civic spirit and an instrument for social peace. Some attempt was made to develop a model institution in Lausanne, but the idea never became very popular, presumably because most municipalities did not wish to bequeath facilities they were constructing to an independent and somewhat autocratic organization.

A third area of government involvement has been in the use of sport as a political weapon. This was foreshadowed by Hitler's refusal to receive the Negro track star, Jesse Owens, at the 1936 Berlin Olympics, but has reached its peak among Communist nations. In such countries, the Olympic Games often seem to be viewed as one more battle in the class struggle against capitalism. East Germany, for example, requires all athletes to belong to a political youth organization (FJD) or the equivalent workers' movement (FDGB). Instruction in Marxist/Leninist philosophy occupies up to a third of the time of coaches and athletes alike, and each participant travels abroad as an ambassador of communism. In proving the decadence of the West, winning is more important than participation, and substantial fractions of limited economies are devoted to the needs of the athlete, with large cadres of professional coaches, substantial expenditures on training facilities, and early concentration of promising candidates in special sports schools.

The Western nations have often ignored political aspects of sports. However, a Canadian Minister of National Health and Welfare wrote in 1962 that 'Canadian participation in international competitive events is emerging as an important aspect of a growing spirit of nationhood.' More recently, the Quebec government has conceived the same idea, and has given strong support to the 'Jeux de Quebec' as a means of developing the French culture and identity within Canadian society. The forms of support offered by Western governments have varied according to local resources and perceived needs, but have included national training centres; national coaches; national magazines, uniforms, and equipment; travel; grants in aid of lost salaries; athletic scholarships; and grants for specific projects of applied research.

Occasionally, there has been more individual political exploitation of the Games, as in the defiant gesture of black militants during the playing of the American national anthem in Mexico City, the slaughter of the Israeli athletes by Arab terrorists in Munich, and disputes over New Zealand rugby engagements and use of the Chinese flag that marred the Montreal Games.

Even the International Olympic Committee has at times used sport as a political weapon. Thus, a regulation passed in 1962 required that the Olympic Games be held only in nations granting free access to all recognized teams. This could well be justified as a means of bringing pressure on countries oppressing black minorities or majorities, but in the event the rule was used to press the case of East Germany for recognition as an independent state.

The role of sports medicine

The physician's role in promoting athletic performance can be traced back to the Greek gymnasium, where we find a three-man team, the doctor with an interest in training (the *gymnastes*), a masseur (the *paidotribes*), and a bath servant (the *aleiptes*) ministering to the competitor.

With the revival of the Games, the physician was again accorded a prominent place in the care of the athlete. The person appointed as team physician was commonly a general practitioner or orthopaedic surgeon who had himself been a sportsman and still enjoyed sitting on the players' bench. However, the classical role of providing advice on training was usually deputed to the team coach, a man who worked on hunches rather than hard facts, and the task of the twentieth-century team doctor was interpreted as the provision of advice on general hygiene (such matters as vaccinations, cleanliness of food and changing areas, and hours of sleep); the treatment of minor medical problems such as stomach upsets, sleeplessness, and colds; the provision of minor psychotherapy; and the primary care of injuries to muscles, bones, and joints (Chapter 10). Appointments to the Olympic Games were at the discretion of the National Olympic Committee, and in many instances were limited by problems of funding. Often, the physician concerned had to travel at his own expense, and sometimes he was required to transport his own equipment to the Olympic site. Canadian athletes made a major outcry about the limited medical coverage available to them in Mexico City, and at subsequent international competitions the Canadian government has made available funds to cover the immediate expenses of a substantial party of physicians and paramedical personnel, including general practitioners, orthopaedic surgeons, and even a team dentist.

Sports medicine quickly attained the standing of a respected specialist medical certification in eastern Europe, the founding meeting of the Federation Internationale de Médicine Sportive (FIMS) being held at St. Moritz in 1928. The FIMS organization is still mainly European based, although it boasts the participation of some forty national federations, including the British Association of Sports Medicine and the gargantuan 4000-member American College of Sports Medicine. The Federation sponsors two-week post-graduate courses in sports medicine, usually in conjunction with a regional contest such as the Mediterranean Games, and every fourth year it holds a

World Congress of Sports Medicine; in 1974, this last event was held in Melbourne, and the 1978 gathering is scheduled for Brazilia.

Baron de Coubertin viewed the progress of sports medicine with some distrust, and spoke of the dangers of invasion by a scientific pedantry, obsessed with a model method for the training of the muscles, 'as closely ruled by discipline and uniformity as any political Jacobinism'. The scientist should learn to be a counsellor rather than a despot, and should pay as much attention to psychology as to the physiological aspects of athletic preparation.

Many athletes also distrusted doctors, particularly those with scientific leanings. There were fears that 'tests' carried out in the laboratory would jeopardize performance on a subsequent day of crucial competition, complaints that the results of tests were rarely made available or interpreted to the athlete or his coach, and cynicism that the poor competitor was tiring his muscles on a treadmill or a bicycle ergometer merely to earn a Ph.D. for the sedentary observer.

Despite these misgivings, the International Olympic Committee soon began to sponsor conferences discussing various questions of sports medicine—the contact points between bodily and moral pedagogy, the laws of sporting hygiene, and the role of psychology in sports performance. Such activity continues to the present day, the Medical Committee under the direction of Prince Alexandre de Merode giving support to conferences for sports physicians in the less-developed nations of the world.

In North America, sports medicine is a relatively recent interest, the American College of Sports Medicine (ACSM) growing to its present membership of more than 4000 in a little over twenty years. Professional groups such as the ACSM and the Canadian Association of Sports Sciences (CASS) have drawn upon a broader base than their medically oriented European counterparts, including in their membership not only physicians but many other scientists with an interest in athletic performance—physical educators, physiologists, biochemists, sociologists, and psychologists. Such an approach has led to a valuable inter-disciplinary discussion of methods of improving athletic performance; however, some more traditional physicians have felt isolated and uncomfortable in such a 'scientific' milieu, and have sought an alternative forum for the discussion of injuries and personal hygiene in sectional meetings of the American Medical Association and the Canadian Medical Association devoted to sports medicine.

Most athletes and their coaches now accept the idea that sports medicine can offer more than emergency care after an injury has occurred. They realize that if they are to enter the top ranks of international competition, they must visit the laboratory not once but many times. Indeed, they must themselves learn something of sports medicine, to the point where they can share a meaningful dialogue with the laboratory worker, establishing deficiencies in their current performance, and working with the scientist to devise an appropriate programme that will rectify their shortcomings.

The development of athletic records

Twenty years ago, the four-minute mile of Roger Bannister seemed incredible. Today, such feats have become almost commonplace among international competitors, and a record-breaker would need to prune over eight seconds from Bannister's exacting time. Progression of performance is seen in almost every sport (Tables 1 and 2). Each Olympics brings a further shortening of winning times for most running and swimming events, with an increase in the heights jumped and the weights lifted. How may we explain this phenomenon, and when may we expect it to end?

Reasons for the performance changes include an increase in the body-size of the competitors (Chapter 4), a more effective and specific selection of participants (Chapter 4), improved training procedures (Chapter 5), and developments in equipment and technique. Athletes have shared in the world-wide increase of stature over the past century. Mechanical analysis suggests that height (H) should have relatively little effect upon the maximum speed of running (Table 2). A taller person can take a longer stride (proportional to H), but this is counteracted by a lower maximum frequency of limb movement (proportional to $1/H$ or $1/\sqrt{H}$ according to different authorities).

Table 1. *The development of selected athletic records*

Event	Record in 1900	Record in 1950	Record in 1975
100-yard run	9·8 s	9·3 s	9·0 s (Ivory Crockett, 1974)
1-mile run	4 min 12·8 s	4 min 1·3 s	3 min 51·1 s (Jim Ryun, 1967)
100-m swim	74·0 s	55·8 s	51.2 s (Mark Spitz, 1972)*
Long-jump	24 ft 7¾ in	26 ft 8¼ in	29 ft 2½ in (R. Beamon, 1968)
High-jump	6 ft 5⅝ in	6 ft 11 in	7 ft 6¼ in (D. Stones, 1973)
Pole-vault	11 ft 10¼ in	15 ft 7¾ in	18 ft 5¾ in (R. Seagren, 1972)
Discus-throw	122 ft 3½ in	186 ft 11 in	224 ft 5 in (L. Silvester, 1968, R. Bouch, 1972)
Ski-jump	116 ft 6 in	442 ft 9 in	554 ft 6 in (H. Wosipo, 1973)
Weight-lift †	4133 lb	4133 lb	6270 lb (Paul Anderson, 1957)

* 49·99 sec, Jim Montgomery, Montreal Olympics, 1976.
† from horizontal trestle, using a back-lift.

In sprint events, the force that can be developed by the muscles is proportional to their cross-sectional area (H^2), while the mass to be moved (body weight) is proportional to tissue volume (and thus to H^3); acceleration (force/mass) thus varies as $1/H$, and the tall person is handicapped over short distances.

In endurance events, aerobic power is theoretically proportional to H^2; the work done in supporting or lifting the body is proportional to its mass (H^3), and air or water resistance varies with the cross-sectional area of the body (H^2). Again, the very tall person has some handicap.

In jumping events, height increases muscle force (proportional to cross-section, or H^2) and the distance through which the muscles can shorten before leaving the ground (proportional to H), although this is offset by the greater weight of tissue to be lifted (proportional to H^3). Advantage is nevertheless gained by the tall person because he is usually lean, and

Table 2. *Influence of body dimensions on development of body performance*

Event	Theoretical relationships to height (H)	Theoretical optimum size	Percentage improvements world records 1900–75
100-yard run	speed = independent acceleration = $1/H$	small	+10·9
1-mile run	aerobic power = H^2 lifting work = $1/H^3$ air resistance = $1/H^2$	small	+9·3
1-hr run	aerobic power = H^2 lifting work = $1/H^3$ air resistance = $1/H^2$	small	+12·0
Long-jump	muscle force = H^2 leverage = H weight = H^3	independent or tall	+18·5
High-jump	muscle force = H^2 leverage = H weight = H^3 centre of gravity = H	tall	+16·6
Shot-put Discus-throw Hammer-throw Javelin-throw	muscle force = H^2 leverage = H ejection = H	tall	+48·6 +83·4 +48·4 +90·8

he also has a high centre of gravity; he can clear a higher crossbar without necessarily lifting his centre of gravity any more than a shorter competitor.

In throwing events, such as javelin and shot-put, the weight of the object to be thrown is constant. However, the available muscle force varies with cross-sectional area (H^2), and leverage is proportional to height (H); furthermore, it is an advantage to release the object as high as possible above the ground. A tall athlete thus has a substantial advantage in all throwing competitions.

In contrast, the gymnast gains from a short body; when performing a chin-up, for example, the leverage exerted by the muscles is proportional to H^3, but the leverage exerted by the body is proportional to weight times length, or H^4.

The actual improvements in world records from 1900 to the present day (Table 2) offer some confirmation of this theoretical analysis. Gain in the running events, where it is an advantage to be short, are only 9–12 per cent, comparable with the 10·2 per cent improvement in one-mile race-horse times for the same period. In jumping events, where there is some advantage to being tall, gains are 16–18·5 per cent, whereas in throwing (where there are many good reasons for being tall), gains range from 48 per cent to 91 per cent. Unfortunately, we do not have details of the body-build of the throwers in 1900, but we do know that the height of the shot-putters and discus-throwers increased by some 8 cm from 1928 to 1964; given a similar rate of change throughout the century, performances proportional to height would improve by about 10 per cent, whereas gains for H^2, H^3, and H^4 would be respectively 21, 33, and 46 per cent. Plainly, size changes cannot account for all of the improvements of performance, even in the unusual case of the throwers.

It is necessary to search entire populations in order to discover individuals with the natural endowments that will enable them to become world champions (page 68); thus, as the search process becomes more complete, top performances inevitably improve. At the beginning of the present century, general social conditions, the rigid enforcement of amateur rules, and the constitution of many athletic clubs helped to keep sports the preserve of a privileged minority. Successive Olympic contests have seen increased participation, in terms of both the number of nations and the proportion of any given nation represented at the Games (Fig. 4). However, there is still much scope for equalization of opportunity; in Helsinki (1952), Karvonen found a participation rate of only 0·09 athletes per million people from nations where the annual per capita income was $60 or less; in contrast, the figure was 8·16 per million for countries with a per capita income of $500–$750. Interestingly enough, the participation rate dropped back to 1·28 per million in the most wealthy nations (per capita income of $750 and over); possibly affluence had sapped the interest of these populations in sport, or the governments concerned felt sufficiently secure not to push participation in the Games as a political weapon.

The present century has also seen more specialization among athletes, with individuals increasingly choosing the sport most appropriate to their body-build. Between 1928 and 1964, the 8-cm increases in height of the shot-putters and the discus-throwers were accompanied by respective increases of 28 kg and 27 kg in body weight; in other words, more of the heavily built athletes were choosing these sports. In contrast, the 5000-m and 10 000-m runners gained 5 cm and 6 cm of height over the same period, with respective weight increases of only 7 kg and 5 kg.

Knowledge of training procedures, including appropriate physiological, psychological, and nutritional techniques for optimizing performance, has increased greatly over the present century, and undoubtedly this new learning has made some contribution to the overall changes in performance. Major changes of philosophy have included the much earlier initiation of training, and a vast increase in the total volume of required preparation. Such developments have been facilitated by the opening of special schools for promising young athletes, the organization of national training centres, the professionalization of coaching, and the provision of various forms of state subsidy to older competitors who neglect their normal employment in order to prepare themselves for international competition. The contribution made by such costly programmes is suggested by the statistics from Helsinki; in nations with a per capita income of less than $200, the points earned per participant averaged from 17·3 to 17·6; with an income between $200 and $750, the figure averaged 27·8, and in nations with a per capita income over $750 it rose to 46·5.

A combination of earlier training and earlier maturation has led to a lowering of the average age of participants in some events; in swimming and in gymnastics, for example, many of the girls now compete between the ages of 14 and 18, and individuals who have the emotional maturity to face the stresses of international competition may actually reach their peak performance in this age range (Chapter 12).

FIG. 5. A comparison between an early ski jumper (1893) and a modern competitor. Note the changes in the skis, the clothing, and the posture of the modern jumper (illustrations reproduced from E. Jokl and P. Jokl, *The physiological basis of athletic records*, by courtesy of the authors and the publisher, C. C. Thomas, Springfield, Illinois).

Changes in equipment and technique have led to notable advances in some sports. A prime example is the ski-jump, where distances covered have increased 376 per cent over the century. In addition to changes in ski construction, competitors now take care to choose more streamlined clothing, and to hold their body in a more aerodynamic posture during the jump

(Fig. 5). The design of racing bicycles has also changed dramatically, and the speed of the paced racer has risen by 12 per cent over the century. The height attained in pole-vaulting showed a steady increment over a number of Olympic contests (4·39 m in 1952, 4·41 m in 1956, 4·57 m in 1960), but there was a dramatic surge to 5·03 m in 1964, following the introduction of the fibreglass pole. Despite a wet afternoon, Tadeusz Sluzarski reached a height of 5·50 m at the Montreal Olympics of 1976. Among the swimmers, Sylvia Ester of the German Democratic Republic pruned more that a second off the previous women's record for the 100-metre free-style event in 1967 when she made the dramatic gesture of peeling off her swim suit before the contest; other swimmers have gained small advantages from shaving hair from various areas of the body.

What of the future? As the times for a given event become shorter, one might anticipate a slowing in the rate of improvement of scores. However, if anything, the rate of improvement has accelerated since the 1950s. A number of factors suggest that the present trend will continue for some years. Equal representation of the nations has yet to be achieved. There are still not too many women following the example of the Canadian ski champion, Nancy Greene, who at a slight 125 lb can carry out forty deep knee bends with a 170 lb bar-bell on her shoulders; 'liberation' (Chapter 11) may well make such arduous training more appropriate for a woman. The potential for discovery of the outstanding individual grows daily as the world population increases in numbers. Marriages such as that between Miss D. Packer (800-metre gold medallist in Tokyo) and R. Brightwell, himself the winner of a bronze medal in the 400-metre event, offer further potential gains from a happily arranged form of selective breeding. Finally, there are climatic variables; often, existing scores have been depressed by poor track conditions, an excess of heat or cold, or a strong headwind, but inevitably the day will come when the physical conditions are ideal for a superlative performance.

4
Shape, strength, and skill

This chapter looks at the body-build of the successful athlete. It discusses biological ingredients of success, adds the seasoning of skill, and finally produces a recipe that combines this very diverse information into a meaningful index of potential performance.

Body-build of the successful athlete

Certain stereotypes of body-build are well known from observation of international competitions—the extreme height of the basketball player, the lithe figure of the gymnast, and the massive body of the weight-lifter. Measurements of such things as height and weight are so simple that everyone is in a position to make an intelligent guess as to the type of sport for which he or she is best suited.

Sports for the short. Japanese athletes took the top five positions at Munich when performing gymnastics about the horizontal bar. In Montreal, Japanese competitors again won gold and silver medals. Such successes are commonly attributed to the small size of the Japanese people. Detailed measurements show that on average, Japanese athletes are not only shorter than Europeans, but they also have different body proportions—the lower part of the legs, the feet, the arms, and the hands are smaller in the oriental competitors. While this is an advantage in making gyrations on the rings and horizontal bars, it is a disadvantage in other events such as the long-horse vault (where the best Japanese competitor finished fourth in Munich and second in Montreal).

Another good choice for the short person seems to be track and field. Most runners are fairly short and relatively light. Sprinters are short with short legs and powerful well-muscled thighs. Marathon runners are also very short, but in this group the characteristic build is of normal legs with a short and extremely lean body. The tallest runners usually elect to participate over distances of about 400 m, but there are remarkable exceptions. Thus the United States distance runner Jim Ryun had a body-build that most of the experts thought suitable for 400-metre events; presumably, the fact that he had a more powerful build than other contestants gave him an important advantage in the final sprint for the tape. Negro contestants have traditionally performed well in sprint and middle-distance events. A British expert on physique, Dr. Tanner, has noted that the negroid races tend to have longer limbs, narrower hips, wider bones, and narrower calves than their 'white' counterparts; the light body is an obvious advantage to the runner, and Tanner has argued that lighter calves help the mechanics of running. The short-legged Indians and Asians might also be expected to do well in sprint events, but in fact their competitive performances have been poor. In these groups, the advantage of limb length seems to be offset by weak leg muscles.

Other possibilities for the short person are association football and field hockey. These are both good games, since people of different shapes and sizes can all find an appropriate playing position—the shortest and the lightest as the wing-forwards, and the tallest and heaviest as the goal-keeper. In baseball, likewise, body weights can range from 65 kg for a lithe infielder to almost 100 kg for a massive pitcher. Fencing and flyweight boxing also attract short and light-weight participants.

The tall athlete. Basketball is the obvious choice of sport for the tall person. An unusual stature and long arms help the contestant guide the ball close to the basket. Figures from both Japan and Brazil show a 12-cm difference of height between top soccer and basketball players. However, because rapid body movements are important in the latter sport, contestants are not particularly heavy relative to their great height.

The best rowers are tall. In this sport, a long trunk and arms are helpful in applying leverage to the oars and in developing a good stroke. Body weight is supported by the boat, and successful contestants are thus quite heavy, with well-developed leg and arm muscles. Kayak paddlers are rather lighter and shorter than the rowers, but nevertheless long and powerful arms give them an advantage in steering through the whirlpools.

Dinghy-sailors also profit from being tall. In their case the boat is counterbalanced most effectively by someone who is heavy in the top half of his body. Knowledgeable sailors boost their natural endowment with the greatest load of clothing permitted by local rules, and, particularly if the weather is warm, they may surreptitiously dowse themselves with water once the formalities of weighing have been completed.

The heavy-weights. Heavy-weights gravitate to the contact sports: weight-lifting, throwing, and appropriate categories of boxing and wrestling. In games such as ice-hockey much depends upon the roughness of the play; some countries field relatively light teams, maintaining the traditions of skill and agility; others, particularly those from North America, seem to rely upon brute force. The urge to 'kill' the opposition by sheer physical weight is most strongly developed in North American football, where professional team members may weigh 100–110 kg apiece. Demands for such unusual weights have created two problems. First, the players tend to over-eat, and are often unduly fat when they report to training camp. Secondly, many team-members despair of reaching the required body-build by legitimate means, and resort to doping with body-building steroid hormones (Chapter 8) is all too common.

In boxing and wrestling, there is the opposite temptation—using fair means or foul in order to compete in a lower weight category than that to which the individual properly belongs. The purpose of the categorization is to ensure a well-matched contest, and attempts to circumvent the weighing procedure are unsporting. The usual approach—going without fluids for a long period—is also stupid (since it weakens working capacity) and it can be dangerous, particularly in a hot climate.

Race and body-build. If body-build is a part contributor to the successes of Negro runners and Asian gymnasts, we are faced with the question as to how far this body-build is a true characteristic of race, and how far it is a result of the environment in which such peoples have lived.

Sports scientists have traditionally accepted the racial explanation. However, we need to be careful in agreeing with conventional wisdom. One difficulty is that selection of contestants can be more rigorous among under-privileged groups. In Britain and many European nations, only a small percentage of potential athletes reach the point of serious participation in the sport for which they are best suited. On the other hand, athletic scholarships have offered a mechanism whereby North American Negroes could move up the social ladder (Chapter 15); team positions have thus been sought eagerly by the majority of Negroes with advantageous physical characteristics.

A second reason for caution is the instability of body-build. In Britain and many other European countries, standing height has increased progressively for several centuries (Fig. 6). A visit to the Tower of London shows that many medieval suits of armour were designed for men who were about five foot (one and a half metres) tall. Data accumulated over the last century reveals that there has been a gain of about 1 cm in average

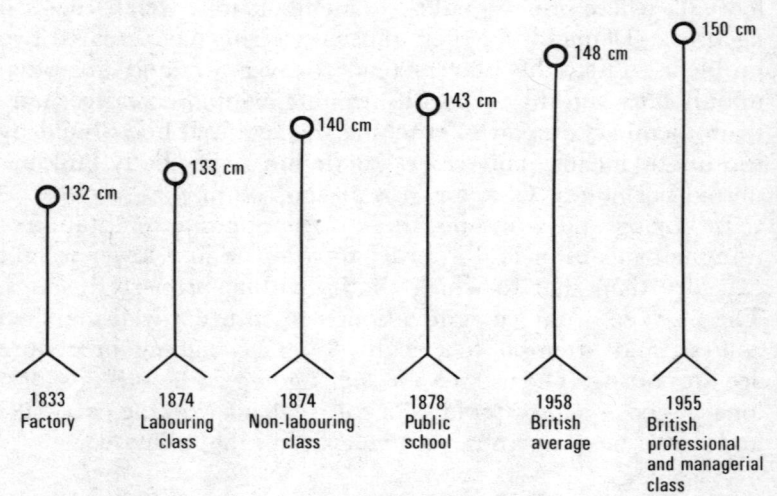

Fig. 6. Changes in the stature of the British twelve-year-old boy, from 1833 to 1958 (based on data of Dr. J. M. Tanner).

adult stature every ten years. One hundred years ago, the average member of the upper class was 10 cm taller than a poor person. However, as the living standards of the workers have improved, the class difference of height has been progressively obliterated. We still do not know all of the reasons for the increase of body-size. Possible influences include changes in diet (particularly an ever-growing consumption of sugar), and an ever-widening circle of potential marriage partners. Until recently, the size of groups such as the Japanese has remained more stable. However, the short peoples of the world have now begun to increase in size even more rapidly than the Europeans and North Americans, and it seems likely that just as the class difference has disappeared in Britain, so the short stature of the oriental will become a thing of the past.

Athletes in general have shared in the world-wide trend to increase of size. Dr. Tanner compared runners from the Olympic Games of Amsterdam (1928) and Rome (1960). Over the intervening 32 years, sprinters had become 4 cm taller and 7 kg heavier, middle-distance runners were 4 cm taller and 10 kg heavier, and long distance runners were 4 cm taller and 1 kg heavier. Nevertheless, the optimum body proportions, such as the ratio of height to weight, remained much the same for the different classes of event.

As standing height has increased, other features of body configuration such as the ratio of leg to trunk length have also changed. There remain some characteristics such as calf-width that apparently have greater racial stability. However, their description is becoming increasingly academic as intermarriage blurs distinctions within multi-racial societies.

Biological ingredients of success

Biological ingredients of top-level performance include strength, endurance, speed, agility, and flexibility. The microscopic features of the muscles also show characteristic differences from one sport to another.

Strength. Sports scientists distinguish several categories of strength. There is the explosive power needed in making sudden movements, the isometric strength developed against almost immovable objects, and the strength needed for repeated strong rhythmic movements.

Explosive power can be estimated simply from the height of a vertical jump; however, the results of such a test depend also on the body weight and height of the individual. In the laboratory, the athlete jumps on a platform that records the force he can develop. Explosive power is important not only to jumpers and hurdlers, but also to sprinters, the bowler in cricket, the pitcher in baseball, discus- and javelin-throwers, and participants in team sports such as soccer, where rapid jumping, turning, and kicking are needed.

Isometric strength is measured by having an athlete tense his muscles against a cable or a strong spring. In some sports, isometric strength is necessary to support the weight of the body. The yachtsman who leans from his dinghy to counterbalance the force of a stiff breeze must make an intense and sustained isometric contraction of the muscles in his thighs and abdomen. The gymnast, the figure skater, and the soccer-player trying to maintain his balance on a muddy field all need isometric strength in certain muscle groups, although excessive development of the upper part of the body increases total weight to the point where the competitor is at a disadvantage. Isometric development reaches its peak in the champion weight-lifter and the heavy-weight wrestler.

The ability to make rhythmic muscular contractions is usually gauged by repeating movements against graded weights. The cyclist needs endurance in his thigh muscles; the rower endurance in both arm and leg muscles.

Endurance. At exhaustion, a cyclist commonly complains of weakness or pain in his legs; we may thus reasonably conclude that his performance has been limited by muscular endurance. However, a distance runner has other complaints—shortness of breath, a staggering gait, and a dimming of vision; in his case, performance is limited by the endurance of the heart and lungs, with the heart no longer pumping enough oxygen to his brain.

Dr. Kenneth Cooper suggested that one very simple measurement of the oxygen transporting power of the heart and lungs was the distance a person could run in twelve minutes (Table 3). The laboratory approach is to have the athlete run uphill

Table 3. *The relationship between the distance an individual can run in twelve minutes and the oxygen transporting power of the blood (based on the data of Dr. Kenneth Cooper).*

Distance (miles) covered in 12 min	Oxygen transporting power (ml per min per kg wt)
Less than 1	Less than 28
1–1·25	28–34
1·25–1·5	34–42
1·5–1·75	42–52
More than 1·75	More than 52

on a treadmill and measure oxygen usage by collecting bags of respired gas in the final minutes prior to exhaustion. Results may be expressed as litres of oxygen transported per minute, or as millilitres per minute per kilogram of body weight. The first type of unit is appropriate for weight-supported sports such as swimming and rowing, but in most types of activity the oxygen cost increases as a person becomes heavier; it is thus a fair penalty to divide his oxygen transporting power by body weight. The penalty is exacted equally whether the weight is fat or muscle. Cross-Channel swimmers are sometimes fat (this helps them to float and protects them against the cold water), and contestants in contact sports such as American football and ice-hockey have difficulty in laying down muscle without fat. However, even the leanest of American football players may have a poor oxygen transport score just because he is heavily built.

The hierarchy of oxygen transport values for the various sports is given in Table 4. Contestants in endurance events—cross-country skiing, very-long-distance running, and distance cycling—have the largest scores. Other vigorous activities—rowing, canoeing, and distance swimming—also attract sportsmen who can develop quite high readings, but scores for participants in team games (association, Rugby, and American football, basketball, ice hockey, volleyball, and baseball) are much poorer.

Speed. It takes a skilful car driver about a third of a second to move his foot from the accelerator to the brake pedal in

Table 4. *The highest reported results for the oxygen transporting power of contestants in various sports*

Sport	Oxygen transporting power (ml per min per kg wt) Men	Women	Sport	Oxygen transporting power (ml per min per kg wt) Men	Women
Cross-country skiing	82	63	Tennis		
3000–10 000 metre running	82		White-water paddling	60	49
Long-distance cycling	80		Gymnastics	60	43
Speed skating	79	53	American football	60	
Orienteering	77	60	Jumping	59	
			Table tennis	59	43
800–1500 metre running	77		Basketball	59	
Marathon	76		Ice hockey	58	
Pentathlon	74		Decathlon	58	
Biathlon	73		Weight lifting	56	
Distance walking	71		Wrestling	56	
			Sprinting	56	45
Canoeing	70		Badminton	55	
Rowing	70		Throwing	55	38
Swimming	70	58	Boxing	55	
Downhill skiing	68	57	Baseball	52	
400-metre running	67	56	Volleyball	52	33
			Rugby football	50	
Field hockey	63		Dinghy sailing	50	
Handball	62		Judo	49	
Association football	61		Archery	—	40

response to a signal such as a red light. The time to initiate a movement can be as much as 5 per cent of the total performance time for a sprint athlete, and small changes in reaction time and the rate of acceleration to maximum speed can have a decisive influence on the outcome of a competition. Fast movements are also necessary for individual sports such as fencing and team games like association football.

For the sprinter, the initiation of movement is fairly simple, since there is only one possible response to the starter's signal; nevertheless, sprint athletes do find certain tricks that enable them to respond faster than an average person. One secret seems to be to concentrate the mind on the starting pistol rather than on the subsequent leg movements, which are in any event well known. In a game such as soccer, the signals initiating a movement are much more complex, and there may be a substantial decision time before the player chooses an appropriate pattern of response; the quick thinker who can store a compendium of effective tactics within his brain and call these into action at instant notice is thus at a premium. The initiation of movement occurs faster if the muscles concerned are tensed in anticipation of the event. However, such tension can lead to a false start, particularly in the sprint swimmer. One possible method of overcoming this problem, first adopted by the United States team in Munich, is the grab start. Instead of hanging poised over the water, the competitor grips the end of the starting board, and in this way can safely build up a substantial tension in his leg muscles.

Acceleration depends upon the weight that must be set in motion. It is thus desirable that a sprinter have a minimum of weight in regions other than the leg muscles. Other critical factors are the amount of energy stored in the active muscle fibres and the efficiency with which this energy can be transformed into forward motion.

A sprinter reaches peak speed within about six seconds, and then gradually slows down until he crosses the finishing line. The loss of speed reflects continuing resistance to movement and a progressive depletion of energy stores. Part of the resistance is internal, energy taken to move the limbs against the natural stiffness of the muscles and joints. This component can be reduced appreciably by a suitable 'warm-up'. External resistance includes friction between the athlete and the ground, and wind or water resistance. Friction can be reduced by improved designs of running shoes (for the track competitor) and bicycle tyres (for the cyclist). Wind-resistance can be minimized by altering body contours (particularly in the cyclist) and choosing streamlined clothing (particularly for down hill skiers). The thinner air at high altitude lowers wind-resistance, and gives an appreciable advantage to sprint athletes; thus, over the short distances many new records were created at the Mexico City Olympic Games (Chapter 9). Shaving of the head can reduce water resistance for the swimmer. It is also important to keep the legs in the horizontal plane when swimming, and for this reason the thighs must be either lightly boned or well-padded with buoyant fat. Women tend to qualify on both counts, and thus fare well in swimming events.

The initial storehouse of energy within the muscle fibre is an organic phosphate called adenosine triphosphate, or ATP (Table 5). Along with other phosphate compounds, ATP

Table 5. *The energy resources of the athlete, expressed in terms of an equivalent transport of oxygen to the working muscles*

Resource	Equivalent oxygen transport (ml per min per kg of body weight)	Time to exhaustion of resource
Phosphate compounds (adenosine triphosphate, creatine phosphate)	165	8 s
Conversion of glycogen to lactic acid	70	40 s
Steady transport of oxygen	50–80	Almost inexhaustible

provides energy at a rate equivalent to a steady oxygen transport of about 165 ml of oxygen per min, per kg of body weight. Unfortunately, all of the phosphate stores can be exhausted by less than eight seconds of maximum activity.

A second resource within the muscle is the carbohydrate glycogen. In the absence of oxygen, this can be partially broken down to lactic acid, liberating energy equivalent to an oxygen transport of 70 ml per min per kg of body weight. However, this reaction is also brought to a halt within about forty seconds. Accumulating lactic acid causes intense breathlessness and inhibits further glycogen breakdown; the affected muscles become weak and painful, and further activity cannot take place except through a steady transport of oxygen. The skilful medium-distance contestant adjusts his pace during the major part of the race so that the oxygen demand of his muscles is kept within the limits imposed by the steady transport of oxygen; only during the final sprint does he call upon the other energy resources. In this way, muscular pain and intense breathlessness are deferred until after he has crossed the finishing line.

Agility. Activities such as figure-skating, gymnastics, fencing, and soccer call not only for speed, but also for agility—the athlete needs to be able to position the various parts of the body with great precision. The control of posture is quite complicated. The brain must make its judgement by synthesizing the sometimes conflicting information reported by the inner ears, the eyes, tension receptors in the muscles and joints, and pressure receptors in the soles of the feet. The importance of the eyes can be demonstrated by comparing how long one can stand on one leg with the eyes open and with the eyes closed.

Laboratory tests of balance use a stabilometer. This is an elaborate form of see-saw or teeter-totter. The athlete stands astride the apparatus for three minutes, and his score is computed from the total time that he can keep both ends of the oscillating board away from the ground. Groups such as skaters, gymnasts, and dinghy sailors have above average scores on such tests. The figure-skater is also very resistant to the dizziness that would disturb most people during repeated fast twirls. This is partly a question of training. The contestant learns to fix the eye on a distant corner of the arena, holding it there for as long as possible before moving to another point of fixation.

Flexibility. The ballet-dancer, the figure-skater, and the gymnast covet a supple body, able to move rapidly through extreme angles. As with most aspects of body function, there are inherited and acquired components. The joints of some individuals favour a wide range of motion. However, a restriction is usually imposed by the rising tension of muscles and tendons before the ultimate mechanical limit is reached. Stretching exercises can extend the potential range of movement allowed by the soft tissues, but care is necessary, particularly in young athletes, since excessive stretching can injure developing bones (Chapter 12).

Muscle structure. Individual muscle fibres are of two basic types. One contracts very quickly, and the other much more slowly. The proportions of the two types of fibre within individual muscles—and other details of muscle chemistry—have been clarified by the Swedish technique of needle biopsy. A large needle is plunged into the athlete's muscle under local anaesthesia, and a thin cylinder of tissue is withdrawn for microscopic and chemical analysis. The fast-twitch fibres have enzymes that enable them to continue functioning if their oxygen supply is interrupted, but the slow-twitch fibres are much more dependent on a steady income of oxygen. Muscles concerned with quick movements have a high proportion of fast fibres, while muscles that maintain body posture contain mostly slow fibres. In any given muscle, the relative proportions of the two fibre types is characteristic for a given class of sportsman. Competitors in endurance events—long-distance runners and cross-country skiers—have a much higher tally of slow fibres than participants in sprint events, ice-hockey, wrestling, swimming, and downhill skiing. This seems mainly an inherited suitability for a particular type of sport. Identical twins have closely similar fibre patterns, and as much as a year of strenuous training does not change the relative fibre counts.

The role of skill

The successful athlete uses many skills. In some sports, the crucial factor is the efficient conversion of chemical energy into human movement. In other events, energy expenditures are relatively small, but there is a need for delicate control of body position, appropriate interaction with other players, and a wise choice between alternative tactics.

Efficient movement. No machine is 100 per cent efficient. A car, for example, takes the chemical energy of petroleum, and converts a proportion into motive power; however, there is also much wastage as heat, noise, and unburnt exhaust gas. The human body has similar limitations. Wastage occurs both during the breakdown of phosphate energy stores (as the muscle contracts) and during recovery (as stores are replenished). Even given a good supply of oxygen to a muscle, efficiency is rarely better than 25 per cent, and if oxygen is not available the maximum possible efficiency drops to 13 per cent.

In some types of activity, the actual efficiency approaches these theoretical limits. Thus an average man riding a stationary bicycle in a laboratory can convert about 23 per cent of the food energy he consumes into mechanical or electrical power. While a top cyclist can develop tricks of pedalling to use more of the body muscles over a longer fraction of the pedal rotation, there is little scope for him to improve the conversion of chemical energy into leg movement. Nevertheless, he can reduce the work to be performed by making an appropriate choice of tyre-width and inflation pressure, and by keeping his body crouched in a position that minimizes wind-resistance while on the road.

The swimmer, in contrast, has a very low efficiency, often no better than 1–2 per cent. There is thus great scope for improvement of mechanical skill in this sport; indeed, we have estimated that in the University of Toronto swimming team at least 80 per cent of differences in performance between sprinters reflects differing levels of skill. Whereas the novice beats the water in a jerky fashion, the experienced swimmer minimizes energy losses by moving his arms at a consistent pace throughout the swimming stroke. The energy cost of supporting body weight is also reduced by keeping the lungs well filled with air, while drag is controlled by skilful horizontal positioning of the legs.

Uphill running is an interesting activity, since the efficiency of a hill climb (40–45 per cent) far exceeds what seems possible from the breakdown and reformation of body energy stores. The explanation of this paradox is that muscles and tendons are tensed as the foot hits the ground, and this provides a substantial part of the force needed for the next stride.

Running on a level track might seem to require fairly little skill. However, if competitors are followed over several years of intense training, track times continue to decrease, despite no detectable gains of body function. We must then conclude the athlete is making a more skilful use of his biological capabilities. Presumably, he has learnt to lift himself less with each stride and has found an optimum stride length for his event, reducing extraneous body movements and contouring his profile to minimize wind-resistance.

Controlled movement. A child who is just learning to play the piano must watch carefully to check where each finger is placed. However, daily practice allows the sensations associated with certain patterns of hand movement to be memorized in a part of the brain known as the cerebellum. Thereafter, the sight of a middle-C on a sheet of music becomes enough to initiate an appropriate sequence of muscle contractions. The playing of the keyboard has changed from a difficult problem, requiring the close attention of the will, to an automatic response needing no conscious thought on the part of the musician. Nevertheless, a severe emotional stress such as performing before a large audience can be enough to disturb the movement patterns pre-programmed in the brain.

Both automation of movement and its occasional deterioration under pressure can be seen in such skilled activities as pistol-shooting, gymnastics, and figure-skating. During a practice session, the Olympic pistol-shooter will nonchalantly approach the firing position, and with a quick movement of hand and arm place a bullet in the centre of the target. Two complete rows of perfect shots are carried out with equal facility, but as the final few targets are approached, the tension rises. The aim becomes slower and less automatic, and accuracy often diminishes.

The pressures of international competition can have a similar effect (Chapter 7). Competitors who have fared very well in regional and national competitions suddenly 'go to pieces' before an Olympic crowd. One example of this was provided by the 1972 Canadian white-water paddling team. During the Canadian national championships of 1971, the first three places were won in the order predicted from laboratory scores such as muscle strength and oxygen transporting power. Nevertheless, the team coach insisted that in Munich the man with the best laboratory score would finish behind the two runners-up. His verdict proved correct. Although faster than his two rivals between gates, the national champion apparently became nervous in the whirlpools, with a loss of his normal skill in manœuvring the boat. He was thus badly defeated, incurring more than twice as many penalties as the other two Canadian entrants.

Group interactions. It is not enough for the team sportsman to be a brilliant individualist. He must also develop the skills that will anticipate patterns of play by his opponents, and learn to work with fellow team-members towards a common objective. The leadership of the team captain, the example of other players, and the attitude of the coach all have a major bearing on group dynamics (Chapter 5).

Tactical skills. Tactical decisions are important in many sports. Even in something as straightforward as distance-running, there is the crucial decision as to when one's opponents should be challenged. If a spurt is made at the wrong point in a race, the contestant may incur the added effort of awkward passing on a bend. Unless he judges his own capacity carefully he may also become exhausted before he has crossed the finishing line.

The use of tactical skills reaches its zenith in dinghy-sailing. Experts have compared the plotting of a racing course to an elaborate game of chess, many possible moves and counter-moves being weighed before a decision is taken. The brain requires sugar for its functioning; we are all familiar with the irritability and poor judgement of the hungry driver. The blood sugar of the dinghy-sailor tends to be used up by the intense isometric contractions of the thigh and abdominal muscles when counter-balancing the boat; the yachtsman is thus at above-average risk of mental fatigue and bad tactical decisions. Perhaps for this reason, we have found a relationship between crew-ratings of tactical ability and blood-sugar readings.

Age and skill. The optimum age of the athlete varies greatly from one sport to another. Girls reach their peak performance as swimmers when in their early teens (Chapter 12). On the other hand, some soccer players such as Stanley Matthews have continued a very successful professional career into their forties. Biological functions begin to deteriorate soon after the age of twenty. The most rapid loss is in speed and agility. Sports that make intense physical demands—cross-country skiing, running, and swimming—are also performed best at a relatively early age. However, activities that require accumulated skills rather than physical excellence may well be won by older contestants (Chapter 13). A further consideration is professionalism. The amateur commonly loses interest in hard training once he senses that he has passed his peak, but a professional soccer player who is earning a high salary is likely to continue to play for as long as is practical.

Developing a performance index

Let us now suppose that we have a thick dossier of information about an athlete—data on his body-build, biological characteristics, and specialized skills. How can this material be combined to yield a performance index of value to the selector, the coach, and the team physician?

One immediate problem is the heterogeneity of our figures. It is as though we were trying to add two apples and three oranges to arrive at a score of five fruit. Height is measured in centimetres, oxygen transport is in millilitres of oxygen moved per minute per kilogram of body weight, and skill may well be an arbitrary score assigned by a coach or team-mate. This problem can be circumvented very simply if all observations are listed in order of magnitude. Let us suppose we are looking at a team of ten white-water paddlers. Height is important to competitive success. The tallest paddler is thus given a score of 10, the next tallest a score of 9, and so on (Table 6). Readings for muscular force, lung capacity, oxygen transporting power, tolerance of an oxygen debt, total weight of lean tissue, and skill as indicated by years of competition are treated in the same way. Adding across the table, we arrive at a cumulative score that reflects the influence upon performance of body-build, biological characteristics, and cumulative experience.

There are a few surprises, but in general the performance index lists competitors in roughly the same order as the coach. Discrepancies may show up a bias on the part of the coach, or they may reveal an unsuspected weakness in the contestant. According to the cumulative performance index, paddler number 3, with a score of 63, was superior to those rated 1 and 2 by the team coach. Canadian national competitions apparently vindicated the performance index, and we suspected the coach of some prejudice against number 3, who was a fairly recent German immigrant. However, the first three paddlers participated in the Munich Olympics, and there the verdict of the coach was substantiated. Contestant number 3 was unable to

Table 6. *Example showing a method used when combining data on body-build, biological characteristics, and skill into a single index of performance. The contestants are Canadian white-water paddlers, listed in the order of overall performance as perceived by the coach. A score of 10 has been awarded for the highest reading on any test, dropping to 1 for the poorest reading*

Contestant	Body-build (height)	Biological characteristics (muscle force)	(lung capacity)	(oxygen transport)	(oxygen debt)	(lean tissue)	Skill (years experience)	Cumulative performance index
1	8	4	6	10	10	8	10	56
2	9	9	9	6	8	7	8	56
3	10	10	10	9	5	10	9	63
4	8	7	8	7	7	6	8	51
5	8	8	7	9	6	9	1	48
6	5	2	3	4	9	4	5	32
7	5	5	4	4	2	3	8	31
8	1	1	1	1	1	1	5	11
9	2	3	5	2	3	5	2	22
10	3	6	3	6	4	2	5	29

sustain his skill under the pressures of international competition, a point not brought out by the laboratory testing.

The method of tabulation used is very helpful in showing areas that need emphasis in a training programme. The first of our white-water paddlers had a poor score on most measures of muscle force, and would thus benefit from exercises designed to increase his musculature. Contestant 2 had a limited oxygen transporting power, thus needing a long-distance running or paddling programme to build up his heart and lungs. Contestant 3 had the psychological problem already noted, but in addition he showed a poor tolerance of oxygen debt; his training plan should thus include frequent crowd exposures and repeated sprints to improve tolerance of the frantic bursts of paddling needed on approaching the whirlpool gates.

Several elements of sophistication can be added to the performance index when it is to be used for more serious scientific study. First, account has to be taken of the fact that tests differ in their predictive value; with the white-water paddlers, for example, the coach's ranking of performance is more closely related to oxygen transporting power than to muscular strength. Allowance for this difference could be made by allocating a higher score (say from 2 to 20) for oxygen transport readings. A related problem is that some tests overlap one another; thus, lung capacity is proportional to standing height, and part of the apparent effect of lung volumes on performance could be due to the hidden influence of height. There are computer methods of eliminating overlap, although in the case of lung capacity we can dispose of height very much more simply by expressing results as a percentage of anticipated figures in a person of the same stature. Lastly, our simple method of converting 'apples' and 'oranges' to a common scale of numbers ignored the magnitude of differences between team members; for example, the contestant scoring 10 for height may have been only slightly taller than the one scoring 9, but both may have been much taller than the person scoring 8. Again, the serious investigator allows for this question, adjusting scores according to the likelihood of their occurrence; an unusual and very advantageous height is awarded more points than a slight difference from a fellow competitor.

5
Mind over matter

In the previous chapter we saw the contribution of physical factors to athletic success, and sensed the occasional dominance of mind over matter. Predictions of the physiologist were sometimes confounded when apparently ideal bodies failed to respond as anticipated in the arena. We shall now look at certain dimensions of the psyche, including ideal personalities for the coach and for different classes of athlete, attitudes of the latter to pain, the role of aggression in contact sports, the importance of intelligence, and group factors contributing to the success of a team.

Personality and attitudes of coach and athlete

The coach. Unfortunately, very few coaches in the Western world have professional training. Some have made serious personal attempts to master the elements of nutrition, physiology, and psychology, but others rely exclusively on their childhood experience of a given sport, attempting to cloak ignorance with a blustering authoritarianism.

The superior coach is typically competitive and ambitious. He is not satisfied with mediocrity in his own life, nor is he prepared to tolerate it in those he is training. Strictness and perseverance must be coupled with a sensitivity to the needs of the individual athlete. The coach must discern what arouses a person's enthusiasm for both training and competition, and must seek to provide the required stimuli, physical and emotional. Empathy must not be carried to excess. Heart attacks are by no means unknown in coaches watching vital contests, and it is quite common for a coach to become so tense as to have a negative influence on the performance of the sportsman.

Intelligence must be matched by skill in communication. A competitor is much more likely to adhere to a proposed game plan if he understands why a particular phase of training is unpleasant, what are the anticipated gains from a procedure, and what are the chances of ultimate success. The good coach should show himself to be familiar with all facets of sports science, encouraging the athlete to share with him in a scholarly study of his chosen sport. Careful records should be maintained—not only track times, but details of diet, simple physiological data, and observations on psychological responses. Log books will be kept regarding not only the performer, but also his rivals, so that weaknesses of technique and temperament in the latter can be exploited in subsequent competitions.

Honesty and fairness are further important personal qualities in a coach. There is sometimes a temptation to soften the apparent demands of training, or to minimize the disappointment of poor results through a series of 'white lies'. However, sooner or later the athlete finds out that he is being hoodwinked, and loses respect for his coach.

An appropriate delegation of authority can be hard for the man who has a menial daily job, and finds in coaching a chance for status and self-fulfilment. There is a temptation to decide every detail of an athlete's life, down to the choice between a twelve- and a sixteen-ounce steak at the dinner table. Some over-burdened competitors may welcome having the minor questions of life resolved in this way, but in more independent personalities much conflict and hostility may arise. The wise coach knows how many decisions can be entrusted to each athlete, and considers one goal of training an increase of personal responsibility among his charges.

The athlete. Although the personality of the coach has had little formal study, much more attention has been directed to the athlete. Nevertheless, progress has been hampered by problems of methodology. One author looked at 400 articles on anxiety, and found that this had been measured in 200 different ways. Another commented that some of the terms used in describing personality had diametrically opposite meanings for different psychologists. Other practical difficulties have included the basing of reports on inadequate numbers of athletes, uncertainties regarding the level of competition under discussion, neglect of the impact of age and education upon manifestations of personality, and cultural changes in such concepts as masculinity and femininity which have occurred since the test methods were devised.

Where it has been possible to describe a characteristic athletic personality, there has still been little agreement as to whether this reflected the attraction of a specific type of person to a given sport, a subsequent moulding of the sample as those with less appropriate characteristics dropped out of competition, reactions of the individual to perpetual hero-worship, or a direct effect of rigorous training upon the development of character.

Perhaps because of these difficulties, formal research studies have not always demonstrated anticipated differences, either between different sports, or between top-level and 'run of the mill' competitors. Nevertheless, sports psychologists are confident that practical ways will soon be found to characterize the personality of top participants in a given event.

One feature noted in many studies of the top athlete is an achievement-oriented personality—a sense of ambition and a desire for dominance. The winner is the type of person who reacts best when the odds are stacked slightly against him. A related attitude is tough-mindedness. This reaches its peak in the racing-driver, but is seen also in other sportsmen, particularly participants in activities calling for aggression, with a risk of injury or death.

Conscientiousness is perhaps the most praiseworthy of athletic characteristics—the individual shows a willingness to persevere in the attainment of goals and ideals larger than himself. Educators would naturally like to know whether a basic tendency in this direction can be reinforced by the full rigours of athletic preparation, but the experiment of following a group of athletes throughout their careers has yet to be carried out.

A low level of anxiety and an ability to relax are important assets in skilled sports. However, a moderate level of anxiety may help the contact sportsman and the man who must undertake very strenuous endurance effort. Trustfulness is particularly vital to the diver, the gymnast, and other athletes who must accept much detailed instruction from the coach. The successful contestant is marked by a willingness to receive both teaching and discipline.

Most athletes have some tendency to extroversion. Performers near the top often play to the audience, but medal winners are more likely to regard spectators as a nuisance, interfering with their concentration. Because of the interaction between personality and arousal by the spectators (Chapter 7), extroversion and the associated acceptance of a crowd are more important in highly skilled sports than in events demanding simply strength or endurance. Formal personality tests suggest that individual sportsmen are dominating, aggressive, self-sufficient, introverted, self-absorbed, emotional, and creative, while team sportsmen are emotionally disciplined, extroverted, practical, and have a liking for group action.

Interesting insights into the make-up of a runner come from books such as Sir Roger Bannister's *First four minutes*. Psychologists have described Dr. Bannister as a very intelligent person, sensitive and easily hurt, with his interests in physical activity emerging from weakness rather than strength—a new objective found amid the unease and uncertainty of adolescence. Bannister himself speaks almost mystically of the discovery of power and beauty in the physical spontaneity and rhythm of running on the seashore, harmony and peace coming from the union of mechanical stimulation with some internal rhythm. He explains how his racing became valued as a source of peer acceptance; 'In the peculiar convention of English schools, it now seemed to me that I would be allowed by my schoolfellows to work harder because I also won races.' He sees perseverance and industry as the main attributes of a runner, and writes of the struggle to get the best from himself, with the growing realization that tiredness was not the same thing as exhaustion. He describes the agony of the final straight, with its need for the stimuli not only of fierceness and confidence, but also of fear—a fear that he first found when running from a gang of bullies as a small boy. Finally, he describes the tense months of waiting that precede a four-minute contest.

Other sports offer very different rewards to the participant.

The rhythmic solitude of long-distance running is in obvious contrast with the noisy bonhomie of the rugger club, the elegant grace of figure-skating, or the movement and power sensed by the sailor. It is thus logical that different types of personality would be attracted to these various classes of activity. One interesting suggestion is that the muscle men—wrestlers, line-men in American football, and weight-lifters—harbour doubts about their anticipated male sex role. Participation in traditional 'masculine' sports could thus be a compensatory form of activity. One investigator asked weight-lifters to interpret ink-blots (Rohrsach test), complete sentences, and carry out other 'projective' tests. Relative to other athletes, the results indicated the weight-lifters were shy, lacking in self-confidence, hostile to both men and women, and concerned to exaggerate their male characteristics. Another study noted that team sportsmen had an above average chance of having an older sister, with attendant difficulties in establishing the usual stereotype of male dominance.

Perception of pain. Casual observation shows that some people make more fuss about discomfort than others, and intuition suggests that the top athlete is one of the group who either inherits or cultivates an exceptional tolerance of pain. This allows an endurance competitor such as Bannister to push himself to exhaustion when he is already fatigued, and likewise permits a contact athlete to return to a game after a fall that would have left many of us crippled for a week.

Attempts to demonstrate an alteration in the perception of effort by the trained person have not been particularly successful. When measuring physical effort, the typical approach of the applied psychologist is to have his subject point to a joint numerical and verbal scale of categories that ranges from very very light to very very hard (Fig. 7). Training reduces the rating of exertion, but it also reduces the associated heart rate response. Thus, if exertion is classified at a fixed heart rate, there is little difference between the trained and the untrained person. There are two additional difficulties when dealing with athletes. The exertion scale was designed for industrial use, the intention being to measure fatigue among employees; the scale is thus reasonably sensitive in its middle part, but is much less

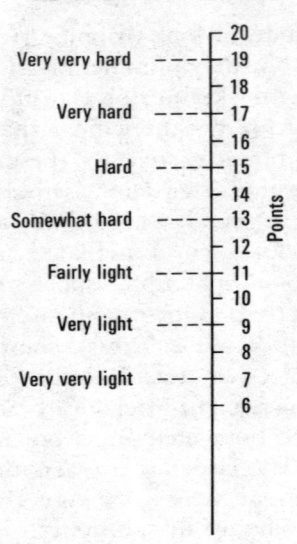

```
Very very hard  ---- 20
                     19
                     18
Very hard      ---- 17
                     16
Hard           ---- 15
                     14
Somewhat hard  ---- 13   Points
                     12
Fairly light   ---- 11
                     10
Very light     ---- 9
                     8
Very very light---- 7
                     6
```

FIG. 7. The rating of 'perceived exertion', according to a scale developed by Dr. Gunnar Borg.

satisfactory at its upper end, where a small increase in the intensity of work produces a large increase of symptoms. Furthermore, the perception of effort at a given heart rate depends upon the type of activity that is being undertaken; most individuals find running easier than cycling, for example. When an athlete visits the laboratory, he is often placed at the disadvantage of performing what is for him an unusual type of exercise. A swimmer may be asked to run uphill, or pedal a bicycle ergometer, and this militates against his describing the task as easy relative to a non-athletic individual's response.

An alternative approach is to ask the sportsman to make assessments of externally induced pain. In one simple technique, a football cleat is placed on the shin bone, under a blood pressure cuff, and the cuff is inflated progressively until the individual protests that the pain has become unbearable. Contact athletes such as football players and wrestlers tolerate more of such pain than tennis-players or golfers, who are in turn more tolerant than non-athletes.

Accepting that the athlete does blunt pain, how is this accomplished? We have noted personality characteristics such as emotional stability and willpower, which might enable him to endure more, but psychologists speak also of a general capacity to reduce sensory input. This is demonstrated by blind-folding a person and having him estimate the width of a bar. Some people ('augmenters') consistently over-estimate its size, while others ('reducers') under-estimate it. 'Reducers' are more extroverted than 'augmenters', they are more tolerant of pain, and they judge time as passing more slowly; the last characteristic is reflected in fast reaction and movement times.

Athletes generally are 'reducers', contact athletes more so than non-contact athletes, and one can demonstrate corresponding differences in time-judgements and reaction and movement times. Such observations have some practical importance, for while the differences of pain tolerance could be explained by a greater motivation on the part of the athletes, it is difficult to see how willpower could alter judgements of size or time.

As with personality, the intriguing question remains as to whether the exceptional pain tolerance of the competitor preceded athletic involvement or was caused by it. It is arguable that the extroverted born 'reducer' suffers from a perpetual lack of stimulation, and thus welcomes movement, speed, and even body contact in preference to sedentary pursuits. On the other hand, it is well recognized that a person can become habituated to a repeated stimulus, and for this reason sport participation probably contributes to the altered perception of physical stimuli.

Aggression. Many people see aggression as a positive attribute, giving the will to survive in a hostile world. However, it becomes an undesirable trait when it drives a man to acts outside legally prescribed bounds, or is directed to destructive ends. The aggressive sportsman is regarded with similar ambivalence. A competitor is roundly criticized if he lacks an aggressive spirit, yet at the same time he is despised if he reveals this characteristic to excess.

Is aggression inherited or acquired? William Golding, in his *Lord of the flies* gives a vivid description of how circumstances could allow average English boys to regress to vicious and aggressive savages. He apparently subscribes to the Freudian view that aggression is an inborn quality. Other psychologists maintain that aggression is mainly a learned behaviour, participation in aggressive activity fostering further acts of aggression with a lesser basis of true anger.

Observation of animals supports the instinctive view. Almost all species have an innate tendency to defend themselves against predators, usually by turning on them in an aggressive manner. Accompanying physiological disturbances emanate from a region of the brain called the hypothalamus—the pulse races, the heart pumps more strongly, and other defence mechanisms are mobilized in what Cannon has called a 'fight or flight' reaction.

While modern man is still faced by occasional predators, culture has decreed that aggressive behaviour should be suppressed. Advocates of sport have thus suggested that physical activity can help to resolve the physiological disturbance, lessening aggressive behaviour in normal daily life. The idea of such a catharsis goes back to ancient Greece. Aristotle believed that a dramatic portrayal of violent acts, with appropriate punishment of the evil-doer, would purge the spectators of dangerous emotions. Current discussion of violence in television indicates that the cathartic value of drama is still far from accepted. There are special problems in applying the concept to participation in violent sport. The 'enemies' are perhaps more clearly identified in the stadium than in other areas of life, but the rules of the contest usually prevent a free release of the emotions. Often, anger must be vented against an outsider, or even an inanimate object such as a punch ball, rather than against the causative agent.

Frustration increases aggressive behaviour, and there are many potential sources of frustration in athletics—the frustration of losing while concealing one's humiliation, of playing well without adequate recognition, of receiving excessive criticism, of being worked too hard, or kept too late at practices. All of these sources of annoyance militate against a successful catharsis.

Experimental analyses have used 'projective' tests, seeing how a player draws or describes something before and after a game. There are obvious semantic problems with such an approach, and no one seems to have tried to find out whether there is any relationship between what is being described as aggressive picture-drawing and objective measures of the mood of a contest such as the number of penalty shots awarded. The pictures may reveal hostility rather than anger and be influenced by feelings of guilt, anxiety, and loss of ego secondary to failures of self-control, rather than by aggressive activity itself. Particularly strong feelings of guilt have been described in boxers, perhaps because overt aggression remains unpunished.

Some psychologists have suggested a distinction should be drawn between hot-tempered anger, induced by and directed towards an external stimulus ('reactive aggression') and the coldly calculated but equally fierce body-check ('instrumental aggression'). The first could well find relief in vigorous aggressive behaviour, but the second is unaccompanied by hostile emotions, finding its rewards in the personal satisfaction of a tackle well executed, the approving roar of the crowd, and the resultant victory. Unless the rewards of instrumental aggression can be given a negative slant (feelings of guilt, crowd disapproval, the award of penalty points, disqualification, and defeat), indulgence of such behaviour is likely to increase rather than diminish the frequency of its occurrence. Most athletes normally view a contest as a form of instrumental aggression, although some competitors freely admit they cannot win unless they see their opponent as an enemy and become angry with him. Further, the distinction between the two types of aggression is by no means absolute. Cold, instrumental aggression can change to hot reactive anger with the taunts of the crowd, the tongue lashing of a coach, or the pain of a body blow.

Bearing in mind these difficulties of interpretation, projective tests have shown no differences in North American football players before and after scrimmaging. There was a diminution in what was regarded as aggression at the end of the season, but this could reflect an increase of guilt for past aggression as the rewarding cheers of the supporters were withdrawn. An apparent diminution of aggression in wrestlers after a contest could be interpreted in the same manner. Violent sport probably helps to restore physiological equilibrium following hot anger, although it is not necessarily more effective than other diversions. On the other hand, coldly calculated acts of aggression yield the rewards that perpetuate the habit. Even where catharsis is apparently achieved, there is no guarantee that the effects will be carried from the sports field into the more complex problems of everyday society. Indeed, hostilities between cities are sometimes increased rather than diminished through sports rivalries.

Professional ice-hockey is particularly plagued by violence. Here, dirty play may no longer be an expression of aggression, but rather the normal, expected behaviour. The young player quickly realizes that the very competitive path to a major league team will be opened to him not for skill in skating, passing, and shooting, but for an ability to violate the rules through tripping, elbowing, fighting, and the use of his stick. Some sociologists have suggested this stems from the low socio-economic background of the average hockey player; in such society, they argue that the recognized virtues are courage, physical strength, resilience, and a willingness never to back down from a fight.

How may the worst effects of aggression be eliminated from sport? In animal societies, one solution has been a ritualistic fight, as between an older buck deer and a young challenger, with subsequent formation of an order of precedence, preserved by threats and avoidance reactions rather than by actual fighting. Sport also offers opportunities to establish orders of dominance, and occasional referees have been tempted to allow fist fights for this purpose. The tendency to aggression is strongest when there are apparent rewards for such behaviour—early wins and a vociferous group of supporters. Much also depends on leadership, whether aggressive or peaceable. In Ontario, the attorney-general has recently reinforced refereeing by bringing court cases against violent professional hockey-players. However, the best solution to violence lies in an adjustment of the reward system, with much less emphasis on winning and gate receipts, and more credit given for a game well played. Above all, the rules of the game must be structured in such a way that misdemeanours invariably diminish the chances of victory.

Intelligence and mental health. Many people have supposed there is an inevitable distinction between brain and brawn, and perhaps in a reaction against such suggestions physical educators have sought to 'prove' that sport enhances the learning process. One review noted that seventy studies had been carried out in 434 high schools, with a fairly equal division of data 'proving' and 'disproving' the intelligence of the athlete. A modicum of intelligence is undoubtedly necessary to become a top competitor in almost any sport, but the more general justification of athletic programmes in terms of their academic virtues has been somewhat deflated by the success of sports for the mentally handicapped!

Intelligence is always hard to define, and the criterion adopted in many published studies has been the fallible evidence of class marks. At some institutions, it is not unknown for athletic scholars to receive special tutoring, or even 'kind' marking to allow them to pass their examinations. More formal tests of intelligence recognize many components, and some attributes such as motor ability are much more likely to be influenced by physical activity than others such as mathematical and verbal skills. Unfortunately, scores depend not only on innate intelligence, but also on self-image—how good an opinion a person has of himself. If the ego of a sportsman is boosted by the adulation of a large group of 'fans', test results may rise relative to true intelligence.

With regard to academic standing, moderate amounts of sport can relieve the boredom of uninterrupted study and provide an arousing stimulus (Chapter 7) that may improve attention in lectures and examinations alike. On the other hand, long hours of physical training can reduce opportunities for study. In one experiment, intramural athletes, that is to say those playing friendly games within the university, had higher marks than non-athletes, but intercollegiate competitors who had to give themselves to more serious training had lower marks than either of the other two groups.

The main determinant of athletic intelligence is probably initial selection. If indeed athletes are an achievement-oriented group, this will be reflected in their attitudes to study as well as to play. Some, like Roger Bannister, may even play in order to be allowed to study!

Are there differences of intelligence between various classes of sportsmen? It is plain that some activities call for more thought than others—the chess-like manœuvrings of a dinghy-sailor, for example, stand in marked contrast with the 'gut' effort of a distance runner. Tradition has regarded the North American football player as one of the lower forms of intellectual life, and at least one study has given a modest confirmation of this impression. The average class marks were 65·9 per cent for all types of athlete, 64·9 per cent for non-athletes, but only 62·9 per cent for football players. Nevertheless, apparent differences of intelligence between the various classes of sportsmen probably arise mainly from factors of personality. In particular, the extrovert, attracted to team sports, makes a less satisfactory student than the introvert.

Another hobby-horse of the professional physical educator has concerned the supposed greater mental health of the top athlete. Much has been made of the unity of mind and body. It has been argued that sport improves physical health, and that it must therefore improve mental health.

In practice, much depends both on actual success and on attitudes towards success. If an athlete senses he is gaining skills that will carry him to the top, this can be very satisfying. On the other hand, failures increase feelings of insecurity, particularly if reinforced by a coach's fierce criticism. The best effects on the mental health of the competitor are likely to occur when the emphasis of his entourage is on sportsmanship, enjoyment, and teamwork rather than winning; when competition is divorced from the pressures of community and national pride; and when losing does not bring automatic blame and rejection.

Unfortunately, top competitions are rarely conducted in such a spirit. The pressures of excessive competition can even give rise to physical symptoms: dizziness, headache, lack of appetite, and nervous tics. A proportion of athletes show above-average concern about minor ailments. However, the physician treating such patients must have the empathy to realize the threat that a common cold or stomach cramp can present to the rightful reward of several years of arduous preparation. It is also fair to add that most athletes are well-adjusted. Those who do not have outstanding personal qualities fall by the wayside during the training period.

Group dynamics. The ability to function as a team is largely independent of the skill of individual players. Nevertheless, in many sports group-skills are more important than individual brilliance.

Group success is contagious, readily infecting even the spectator. However, too frequent victories can cause a disastrous euphoria. The objective of a team shifts from winning a sequence of games to mutual admiration—commendable in friendly sport, but hardly conducive to victory in the cup-final. The loss of an occasional match can weld a team together, and re-orient it towards victory. On the other hand, repeated losses cause a precipitous fall of group morale, with mutual dissatisfaction, loss of cohesion, and a search for scapegoats. Some hostility may show players that they should concentrate on the game rather than on friendship, but excessive conflict dissipates the energy of the team, with poor performance by individual members. The coach should seek to channel hostility into physical performance, insisting that individual team-members assume their share of responsibility for any failures. Isolated members must be brought back within the group, the over-dominant controlled, and a spirit of co-operation re-established. In particular, the correct balance must be struck between the opposing objectives of becoming a mutual admiration society or a ruthless band of robots set to win at all costs.

The leader plays a critical role in any sport. Some are appointed by outside authority, such as a government-selected national coach. Some are self-appointed, stepping into a power-vacuum within a club. Some emerge naturally from a consensus among the players. The last type is the most effective. Such a leader is usually more capable than his team-mates, and in contact sports he may also be physically larger. However, he must not be too obviously superior to his fellow players, or his effectiveness will be lost.

6
Choosing your parents

In this chapter, we shall look more closely at the question of 'choosing our parents wisely', and will try to partition responsibility for athletic success between inheritance, childhood nurture, and more immediate training. The topic is of vital concern to Olympic strategists. If the genes are dominant, then the key to success lies in mass testing, exhaustive searches of the national population for champions already hidden in our midst. On the other hand, if nurture and training are the major factors in athletic victory, government priorities could well become the provision of coaches and training facilities to allow adequate preparation of any young person with the time and the inclination to pursue a particular sport.

The inherited component of success

How easy is it to chart the genetic profile of a successful athlete? Biochemists now have the capacity to relate chemical architecture to man's development and function, to describe the characteristic chains of nucleic acids within the chromosomes of the cell nucleus that set the body's patterns of protein formation. However, the sports scientist has looked at the inheritance of athletic success with much simpler tools. Perhaps for this reason, we still await a clear-cut answer on the relative importance of nature and nurture.

Isolated communities. One possible way of studying inheritance might be to examine small and isolated communities. Just as a pure breed of dog can emerge by careful matings of a small colony over many generations, so in man a closed settlement of perhaps a couple of hundred people might give rise to a population with a much reduced variation of inherited characteristics. Data to answer this question has become available over the last several years, as investigators associated with the International Biological Programme have tested tribes living in remote Arctic settlements, small tropical islands, and secluded mountain valleys. Unfortunately, the quantities likely to influence athletic success—such as the oxygen transporting power of the heart and lungs—have varied just as much as in large cities.

For what it may be worth, this strand of evidence speaks against a strong influence of inheritance. However, even if variation had been less in the isolated communities, much further work would have been needed to establish the importance of genes relative to environment; in particular, it would have been necessary to prove that variations of childhood nurture and subsequent life style were as great in the closed society as in a major metropolis.

Blood grouping. The determination of blood groups is another trick of the geneticist well known in legal battles over paternity. Medical problems such as a high blood pressure and a liability to heart attacks seem linked to people with an unhappy 'choice' of blood group. The inference is that the genes responsible for blood grouping and those that determine liability to certain diseases are inherited as a 'package deal'. It is fairly easy to see how this could happen with some diseases—the malfunction of a single biochemical reaction could lead to the accumulation of an excess of materials such as cholesterol within the body. But the factors determining athletic success are much more complex, making it less likely that they can be described by a single, blood-group-related genetic package.

An experiment of this type was carried out in one Eskimo community a few years ago. The population was carefully divided into three groups—those with high, average, and low levels of working capacity, and a wide variety of blood groups was determined. Again, the answer to the question of inheritance was negative—there were no differences of blood groupings that could be related to differences of physical fitness and working capacity.

Looking at twins. A comparison of identical and dissimilar twins is perhaps the commonest method of studying human inheritance. Let us first see how the geneticist uses this method. He assumes that in identical twins, the variability of any measurement reflects the joint effects of technical errors and environment. In dissimilar twins, the variability is greater, owing to the added influence of inherited differences (Fig. 8). Technical

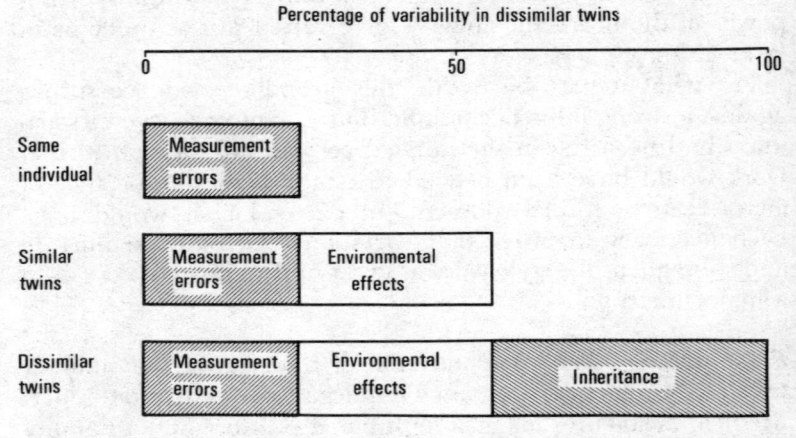

FIG. 8. The use of twins to apportion the variability of data between environmental effects and inheritance, taking into account measurement errors. Measurement errors are determined by the repeated testing of the same individual. The residue of variability in dissimilar twins is apportioned between environment and inheritance by a comparison with the variability encountered in similar twins.

errors can be estimated by repeating observations on the same individual. The effect of genes is found from the *difference* in variability between similar and dissimilar twins, and finally the environmental contribution is calculated as the variability found in similar twins after subtraction of the component due to technical errors.

Stated in such terms, it seems a simple enough mathematical exercise. However, there are several pitfalls in the practical application of the method. One big weakness is the assumption that technical errors and environmental differences are each equal for the two types of twins. In fact, environment is better matched for similar than for dissimilar twins. Mothers think it 'cute' to dress such children in the same style of clothing, to buy them identical items of sports equipment, and so on. Further, we are trying to discover the relative importance of inheritance and environment in the general population rather than in a small sample of twins, and there can be little argument that ordinary individuals encounter a wider range of environment than any pair of twins, similar or dissimilar. The manipulation of variability must thus be regarded with some suspicion.

Application of twin techniques in sports medicine has been limited by the small number of individuals who are both twins and athletes. Dr. Vassilis Klissouras of Montreal gathered together fifteen pairs of similar twins and ten pairs of dissimilar twins. Similarity of the twins was established not only from outward appearances (hair colour and texture, shape of the ear lobes, eye colour, and iris patterns) but also by a comparison of finger-prints and a biochemical examination of the blood. Various measurements of fitness such as the oxygen transporting power of the blood were then completed, and a formal analysis of variability was carried out. The answers suggested that as much as 94 per cent of the components of fitness that they measured was inherited! However, it seems clear from the original report that the chances of reaching any other conclusion were small, even before the experiment began. The authors freely admitted that the children studied all had 'similar upbringing, living standards, and leisure-time activity'. The results thus have limited application to the world outside the laboratory, where unfortunately upbringing, living standards, and leisure activities are seldom equal.

The difficulty in reaching reliable conclusions from this type of study was underlined when Dr. Klissouras carried out a similar experiment in Jyvaskyla, Finland. Again, he applied a wide range of physiological fitness tests, but this time he calculated that almost *all* of the variability was due to environment rather than inheritance.

An alternative approach is to see what effect training has on one of a pair of similar twins, using the other as a 'control'. At the age of thirteen, Klissouras found that both trained and untrained partners made large gains of oxygen transporting power over a ten-week study, the increases amounting to 16 per cent and 13 per cent respectively. This suggests another problem in dealing with twins—presumably, the partner that the laboratory hoped was 'untrained' shared in the programme of added physical activity when the back of the investigator was turned. In support of this suggestion, the effects of training became more distinct in older twins, where the outside activities of the partners were presumably more independent. Thus, at the age of sixteen, respective changes over a ten-week programme were 21 per cent in the 'trained' group, and only 3 per cent in the 'untrained' controls. One pair of twenty-one-year-old twins volunteered for testing. Up to the age of fifteen, they had both been very active. However, at the time of examination, one had become a rather sedentary salesman, spending a great deal of time in his car and participating only occasionally in such unorganized sports as swimming and golf. By a happy chance, his brother had continued year-round training for Canadian football and ice-hockey; thus the latter now had an advantage of 47 per cent in terms of oxygen transport, and of 61 per cent in terms of his tolerance of oxygen lack ('oxygen debt') in the muscles. However, both boys still had identical slow resting heart rates of fifty-four beats a minute.

These examples are enough to show that although in theory twins provide most of the answers to genetic problems, in practice results are conflicting. Some twin studies suggest inheritance is very important for a high level of fitness, while others show major responses to training with almost no effect from the genetic make-up of the individual.

Family relationships. One way around the shortage of twins is to extend the genetic analysis, comparing parents with each other and with their offspring. Some years ago, the American expert on body types, Dr. Stanley Garn, pointed out that the heavy, muscular build needed for contact sports was much more likely to be found in the offspring of large-framed parents than in the progeny of either large- and small-framed parents, or of two small-framed parents. His observation immediately conjures up Orwellian visions of an unscrupulous government insisting upon marriages between successful competitors in specific events. But 'Big Brother' is hardly needed to induce such unions; the humbler darts of Cupid seem likely to produce the same end-result, given the ever-increasing female participation in international competition.

Formal comparisons of parent with parent, parent with child, and child with brother or sister have yet to be carried out with respect to characteristics of interest to the sports scientist. However, use of the method in certain branches of medicine has brought to light another problem. Despite almost equal genetic contributions from the two parents, children quickly show more resemblance to their mothers than to their fathers. When choosing our parents, it is much more important that our mother have the attributes of Diana than that our father be a veritable Apollo. The greater maternal influence reflects not only care fostered on the child after birth, but environmental experiences transmitted to the unborn child. A father who smokes, for example, is damaging his own health and polluting his house for others who live there; however, the mother who smokes is also assuming the responsibility of exposing her unborn and highly susceptible child directly to the toxic fumes of carbon monoxide found in cigarette smoke.

A pragmatic approach. A pragmatic approach to the importance of genes is to test whether one could produce a top athlete simply by a process of exhaustive selection. Let us suppose, for example, that we wished to win an international cross-country ski championship. This type of event calls for vigorous activity of most of the large muscles in the body, and one of the main requirements of success is an outstanding oxygen transporting power on the part of the heart and lungs. The current record, found in a Finnish contestant, is about 92 ml of oxygen pumped per min per kg of body-weight. To ensure success, we would thus like our entrant to have a physiological capability of at least 96 ml per min per kg.

The ordinary, rather sedentary, working-class young man in Toronto has, on average, a score of no more than 48 ml per min per kg. Having tested quite a large sample of the population, we know the effects of an exhaustive search (Fig. 9). Every sixth candidate has a score of 56 ml per min per kg, every fortieth man achieves 64 ml per min per kg, and about one in 2000 reaches 72 ml per min per kg. There are mathematical procedures for estimating the results of a yet more exhausting

CHOOSING YOUR PARENTS

Oxygen transporting power (ml of Oxygen per minute per kilogram of body weight)

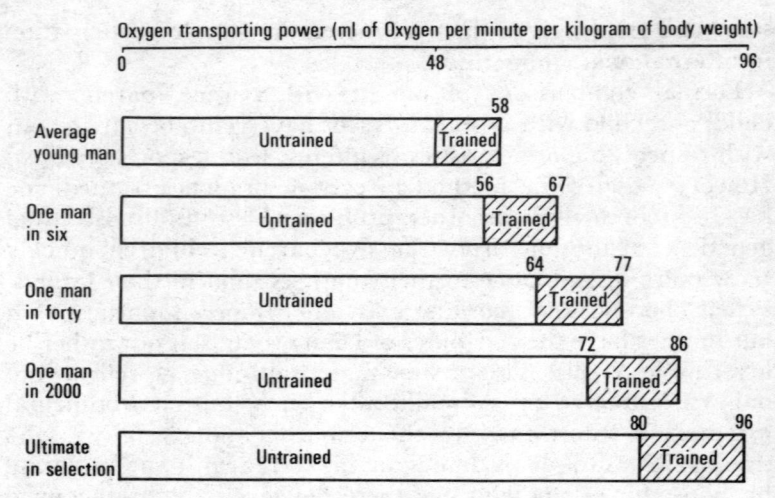

Category	Untrained	Trained
Average young man	—	58
One man in six	56	67
One man in forty	64	77
One man in 2000	72	86
Ultimate in selection	80	96

FIG. 9. A diagram showing the relative importance of training and an exhaustive search of the population in the emergence of an athlete with an exceptional oxygen transporting power.

search of a population, but it does not take great intuition to see that a limit is likely to be reached at about 80 ml per min per kg. Searching has in fact realized only about two-thirds of our objective. Fortunately, the residue can be made good by rigorous training; this augments oxygen transport by at least 20 per cent (from 80 ml per min per kg wt to 96) possibly producing rather larger gains in those individuals who have low initial scores.

We might thus conclude that two-thirds of the difference between the average person and the top long-distance athlete is inherited, and one-third is due to training. However, the contribution of the genes has probably been over-estimated in this simple calculation, as some of the differences found in the general population are due to environment rather than heredity. Thus, in one population of British servicemen, we estimated that more than a third of differences in pulse responses to physical activity was due simply to variations in the amount of physical activity undertaken by the individual soldiers.

There is still scope for an imaginative scientist to provide a more convincing answer, but it appears unlikely that inheritance accounts for much more than a half of differences between the sedentary person and the fit athlete.

The environmental component

The successes of distance runners such as Kip Keino from the mountains of Kenya have drawn attention to possible long-term effects of environment upon the performance of the top athlete. A man born in the mountains, for example, seems to perform well at altitudes such as Mexico City (about 2240 m), and may even have an advantage in competitions at sea-level. Often, we think of environment in a more immediate sense, such as the difficulty in sustaining world records on a hot and humid day. Strictly speaking, environment includes all influences other than heredity—the stimulating or depressing action of various drugs, interactions with the crowd, diet, training, and so on. Many of these topics will be discussed elsewhere. In this section, we will consider briefly the influence of environment upon inheritance, the consequences of a life-long sojourn in an adverse environment, and possible advantages gained from training camps in exotic resorts.

Environment and inheritance. The giraffe provides a good illustration both of the way in which environment can lead to the development of an unusual body form, and also of the two suggestions made to account for this phenomenon. Lamarcke proposed that some creature of the forest stretched his neck to reach the tender shoots on the higher branches when food was in short supply, and this unusual characteristic was transmitted to his offspring. In contrast, Darwin held that a proportion of the species were born with a tendency to long necks, and this gave them an advantage in the struggle for life. Thus, over a series of generations, a long-necked species tended to emerge. Lamarckian views had a brief resurgence in Russia around 1950, through the writings of Dr. Lysencko, a wheat-breeding botanist. However, most scientists now accept Darwin's ideas as the correct explanation of the many ways in which natural species have succeeded in adapting to unusual habitats.

Do similar adaptations occur in man? Were there unusual changes in the genetic code ('mutations') at some point in history, permitting small segments of the human race to colonize unusual environments such as the extreme cold of the Arctic, the steaming heat of dense jungles, and the rarefied atmospheres of high altitudes? And if so, would this type of adaptation afford to the peoples concerned an advantage in current athletic competitions?

Anthropologists are much less secure in their beliefs than was the case a few years ago. Take the question of standing height and related body measurements. Elaborate theories had been proposed to account for racial differences of body-size. The Bergmann–Allen laws, for example, related stature to the distance from the equator. It was argued that the lanky individual could dissipate body heat readily, giving an advantage in the tropics, while a short and compact body form helped to conserve heat in the Arctic. Explanations were readily forthcoming for exceptions to the laws; thus jungle pygmies needed to be small to crawl through narrow gaps in the undergrowth. Unfortunately for the theorists, body form has not proved a stable criterion of race. Groups such as the Japanese, the Lapps, and the Eskimos, historically short peoples, are now rapidly approaching the height of North Americans and Western Europeans. Careful observers are thus beginning to suspect that body-size depends more upon nutrition and other aspects of environment than upon inheritance.

Could natural selection ever work in man? Body peculiarities tend to be very specific, and an advantageous shape for one type of activity may be a severe handicap in other forms of endeavour. While the giraffe enjoys shoots from the top of the tree, there must be times when he wishes his neck were shorter. In the same way, a man well-endowed to be a heavy-weight wrestler is at a substantial disadvantage in distance-running (and vice-versa!). Such specificity does not matter to the athlete, provided that he has chosen a suitable mode of competition. However, the challenges faced by primitive man are diverse rather than specific, and there is no guarantee that an inherited peculiarity advantageous on one day would not prove an embarrassment later in the week. Further, as in many athletic contests, skill and motivation can triumph over a powerful body-build. This was brought home to us in our studies of the Eskimo hunters at Igloolik in the North West Territories. One wizened old inhabitant set 48 traps, and by a seven-mile sled journey caught 21 foxes in less than 24 hours. A second man, seemingly much more powerful, set 24 traps on each of two occasions. He journeyed an exhausting 100 miles over the ice-floes, and came home empty-handed. Clearly, the first man was a much more skilful hunter, and although his physical inheritance might have been judged disappointing, his brain would allow him to survive in a season when his stronger companion might well die of starvation.

The other question now emerging is uncertainty regarding the strength of evolutionary pressures. Starvation, for example, has not been as common a threat as is sometimes supposed. According to Lee, the very primitive !Kung bushmen of the African desert can survive quite well by working an average of $1\frac{1}{2}$ days per week. Those who are physically weaker or less clever at finding food can easily compensate by increasing their labours to 2 or 3 days per week. Even in the bleak hunting grounds of the Arctic, it is rare for the hunter to spend more than 3 days out of 7 away from the settlement. Warfare has provided a more effective method of eliminating weaklings in some tropical islands, and in most primitive societies disease has played a selecting role, particularly in the first year of life.

Despite these various uncertainties in evolutionary theory, some regional peculiarities are known, features that cannot be induced by a temporary residence in the adverse environment. Thus men such as the Sherpas, born at very high altitudes, show an unusually small increase of breathing in response to oxygen deprivation; it appears that the oxygen pressure detectors in their neck arteries ('carotid chemo-receptors') have a reduced sensitivity to changes of oxygen pressure in the arterial blood. In consequence, the high-altitude natives are spared the discomforts of over-breathing that sometimes beset the athlete newly arrived in such places as Mexico City. However, it is less certain whether this functional peculiarity is an advantage when competing at sea-level.

Adaptations to a tropical climate are not clearly identified. Ladell suggested that when vigorous activity was required in the heat, Nigerian soldiers fared no better than Europeans who had spent a few days adjusting to the climate. One interesting adaptation to a cold environment seen in the Eskimo is an altered distribution of sweat glands. During vigorous exercise, sweating occurs freely over the face, but the rest of the body remains almost dry. This feature of body function is important to Arctic survival, for if the clothes become soaked with sweat, they lose their insulating properties and frostbite rapidly follows. Canadian ('white') troops are well aware of this problem and find that when on an Arctic manœuvre they cannot prudently move at more than a brisk walk. In any distance competition under Arctic conditions, the Eskimo would have a real advantage, but on the other hand the lesser use of the body surface for sweat evaporation would restrict his performance in a tropical climate.

The International Biological Programme has made comparisons of many physiological measurements between different groups of primitive tribespeople. There is some suggestion that groups living in the mountains and in the cold northern regions have higher scores than tropical peoples with respect to measures of endurance such as the oxygen transporting power of the heart and lungs. However, it is difficult to be certain that this is not due to differences in current patterns of physical activity between the three environments, rather than to any more permanent inherited adaptations.

Long-term adaptations. Several years of life in a mountainous region produce a number of changes in body function; we will discuss three. The number of red cells in the blood is increased, sometimes by as much as 20–30 per cent; given a proportionate rise in the haemoglobin content of individual red cells, the implication is that 20–30 per cent more oxygen can be carried for every litre of blood that is pumped around the circulation. When the athlete first arrives at high altitude, the oxygen content of the blood is reduced by the rarefied air, and the increase of red cell population does much to compensate for this difficulty. There may also be some competitive advantage during a brief visit to sea-level; however, such gains of performance are at best transitory. The red cell count drops to normal within about two weeks of a return to sea-level, and even in the interim it is by no means certain that the thick and sticky nature of the high-altitude-adapted blood does not restrict the maximum pumping ability of the heart.

A second important adjustment at high altitude is a reduction in the sodium bicarbonate content of the blood and tissues. The acidity of the body depends largely on the ratio of bicarbonate to carbon dioxide content. In the early days at high altitude, attempts to compensate for the thin air, by deep breathing, pump too much carbon dioxide out of the tissues; they become alkaline, and normal function is impaired. However, once the bicarbonate levels have dropped, greater ventilation of the lungs can proceed without difficulty. The main disadvantage to the competitor, both at altitude and at sea-level, is that the bicarbonate is also required to mop up the acids formed when the rate of working of the muscles exceeds their immediate oxygen supply; thus, altitude adaptation tends to impair middle-distance events where an oxygen debt must be tolerated.

The third adjustment to high altitude is within the muscle fibres, where the concentrations of many enzymes increase over the course of one to two weeks. This is plainly of some advantage to competition both at high altitude and at sea-level.

Prolonged residence in the tropics produces a number of the changes associated with vigorous physical training. This is hardly surprising, since one of the consequences of sustained activity is a general increase of body temperature. The normal resting value is a little over 37 °C. However, readings as high as 41 °C have been described not only in top-level marathon runners but also in middle-aged coronary patients running a similar distance. One of the prime adjustments to a warm climate seems an earlier and more copious secretion of sweat when exercising at any given percentage of maximum effort. As a result, the heat produced by the exercise is dissipated by evaporation of sweat rather than by pumping of blood to the skin. This means in turn that the heart can pump less blood in moderate effort, and that during maximum exercise a larger proportion of the heart's output can be directed to the active muscles. Many international contests are run under very hot conditions. Heat exhaustion is quite common, and deaths due to over-heating of athletes are not unknown (Chapter 9). The competitor from a tropical region is thus at an advantage in any sustained form of activity unless the event is contested under cool conditions.

Prolonged residence in the Arctic also leads to adjustments of body function. Shivering and discomfort are less at any given temperature, while the blood pressure and the pulse rate rise less if the hands or the face are suddenly exposed to cold air or cold water. Athletes are rarely cold, even in Winter Games, and changes in the response to cold have little influence upon the chances of an Arctic resident who competes under more temperate conditions. The one exception to this generalization is the cross-channel swimmer. The casual bather at Folkestone or Dover knows that the English Channel is quite cold (5–10 °C) even in summer, and on an eight-hour trip from Calais to Dover tolerance to feelings of cold with a resistance to shivering must be of some benefit.

Exotic training camps. Exotic training camps are quite popular with officials. Who can argue against two weeks at St. Moritz? However, it is less clearly established that periods spent in such delightful surroundings are helpful to the performance of the athlete.

The idea of organizing training camps at mountain resorts was first conceived in the years before the Mexico City Olympics. Athletes and their advisors were concerned about a possible deterioration of their performance in Mexico, and many teams spent several weeks attempting to adjust to such altitudes. Performance was poor in the first couple of days as a result of the headache, nausea, and vomiting of mountain sickness (Chapter 9); however, this passed as the bicarbonate levels of the body were reduced. The red cell production of the body was stimulated immediately, but the full changes of the permanent resident were seen only in the minority who passed several months at high altitude; in the first two or three weeks, further deterioration of performance occurred because fluid was lost from the body and the heart in effect lacked blood to pump around. One might suppose that the best preparation for a Mexican contest would be to spend several months at altitude, giving time for full development of additional red cells and replacement of missing fluid. Unfortunately, even if it were permitted by international rules, such a luxury would rarely be possible for the true amateur who must work for his living. Further, there is no guarantee that the sacrifices involved would bring the desired reward. Prolonged absence from home and family has a negative effect on many athletes, and interruption of normal training schedules might more than outweigh the theoretical advantages. There seems to be much to commend the alternative of competing about three days after ascent. This arrangement allows time for recovery from the journey and any subsequent mountain sickness, provides opportunity to explore the field of contest, and permits practice of the altered pace needed in the new environment; at the same time, it avoids the gross deterioration of performance sometimes seen in the second and third weeks at high altitude.

Since the Mexico City games, some teams have had the notion that mountain training might also give an advantage during sea-level competition. If this were true, timing would be crucial. Two or three days would be needed to allow for re-adjustment of such things as bicarbonate and blood volume, if the contest were delayed by more than about two weeks most of the increase in red cell count produced by the high-altitude camp would have disappeared. In practice, negative factors such as interruption of training seem to outweigh the theoretical benefits of high-altitude training. There may even be medical dangers, and two German athletes reputedly sustained heart attacks while at high-altitude camps. A recent meeting of the British Olympic Association thus ruled firmly against further use of this practice.

No-one seems to have proposed temporary camps in the jungle or the Arctic as yet. A great deal of heat adaption could occur during a two-week stay in the tropics, and in theory this could benefit the distance performer; however, in practice, interruption of training with depletion of body fluids and minerals might cancel out the changes favourable to success. Many of the body's adjustments to cold also occur over the space of about two weeks; however, it is hardly necessary for the very-long-distance swimmer to go to the expense of visiting the Arctic. He can gain the necessary exposure to cold simply by swimming in deep sea water rather than in a heated swimming pool.

The role of training

Secrets of preparing the athlete for major competition will be discussed later (Chapter 7). Here, we are concerned simply to relate the dividends of an effective training schedule to genetic endowment and to other environmental influences.

The training response depends on the individual's starting point. Absolute zero is complete bed rest, the ultimate in sedentary lifestyle. All of the body muscles are wasted, attempts at walking produce dizziness and severe shortness of breath, and X-rays show a marked loss of calcium, particularly from the weight-bearing bones. Scientists have not carried out any formal training experiments on permanent invalids, but have followed normal sedentary individuals and athletes during several weeks of enforced bed rest and the subsequent recovery period. Astronauts, temporarily deprived of gravity and confined to a small space capsule, have provided another example of deconditioning and recovery. Heart attacks and leg injuries again lead to weeks or even months of immobilization. Similar changes of body function are seen in all of these conditions. By way of example, we may take the oxygen transporting power of patients attending our cardiac rehabilitation programme. When we first see them, their oxygen transport level is only about 70 per cent of that for a sedentary person of the same age. However, a year or more of hard and progressive training pushes the figure to 110–115 per cent of normal, a 50–60 per cent increase relative to the hospitalized base-line. Compulsory bed rest likewise reduces the function of an ordinary person by 20–30 per cent over 2–3 weeks; renewed activity gives recovery of the starting values within 2–3 weeks, and if the exercise is continued there may be a further 20 per cent gain of oxygen transport over the next 6–8 weeks. The occasional scientist, bitten by the fitness bug, has continued to exercise for several years, and in some instances has succeeded in reaching a point 50 per cent above a sedentary starting line. This seems the ultimate in possible training response.

Unfortunately, the dividends of a given training schedule diminish progressively as the final ceiling is approached. Athletes naturally start serious training nearer to their ceiling than truly sedentary people, and perhaps for this reason can rarely augment their pre-season oxygen transporting power by more than about 20 per cent. Nevertheless, the effects of training should not be scorned. Most races are won or lost by a much smaller margin than 20 per cent. Further, a 20 per cent change in a physiological score such as oxygen transport or muscle strength often has a much larger influence upon performance—

it can convert a contest from the threatening situation where an athlete is outclassed, forced to perform at a pace that is more than he can sustain, to a confident demonstration of ability where the competitor can plan his tactics knowing that he has a reserve of power in hand. Finally, training makes a large difference to the efficiency of movement at all stages of a race; in a highly skilled sport such as swimming, a well-trained competitor may burn only a quarter as much oxygen as an indifferent performer who is attempting to swim at the same speed.

Implications for athletic selection

It is premature to state the precise contribution of heredity to performance. Nevertheless, we may suspect that parentage accounts for about 50 per cent of most components of athletic prowess. Those of us who are indifferent performers can enjoy recreational sport, knowing we have a reasonable alibi for our consistent lack of success. But if government or sporting associations want to increase a nation's share of Olympic medallists, it will not suffice to submit candidates such as ourselves to a rigorous training programme. The best-endowed competitors must first be found for each sport.

What principles can be suggested to expedite national screening? In a free society, the individual must himself want to undergo training for a specific sport. A coach cannot arbitrarily take ten teenagers with certain characteristics proposed by sports scientists and order them to become sprint swimmers or long-distance cyclists. However, the problem of gentle persuasion may not be as difficult as it appears. Human nature is such that we enjoy doing the things at which we excel. So it may merely be necessary to kindle interest in the type of activity for which the person is best suited.

Specific training is most effective if commenced while the child is still growing, and early specialization is thus to be encouraged. Prime responsibility for correct counselling of the student must rest with the teacher of physical education. The likely adult build of a class-member can be decided from inspection of the parents and a consideration of the present size of the child relative to its maturity; children who mature early generally reach a smaller final size than those who mature late.

Enquiry can also be made regarding the sports skills of the parents. The school athletic programme should rotate the student through a wide range of sports at an early age, so that appropriate interests are stimulated and potential stars identified. About once every second year, such intuitive allocation of students should be supplemented by more formal counselling, based on the results of field tests suggested by the sports scientists.

Subsequent selection could come jointly from a sequence of well-structured regional and national competitions and a system of tests of increasing sophistication; at each level of competition and testing, the top 10 per cent of candidates could be advanced to opportunity for greater training. The concept for a country such as Canada is illustrated in Fig. 10. Let us suppose we have a total population of 500 000 twelve-year-old children. For each of as wide a variety of contests as possible, individual recreation leaders and physical education teachers would use the criteria we have discussed above to pick out the best 10 per cent of their class; this group would then move

```
              500 000 Children aged twelve
              /                \
    250 000 Girls          250 000 Boys
       |                       |          Counselling by recreation leaders and
       |                       |          physical education teachers, simple field
       |                       |          tests, experience of a wide variety of sports.
     25 000                  25 000
       |                       |          Municipality
       |                       |          Competitions and careful field tests.
      2500                    2500
       |                       |          Metropolitan Regions
       |                       |          Competitions and simple laboratory tests.
       250                     250
       |                       |          Provincial Training Camps
       |                       |          Competitions and detailed laboratory tests.
        25                      25        National Training Camps
```

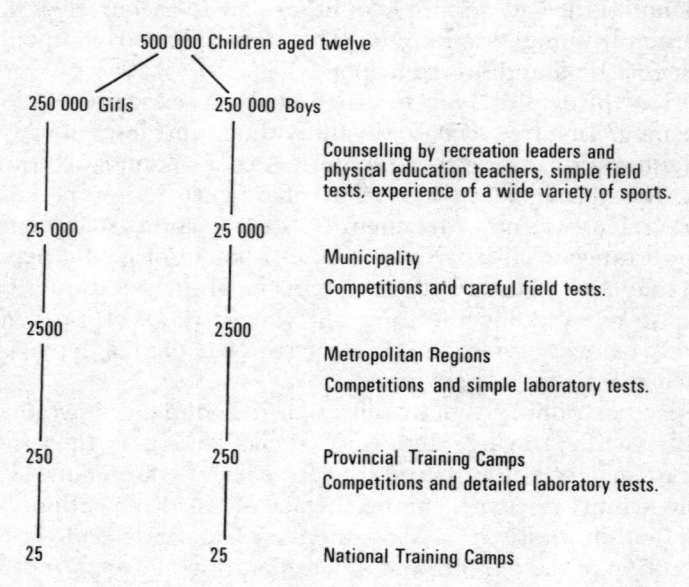

Fig. 10. A possible scheme for the selection of children with inherited athletic skills for advanced training.

forward to competition and training at the level of the municipality. Once again, 10 per cent would be selected, moving forward for further competition and training within the nearest Metropolitan Region; criteria of selection would again be contest results and carefully administered field tests. Each Metropolitan Region has within it a University department of physical education, so that further advancement could be based on a combination of competition results and simple laboratory tests. Each of the ten Provinces could establish summer training camps with more sophisticated testing and preparation available for the best 10 per cent of the metropolitan candidates, and a final stage of selection would carry forward two or three children from each province to a national training centre.

In such a system, selection arises out of a scheme of progressive training; although priority of funding is given to the search process, subsequent preparation of likely candidates also becomes important. The critical stage is the first screening within local recreation programmes and school systems, and a substantial increase of both staff and physical facilities may be needed to permit objective evaluation of aptitudes for all students, while providing them with opportunities to experience a wide variety of sports. However, at least within the major metropolitan areas, much could be accomplished merely by making better use of existing facilities, bussing students and specialized items of equipment between different parts of a city. Some capital investment would be needed for the development of National and Provincial Training Camps, despite occasional legacies from such events as the Olympic Games, the Pan American Games, and the Commonwealth Games.

Perhaps more important, there would need to be a major upgrading in the educational background of those responsible for selection and training. A stop-watch and an iron will to force pupils to repeat a particular manœuvre *ad nauseam* could no longer suffice. Unhappily, a proportion of coaches seem psychologically unsuited to their task; far from helping the child, they seek to experience through him triumphs they themselves were unable to realize. The majority are of course sincere and dedicated volunteers, but their enthusiasm is rarely matched by their knowledge. Voluntary education programmes have had little success, and the time is at hand when there should be a rigorous certification system. At all levels of competition, coaches, trainers, and sports physicians alike need a clear understanding of the mechanisms of success in terms of body mechanics, psychology, physiology, and nutrition, together with instruction in using such principles in selection and training.

Better facilities and better staff will undoubtedly cost money. However, an increase in the physical activity of the population is a major health goal of most Western nations, and a boosting of activity should be an important by-product of a selection and training system that identifies the physical aptitudes of the individual and gives him the necessary preparation to realize his inherited potential.

7
Preparing the athlete

When an athlete fails to win a major competition, he often blames his poor performance on some fault in the long-term game plan of his coach. The latter must organize diet and physiological and psychological preparation in such a way that optimum condition is reached on the day of contest. Either over- or under-preparation can have adverse consequences for performance.

Diet

Fuel for movement. Food provides the fuel to sustain movement. As we saw in Chapter 4, the phosphate energy stores within the muscle fibres are so limited that they can be exhausted in a mere eight seconds. Continuance of activity depends on the ability of the body to rebuild the energy-rich phosphate compounds by the breakdown of carbohydrate, fat, or protein.

In the short term, it is possible to draw upon the body's stockpiles of these fuels. Individual days may be marked by a substantial shortfall or excess of Calories.* However, except in cases of starvation, there is soon an appropriate modification of food intake, and accounts are balanced over the course of one or two weeks.

Immediate resources during activity include glycogen and fat within the muscle fibres, glycogen in the liver, and any foods taken during the period of competition. Residual needs are met by drawing upon body reserves of body fat and protein (Table 7).

Muscle fibres store glycogen and fat to a total of about 2000

* 1 Calorie = 1000 calories = 1 kilocalorie = 4·19 kilojoules.

Table 7. *Energy stores of the athlete*

Source	Site	Quantity of stored energy	Minimum time to exhaustion
Phosphates (adenosine triphosphate, creatine phosphate)	Muscle	7–10 Cal	8 s
Glycogen	Muscle	1600 Cal	1–2 h
	Liver	400 Cal	1–2 h
Fat	Fat deposits †	50–70 000 Cal	20–40 d
Protein	Mainly muscle †	10 000 Cal	40 d

† Complete depletion of body fat and protein is incompatible with life; the quantities cited are the maximum proportions of the reserves that can be mobilized.

Cal. This provides enough energy for one and a half to two hours of steady, near-maximum activity (such as marathon running or distance-cycling) or a series of shorter sprints (where only the glycogen is used). Once such foods within the muscles have been exhausted, continuation of exercise depends on the carriage of fuels to the active tissues via the blood stream. The liver contributes further carbohydrate (a maximum of 100 g glycogen, equivalent to about 400 Cal). The rules of some contests also permit the taking of nutrients during an event. Water loss is usually a more serious problem than the depletion of energy stores, and any fluid provided should thus be sufficiently dilute to allow rapid absorption by the stomach and intestines. Athletes can drink about 800 ml per h of a 2·5% glucose solution, obtaining from it about 80 Cal per h. Food intake becomes more important than water in very long events, such as a cross-Canada race. Drinks rich in fat and protein (such as instant breakfasts) enable a runner to absorb about 400 Cal per h, although the intake of water drops to about 250 ml per h.

Many athletes feel a compulsion to eat large steaks. It is thus a little surprising to find that almost no protein is used as an energy source even during prolonged exercise. Our middle-aged runners burnt a total of 3700 Cal over a marathon race, but only 200 Cal of this total came from protein. Such a loss could be made good by eating a little over 200 g of roast lamb or beef.

Replenishing the stockpiles. The long-term diet of the athlete should meet his caloric needs, using food of adequate quality. Whereas a sedentary office worker may require only 2500 Cal per day, a football player or a man running across Canada can use upwards of 6000 Cal, and a long-distance cyclist may consume as much as 10 000 Cal per day.

Some athletes have an insufficient intake of calories. This may be deliberate policy on the part of a wrestler or a boxer who is unfairly trying to make a lower weight category than is appropriate to his body-build. Some distance runners also have reputedly starved themselves in an attempt to ease the work of running by burning away 'unwanted' muscle from the upper parts of their bodies. Many athletes find real or imagined difficulty in eating or drinking while they are moving, and in very-long-distance running or cycling events the race may occupy so much of the day that there is insufficient time to eat the necessary calories. A small deficit (100–200 Cal per day) can be helpful in trimming away unwanted fat, but larger discrepancies inevitably lead to a loss of muscle. Whether deliberate or accidental, such starvation is plainly undesirable.

An excessive intake of calories may occur between seasons. Some athletes become accustomed to eating large meals, and find it difficult to divest themselves of this habit when they are not in training. The contact sportsman, in particular, may arrive at his training camp carrying as much as 10 kg of excess fat, a problem that could have been avoided by greater activity and a more watchful diet out of season.

The quality of the diet refers to its composition. It should provide adequate amounts of those protein and fat constituents that the body is unable to manufacture itself, together with sufficient vitamins and mineral elements. The average sedentary person in the western world eats about 12–15 per cent of his calories in the form of protein, about 40 per cent as fat, and the rest as carbohydrate. We have noted that many athletes eat much more protein than the average person. This may be justified in sports where a large muscle mass has to be developed. The American footballer who weighs 110 kg may have gained 30 kg of muscle over a year of intensive training. Even on the unlikely assumption of 100 per cent efficiency of conversion of flesh into flesh, he would need to eat 600 g of additional meat every week of the year when weight was being gained. On the other hand, the endurance athlete often carries little more flesh than a sedentary person, and also burns little protein during his event. His protein requirements are thus no greater than those of the average citizen, and it is not surprising that successful competitors have included vegetarians and entrants from the Third World (where animal protein is often in short supply).

Current advice to the ordinary citizen is to restrict his intake of animal fat, since there is some evidence that an excess of such fat increases the blood cholesterol, thereby enhancing the risks of heart attacks and other forms of vascular disease. However, an athlete with a large daily caloric output needs fat if his total food intake is to be kept to a reasonable bulk. Whereas protein and carbohydrate yield only 4 Cal per g, each gram of fat provides about 9 Cal of energy. Fortunately, if the daily energy expenditure is large, a high-fat diet can be tolerated without an increase of blood cholesterol.

Alcohol. Alcohol is a further source of energy, with a yield of about 7 Cal per g. The consumption of alcohol immediately before an event to deaden pain or 'steady the nerves' is regarded as a form of 'doping', and has led to the disqualification of some competitors (see Chapter 8). Arguments for and against the consumption of moderate amounts of alcohol during leisure hours follow a similar pattern to those encountered in the general population. However, there are several reasons why the athlete should approach the use of alcohol with more caution than a sedentary person:

1. Statistics show that athletes have a predisposition towards violent deaths (Chapter 10). Their propensity for taking unnecessary risks is likely to be exacerbated by even moderate doses of alcohol.
2. Considerable fluid depletion is incurred over a day of vigorous activity. If the athlete develops the habit of replac-

ing the lost fluid by alcohol, addiction could soon supervene.
3. Athletes are exposed to much stronger psychological pressures than the average individual. There is thus a danger of seeking escape from such pressures in alcohol, again with rapid progression to addiction.

Vitamins. The majority of athletes have a great belief in the value of dietary supplements, especially vitamins. The reasoning seems that if small quantities of vitamins are good for the average performer, large doses will produce an international champion! Unfortunate competitors have at various times been persuaded to include in their diet such items as queen-bee extract, seaweed cakes, rice polishings, celery-leaf powder, wheat-germ oil, liver pills, yeast, large quantities of fortified cereals, and various more specific vitamin preparations. The power of faith is such that performance has sometimes been improved thereby. However, the gain has usually had a psychological basis, and has not been duplicated when neither the athlete nor his coach knew whether the capsules administered contained the vaunted dietary supplement or some inactive substitute.

One manifestation of Vitamin A deficiency of concern to the athlete would be a blocking of the sweat glands in the skin by horny plugs. In addition to carrots, Vitamin A is found in such items as tomato juice, melon, and canteloupe, all popular items on the training table. Many athletes thus eat ten times the body requirement of Vitamin A in their normal diet.

The B group of vitamins, such as thiamine, riboflavine, and miacin, are closely involved in energy-producing reactions. The body-needs thus rise with total caloric expenditure. However, if the added energy requirements of the competitor are met by a good mixed diet rather than by 'empty calories' such as glucose, alcohol, or sweetened soft drinks, then the necessary additional vitamins will be provided by normal food without supplementation.

Vitamin C (ascorbic acid) is concerned with the healing of injuries, and very large doses may reduce the period of disability from the common cold. It has been argued that athletes suffer more minor injuries than the average person, and thus need more Vitamin C; however, the quantity of the vitamin needed to ensure rapid healing is extremely small. We have found no difference in the number of injuries or in the duration of disability when distance runners take large doses of Vitamin C. The possible influence on the course of respiratory infections is a more valid argument, since a cold can make the difference between victory and defeat. On this basis, some athletes take as much as one gram of Vitamin C per day.

Vitamin E contributes to the normal health of muscle in some animals. However, its precise role in the human body remains a mystery. There are substantial amounts of the vitamin in normal food, and although additional dosage is popular among athletes, there is no evidence that such treatment helps performance either in the laboratory or on the track.

Fluid and minerals. Immediate needs for water, sodium, and potassium are considered in Chapter 9. Anaemia can be a problem in distance-runners and other endurance athletes, and there has been speculation that iron losses in the sweat are at least partly responsible. Unfortunately, it is difficult to make laboratory measurements of the iron content of sweat, since the fluid is readily contaminated with iron-rich cells from the skin. Estimates of iron losses by this route show a 300-fold range. Taking the highest figures, a man who was sweating hard all day could lose 14 mg of iron. The average diet provides only about 12 mg per day, of which a mere 1 mg is absorbed. Thus, the regular repetition of a 14 mg loss could certainly lead to a progressive iron-deficiency anaemia. In support of this suggestion, our data have shown below-average blood-iron levels in distance runners, with a further drop in readings over the course of a marathon race in which much sweat was produced. There may thus be advantage in the athlete's increasing his intake of iron through the choice of such foods as liver. Cereals are also rich in iron if they are not unduly processed, but they contain phytic acid which prevents absorption of the mineral by the body.

Fracture of the long bones from the repetitive stress of running is a common problem in the older athlete. However, this type of injury probably reflects a deficiency in the organic constituents of the bone rather than a lack of minerals such as calcium. Certainly, I have encountered stress fractures in runners who were regularly eating two or three times the recommended dietary allowance of calcium.

Immediate preparation. Since the most convenient fuel for activity is the glycogen within the muscle fibres, the endurance athlete gains some advantage from boosting such stores immediately before a major contest. Scandinavian scientists have developed forms of dietary manipulation that can approximately double the glycogen content of the fibres. The most successful technique (Fig. 11) involves one or more bouts of vigorous and sustained effort, which thoroughly depletes the muscles of

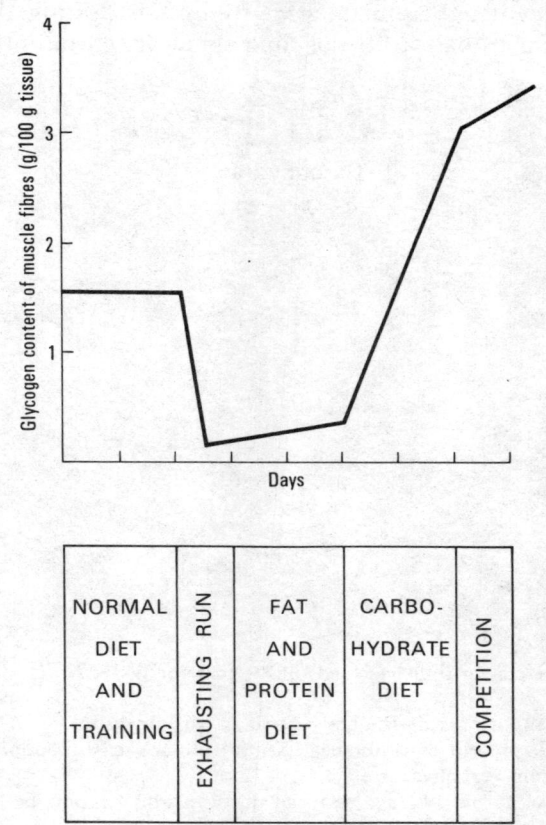

FIG. 11. A regimen to boost the glycogen content of muscle fibres, as suggested by Dr. Bengt Saltin.

glycogen, a period of two or three days on a protein and fat diet, which further augments the hunger of the muscle cells for glycogen, and a final two days of carbohydrate-rich foods immediately before competition.

Most athletes avoid a heavy meal for several hours before a contest. Digestive activity diverts blood from the muscles to the stomach and intestines. It is also uncomfortable to perform physical activity with a full stomach, and in some individuals vomiting may be induced. The optimum timing seems to take a light and not-too-sugary meal between two and three hours before an event. If the day is hot and a heavy sweat loss is anticipated, it is helpful to start by over-hydrating the body, drinking up to half a litre of fluid some fifteen minutes before

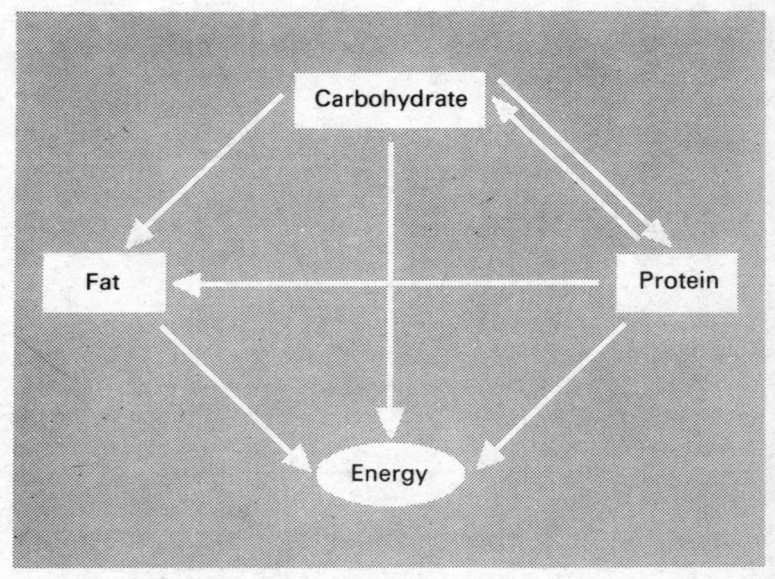

Fig. 12. Inter-convertibility of foodstuffs within the body. Note that:

(1) fat cannot provide the body-needs of carbohydrate;
(2) a few protein constituents 'essential amino acids' cannot be built up from carbohydrate;
(3) a few forms of fat 'essential fatty acids' cannot be built up from carbohydrate;
(4) fat is burnt incompletely if too little energy is drawn from carbohydrate.

the race or game begins. In longer events, further fluid should be taken at regular intervals, as the rules allow. Dilute solutions (such as 2·5% glucose) empty most quickly from the stomach, and are to be preferred unless the need is to absorb calories rather than fluid.

Over-view of diet. The majority of foodstuffs are inter-convertible within the body (Fig. 12), and any good mixed diet can lay the groundwork for athletic success. Standard fare provides not only the protein and fat constituents that the body is unable to manufacture, but also the necessary complement of minerals and vitamins (with the possible exceptions of iron and Vitamin C). Although the athlete requires more vitamins than a sedentary person, his increased appetite takes care of this need. Indeed, the very sedentary person who eats little of any food is at more risk of deprivation of essential elements than a cyclist who is consuming 10 000 Cal per day.

Nevertheless, many competitors continue to express strong preferences for unusual foods, and if such fads can be humoured without endangering the overall balance of nutrition, some psychological advantage may be gained.

Physiological preparation

Training objectives. Athletic preparation is sport-specific. The objective is to bring the various systems of the body as close to peak efficiency as is mutually possible with respect to the performance of the chosen sport. Such a goal is in contrast with the fitness plan for an ordinary person, where the concern is for the overall development of both body and mind. An adolescent who has prepared himself for an international swimming competition by spending every moment of his leisure in the pool may have become in consequence a social misfit. Likewise, a 200-kilogram wrestler may be in top condition for heavyweight wrestling, yet poorly prepared for any incidental running he may undertake in ordinary life.

Adaptations occur in response to the frequent repetitions of either the chosen activity or its training equivalent. In different sports, the emphasis falls on the development of endurance, of anaerobic capacity and power, and of strength (Fig. 13). Some

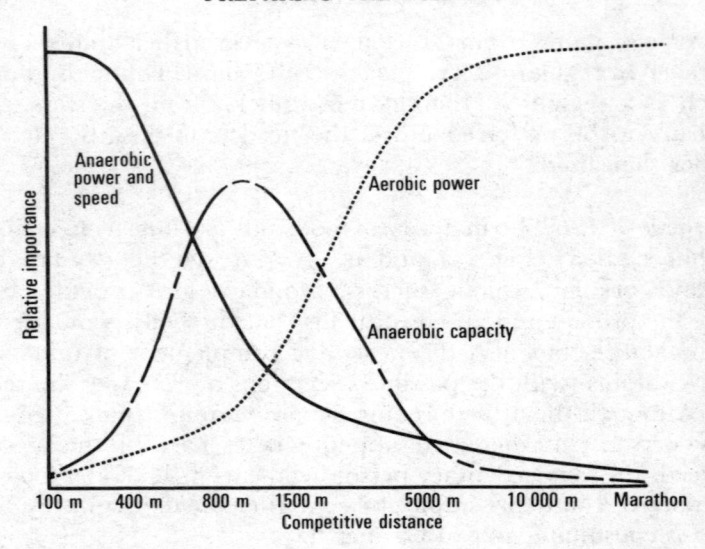

FIG. 13. The types of training most needed by track athletes.

changes, such as altered behaviour of the brain and nerve pathways, are realized over the course of a few weeks. Other developments, particularly the growth of muscle and the strengthening of bones, can take months or years to complete.

Endurance training. Endurance training aims at increasing the oxygen transporting power of the competitor. Gains of 5–50 per cent may occur, the largest changes being seen in an athlete who has been bed-ridden for some months owing to disease or injury. Improvements of condition in a normally active but out-of season competitor are rarely greater than 20 per cent (Chapter 6).

The main responses are found in the heart and circulation. The resting heart rate becomes slower, and more blood is expelled with each beat. The latter change is largely responsible for the gains in oxygen transport. Nervous adjustments stimulate the heart muscle to contract more vigorously, while at the same time the filling of the heart chambers between contractions is encouraged by an increased total volume of blood and a shift of blood from the reservoir veins of the legs towards the heart. Over a longer period, the muscle of the heart wall also thickens, and attendant arterial and capillary blood vessels undergo development.

Better use is also made of the available pumping force of the heart. As training proceeds, more oxygen is extracted from the blood during circulation. Whereas a sedentary person can extract no more than 70 per cent of the available oxygen even during maximum effort, the well-trained athlete can take out as much as 85 per cent of the total. There are two main reasons for this gain of circulatory efficiency—a greater quantity of enzymes in the active muscles, and diversion of blood away from regions of low oxygen extraction, such as the skin and kidneys. The well-conditioned athlete can function with a smaller relative skin blood flow because he is thinner than a sedentary person and he has developed an ability to dissipate body heat by early and more vigorous sweating.

Some aspects of lung function are also improved by endurance training. The respiratory rate becomes slower and the volume of gas breathed smaller at a given rate of working; in other words, the lungs are extracting more oxygen from each litre of oxygen that is breathed. Strengthening of the chest muscles may lead to small increases in both the static lung volume and the dynamic bellows function of the chest, while the greater maximum blood flow through the lungs expands the capillary vessels, facilitating the exchange of oxygen between the air and the blood.

The practical consequences of endurance training include not only an increase in the maximum possible rate of performing endurance type work, but also an enhanced tolerance of just sub-maximum effort.

Anaerobic training. The athlete who intends to perform over short distances places his main training emphasis on anaerobic effort, with a view to developing what are termed anaerobic capacity and power. Table 8 may be helpful in understanding these two determinants of brief performance.

Anaerobic capacity is particularly important in events lasting from ten to sixty seconds. It is a measure of the total 'oxygen debt' an individual can accumulate through the breakdown of high-energy phosphate compounds and the conversion

Table 8. *The energy resources of the athlete, expressed in terms of an equivalent transport of oxygen to the working muscles*

Resource	Equivalent oxygen transport (ml per min per kg of body weight)	Time to exhaustion of resource
Phosphate compounds (adenosine triphosphate, creatine phosphate)	165	8 s
Conversion of glycogen to lactic acid	70	40 s
Steady transport of oxygen	50–80	Almost inexhaustible

of the stored carbohydrate glycogen to lactic acid. In terms of an equivalent oxygen supply, anaerobic capacity is typically about seventy millilitres per kilogram of body weight. The ultimate limit is set by the accumulation of lactic acid within the contracting muscle fibres; the rising acidity of the tissues brings to a halt the chemical processes concerned with muscular movement. The more usual practical limit is psychological, a reaction to the sensations of pain, weakness, and fatigue in the active limbs. Appropriate patterns of training can boost the anaerobic capacity in several ways:

1. The blood volume and the total weight of lean tissue may both be increased. Thus, even if the anaerobic capacity were to remain at seventy millilitres per kilogram, the total oxygen debt would rise as a result of the augmentation of body weight.
2. Amounts of high-energy phosphate compounds within the active fibres are increased, and the content of the red oxygen-storing pigment myoglobin also rises.
3. Through frequent repetitions, the athlete becomes accustomed to the sensations of anaerobic effort, and carries himself to a higher final lactate concentration before deciding that he is exhausted.
4. The bicarbonate content of the tissues may rise, thus providing a 'buffer' to mop up lactic acid as it is formed, reducing unpleasant sensations, and delaying the ultimate inhibition

of muscular contractions brought about by the rising tide of acidity within the active muscle fibres.

Anaerobic power is needed especially in events lasting less than ten seconds. It depends on initial stores of the high-energy phosphate compounds, and the maximum rate at which these can be broken down by the active tissues. Anaerobic training tends to improve both the size of the stores and the speed of energy release, to the point where a well-prepared sprinter has about 30 per cent more anaerobic power than a sedentary person per unit of body weight.

Strength training. Strength training may be rhythmic, for example, ten repetitions of a weight-lifting exercise, or isometric, where the muscles are tensed against a strong spring or other device resisting movement. The gains of strength that develop during conditioning are somewhat specific to the type of exercise that has been undertaken. Rhythmic effort increases the loads that can be lifted, and particularly if lighter loads have been used increases endurance in terms of the number of repetitions that can be tolerated. Isometric training increases the maximum force that can be developed against a rigid obstacle, and particularly with repeated holding of sub-maximum efforts increases the endurance time of the tensed muscle.

Initially, gains of strength have a regulatory rather than a structural basis, and despite a dramatic improvement of performance it may be difficult to show any change in the dimensions of the muscles concerned. We must presume the body learns to produce more powerful contractions by calling upon a greater number of existing muscle fibres and using them more effectively. If training continues for several months or years, there is ultimately a substantial increase in the bulk of muscle tissue. The size of the individual fibres increases, and there is a corresponding development of the capillary blood supply, while the ratio of active, contractile tissue to the infrastructure of fat and supporting elements is much improved. At the same time, the calcium content of the exercised bones is increased, and where necessary their internal architecture is modified to give them greater strength; in a tennis player, for example, the bones of the serving arm become much more robust than those on the opposite side of the body. Cartilage covering the joint surfaces is thickened and becomes more resistant to compression, and the flexibility of the joints that are used is increased.

Sport as a training tool. The most satisfactory method of athletic preparation is frequent repetition of the intended activity. This is particularly true of the highly skilled activities, but applies in lesser measure to all sports; cycling or laboratory exercise on a bicycle ergometer, for example, are less effective means of preparing a runner than an equivalent expenditure of time on the track. This follows necessarily from the very specific nature of body responses to a training programme. Cycling builds up a different group of muscles from those needed in running, and vice versa. The added tissue is a handicap in all except the contact sports, and in some marginally nourished competitors the inappropriate development may rob other more vital areas of needed nutrients. More commonly, the main difficulty is an ineffective use of valuable training time.

There is much learning to any sport. Improvements in the rate of reaction to the starter's pistol and efficiency in subsequent motion can be acquired and impressed upon the appropriate segments of the brain only by relentless repetition of the competitive sequence.

What, then, are the arguments for use of other types of training? Perhaps the most obvious is a seasonal problem. Much painfully won fitness can be dissipated through a few weeks of inactivity, and if the local lake is covered by ice for three months of the year, the serious rower cannot afford to ignore other activities that may help to maintain his condition during the winter months. Injury is a second common reason for temporary abandonment of actual sport participation. A minor tendon tear or inflammation can restrict normal movement for several weeks, while a fracture of the leg can put the fittest athlete in plaster for several months; in either case, exercises for the uninjured regions can help maintain the general condition of the body, while specific isometric exercises and/or electrical (faradic) stimulation can do much to conserve the function of the muscles within the plaster. A third possible reason for gymnasium-based training might be to correct a basic defect in the constitution of a competitor. Let us suppose that a paddler has participated faithfully in his water practice, yet after several months a laboratory test profile (Table 6, p. 47) shows a startling deficiency of leg strength relative to other team members; it might then be reasonable to propose specific weight training for the leg muscles in order to rectify this deficiency. Boredom has sometimes been advanced as a fourth reason for changing the pattern of training. This may be appropriate for a recreational sportsman, but if a top-level athlete lacks the self-discipline to continue with the most effective form of training, he is unlikely to excel in major competition.

If alternative forms of exercise are adopted, it is probably preferable to choose formal gymnastic manœuvres rather than simulators or other forms of sport. Unfortunately, it is very difficult to devise a realistic simulator for most classes of event: water-skills, for example, are very different from those required in operating the average rowing machine, and there is a danger that the various details of techique painstakingly mastered and stored in the brain during a summer of rowing will become confused and valueless through a winter of practice on a superficially similar gymnasium-based rowing machine. Likewise, it can be appreciated that a tennis player who attempts to maintain his condition by playing badminton during the winter months will approach the new season with a distorted 'feel' for his racquet.

Other types of training. Cardio-respiratory endurance can be developed by continuous running or fast jogging. The effectiveness of the stimulus depends largely on the intensity of training relative to the initial fitness of the individual; an athlete who is already bringing his heart rate to 170 beats per minute throughout an hour and a half of fast hockey will do little for his condition by thirty minutes of jogging at a pulse rate of 130 beats per minute. Other variables are the frequency and duration of effort. The modern trend is to make large demands in both areas, five or six hours of preparation per day being commonplace in serious endurance preparation. A more recreational athlete could well start his conditioning by running for thirty minutes five or six times per week at a speed sufficient to increase his heart rate 70 per cent of the way from rest to its maximum value; as condition improved, he could then increase alternately the speed of running and the distance covered during individual training sessions.

Interval training intersperses bouts of quite high speed running with recovery periods when the subject jogs at a more leisurely pace. A typical early-season sequence for a young runner might alternate three quarter-mile runs at a pulse rate of 180 beats per minute with three quarter-mile stints of slow jogging. Depending on the intensity and duration of the more vigorous phase and the length of the recovery period, interval training could develop cardio-respiratory endurance, anaerobic capacity, or anaerobic power. In general, it is more effective than continuous running in improving performance at top speeds, but it is less beneficial in adapting a person to submaximum effort (as may be required for example in a marathon race).

Circuit training is popular in preparation for contact sports such as rugger. Eight to twelve 'stations' are arranged around a gymnasium, and a different form of activity is carried out at each. A well-devised general circuit might include a track for jogging, and equipment to exercise arm, shoulder, back, abdominal, and leg muscles. The programme is self-paced, the individual deciding how many repetitions he can make at each station before he is exhausted. Having set himself an appropriate target, he moves three times around the circuit, performing half the maximum possible number of repetitions at each visit. On subsequent days, he attempts to improve both the speed of movement around the circuit and the number of repetitions performed at each station. As might be anticipated from the nature of the exercises, muscle development is greater, and gains of cardio-respiratory endurance are less than for continuous or interval-type work.

If strength is to be developed, most athletes prefer weight training to isometric exercises. The programme adopted may be general, in an attempt to develop bulk for contact sports, or specific to a given sport. A rower, for example, would concentrate on leg-presses and arm-pulls, whereas a sailor would attempt to build up the thigh and abdominal muscles needed to support the body when counter-balancing the boat. Individual coaches all have their favourite combinations of 'sets' and 'repetitions' of the weight-lifting manœuvres—a typical plan for a recreational athlete might use half the load that could be lifted ten times, making three sets of ten repetitions of the movement in the course of a daily training session.

A one-year game plan. Let us suppose that an athlete has just completed a reasonably successful four-month season. What plan should be adopted to ensure that he is in peak condition for the following year? The first requirement is a one-month holiday from his chosen sport (Fig. 14). However, this must be a time of active relaxation and recuperation. It is important to avoid both a gross deterioration of physical condition and the adoption of leisure sports that will interfere with competitive skills. Good overall exercises include swimming, hill-walking, and wilderness canoeing, as circumstances and interests may suggest. When training is resumed, there is scope for a three-month period of general endurance and strength training, seeking to correct personal deficiencies in the performance profile, but during the final four months efforts must be concentrated

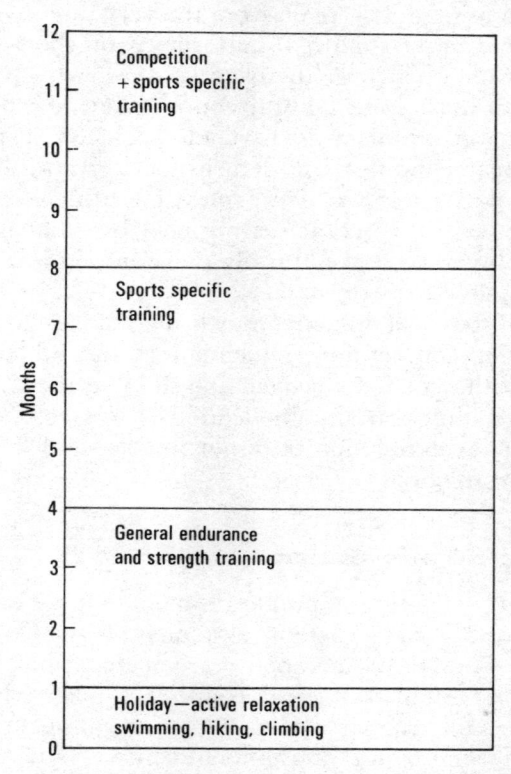

Fig. 14. A one-year training plan for the competitive athlete.

on the chosen sport, repeated as often as body, mind, and clock will allow. Some training should continue throughout the active season, as competitions rarely occur with sufficient frequency to develop or even to maintain peak condition.

The needs for rest must be gauged carefully in terms of morale and the necessity of avoiding minor injuries. Work-outs should not be so intense that a competitor is physically or emotionally exhausted at the commencement of the next day's training session. Two days of rest should precede major competitions, thus allowing opportunity for the stabilization of tissue fluid and mineral balances, and replenishment of glycogen stores in the muscle and liver.

Over-training. Much was once written on the dangers of over-training an athlete. It is plain from the very intensive schedules that are currently followed that many of these fears were groundless. Nevertheless, there are reasons why performance can deteriorate despite faithful continuation of training. The most common problem is psychological. As a person approaches peak condition, the returns for a given training effort become progressively smaller. Unless the athlete is advised of this, he is likely to become discouraged by what he sees as a passing of his peak, and naturally once morale is sapped there is a real decline in performance.

A second source of difficulty may be an inadequate rest period before major competition, which forces the athlete to enter his event with depleted glycogen and fluid reserves. A relentless training schedule can finally lead to a loss of performance through the accumulation of minor injuries and inflammation of the active tendons.

Psychological preparation

The proper psychological preparation of the athlete is probably more important than dietetic and physiological conditioning combined. Sometimes, competitors who have had ideal diets and the best of physiological training 'choke' when on the track, miss vital chances, or show an alarming loss of group skills when faced by an international contest. Other performers are poorly nourished and have little formal preparation, yet go on to win by an apparently superhuman effort when every objective piece of evidence suggests that they should have given up the unequal struggle.

Eastern Europe has had a strong interest in the influence of the mind on performance since the time of the great Russian psycho-physiologist Pavlov. One may thus wonder how far team psychologists have contributed to the successes of Eastern European countries in major competition. Unfortunately, details of the methods used are not generally available to Western readers. In the rest of the world, understanding of the psychology of sport remains in its infancy. Certain topics, including personality, perception of pain, aggression, intelligence, and group interactions were discussed in Chapter 5. In this chapter, we shall look briefly at the way skills are perceived and learned; we shall consider the factors that motivate the athlete to undertake arduous training; and we shall decide how a psychological peak can be realized on the day of a crucial competition.

Perception of skilled movements. We saw in Chapter 4 that in making a skilled movement such as a powerful tennis serve, the cerebellum of the brain co-ordinates information from tension receptors in the active limb with reports from the eyes, ears, and elsewhere, translating the whole sensory input into a precise and relatively automatic instruction of force that is transmitted to the appropriate muscles of the arm.

While much can be done to train this system, there are clear inequalities of inheritance. The top athlete is generally endowed with a greater inherent sensitivity of his receptor organs. Not only can the muscles detect smaller changes of tension, but the eyes function better: there is a clearer perception of depth, more can be seen from the corner of the eye, and more is taken in by a single glance than would be possible for the average person. If one watches a cricketer tracking the path of a ball, for example, one is impressed with the unusual smoothness of the eye movements.

Nevertheless, even the skills of the athlete can be confounded. Performance is undermined by fatigue, and it is particularly important not to persist with training in the face of extreme fatigue, for then the brain may start to learn incorrect patterns of movement. The response may also become confused if a parallel but different activity is practiced immediately before competition. Sometimes, an attempt is made to take advantage of such confusion. A baseball player, for example, may warm up by swinging two bats simultaneously. The logic seems to be that when he reverts to a single bat, this will feel lighter and he will be able to swing it faster. Basketball players also may sometimes engage in practice with a lighter ball in an attempt to increase accuracy with one of normal weight. However, the wisdom of confounding the regulating centres is dubious, and liable to give rise to an incorrect response at an inopportune moment.

Misperception of time is likely if a person is highly motivated and tense. In such circumstances, a fraction of a second seems an eternity, and false starts and missed strokes become commonplace. In team sports, several objects are often in simultaneous motion, and the natural tendency is for attention to be focused upon the most rapidly moving of the group. The eye of the fielder in cricket or in baseball may be drawn to the running players, and much practice under conditions of actual play is needed to keep his eye on the ball.

Learning of skills. Learning is accompanied by an increase in both the speed and the accuracy of performance, with a progressive decrease in errors of both commission and omission. As with physiological preparation, performance shows a characteristic curve of improvement (Fig. 15) and the athlete should be aware of this if he is not to be discouraged by apparent lack of progress. In the early stages of training, nervousness and the inherent difficulty of the task may lead to rather slow learning. Rapid improvement commences as appropriate techniques are discovered, but the final approach to a peak of skill can again be quite slow. Intermediate plateaus may develop because the coach has suggested some slight alteration in approach, or the athlete is in process of building up a complex skill from several simpler items of technique. Finally, fatigue and boredom can slow learning to the point where performance actually deteriorates.

In the early stages of preparation, it is usually most effective to concentrate on 'mass' practices; fast physiological gains are obtained thereby, and the competitor is encouraged by the

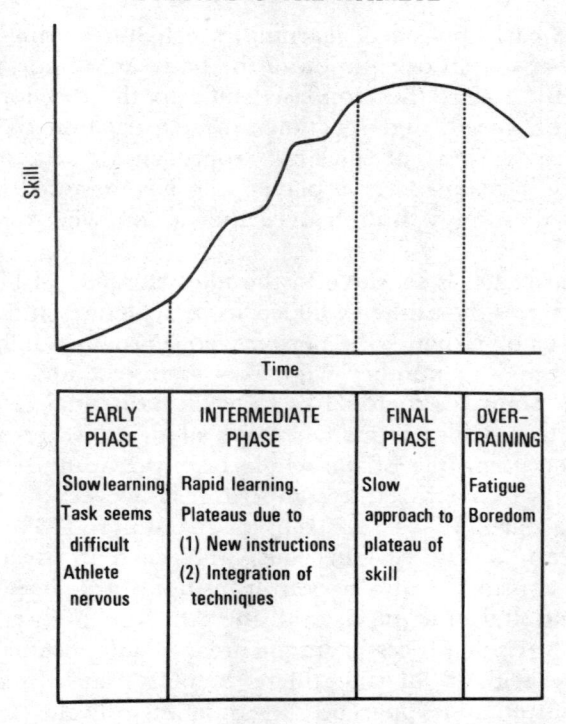

EARLY PHASE	INTERMEDIATE PHASE	FINAL PHASE	OVER-TRAINING
Slow learning. Task seems difficult Athlete nervous	Rapid learning. Plateaus due to (1) New instructions (2) Integration of techniques	Slow approach to plateau of skill	Fatigue Boredom

FIG. 15. The time course for the learning of a complex athletic skill.

rapid strides in his condition. Later, practices should be more widely spaced. Massed practice is particularly effective with sports that are interesting and highly motivating, whereas spaced practice is helpful for sports that are difficult, physically taxing, or rather uninteresting. Cratty cites the example of a basketball team who were given three days of massed practice—undiluted demonstrations and rehearsals. At the end of this time, they were not only thoroughly exhausted; they had improved less than a second team who had done nothing! The detrimental effects of fatigue and boredom are best counteracted by adding novelty to the practice sessions, allowing longer rest intervals, and spacing practice sessions more widely. Since there is some transfer of training between opposite limbs, it may also be possible to practice with the opposite arm or leg when one has worked to exhaustion.

In the early phases of learning, mechanical principles and the correct spatial orientation of the body are important items of content. Later, the emphasis shifts to the development of movement, speed, and reaction time. Instruction should emphasize a variety of possible approaches to a problem, especially in team sports: a player who has mastered five techniques will surely triumph over the person who knows only two.

A good coach is sensitive to the idiosyncracies of his pupils. He recognizes the athlete who learns by watching and the man who learns by moving, the person who synthesizes information and his opposite number who likes to dissect and analyse a problem. Some instructors like to teach individual elements of the required skills through a series of drills, whereas others recommend learning of the whole task, providing it is not so complex as to overawe the competitor. However, the performance of a partially learned complex manœuvre at competitive speeds can be quite dangerous, and current psychological theory seems to favour a smooth transition through short steps, imperceptible to the pupil, until the skill is finally mastered.

If the learning process is fragmented, it is important to build 'cognitive bridges' for the athlete, helping him to understand how a simple and apparently meaningless routine can contribute to his final objective. Not only is motivation improved thereby, but people have a knack of remembering a skill that they appreciate will later be required. Any drills that are used must resemble the corresponding components of the sport very closely, or the motor controls of the brain will become confused. In planning a daily routine, the coach must weigh carefully not only the positive components of a given drill, but its possible negative influences on ultimate performance. Negative effects are particularly likely if the signal triggering the movement is the same in the drill and the sport, but the movement pattern differs in the two situations.

Within any given conditioning session, items practised early are learned the most effectively. If a task is left incomplete, a 'need tension' builds up in the individual, and this encourages learning. One way of exploiting this with an athlete is to pose performance questions, to be solved at the next session.

Armchair sportsmen can take some comfort from the fact

that skills such as gymnastics, diving, and ball-striking improve with 'mental practice'—a period of intense thought, particularly when linked with the watching of other competitors. Unfortunately for the lazy, the method is only really effective when interspersed with physical practice. Mental rehearsal of a complex movement sequence is also helpful immediately before its execution, as when carrying out a difficult dive.

Forgetting begins as soon as a practice session is over, and indeed occurs most rapidly in the first few minutes of relaxation. Control of forgetting is thus a further important aspect of the development of skill. Memory is improved if the coach emphasizes the subsequent need of the skill that is being taught. Other approaches are to schedule a further practice before too much skill has been lost, to facilitate retention through 'mental practice', and to allow for lapses of memory by an initial 'overlearning'.

Motivation. Current theories of motivation are based largely upon the observations of Dr. Skinner, using pigeons and other small animals. Skinner demonstrated that a tangible reward such as a food pellet was a powerful stimulus to the animal, encouraging it to press a foot-switch in response to a signal light. Punishment also modified behaviour, although less certainly; a rat could be taught that if it did not jump smartly to the opposite side of its cage when a signal was given, an uncomfortable electrical shock was applied to its back-side.

The underlying principles of these two types of experiment have been used to interpret human behaviour, in some instances with remarkable success. When dealing with the athlete, the Skinnerian psychologist would suggest that we should decide on an appropriate system of rewards or punishments, and administer such stimuli according to a suitable schedule. Unfortunately for the gifted rat psychologist, man is an individualist, and not everyone gets very excited when given a food pellet. The coach must thus first discover what 'turns on' an individual competitor at any given point in his career.

The traditional reward for the human species has been money, which is most effective when it is dispensed with uncertainty as to frequency and amount, as in the almost unexpected production bonus, and the occasional jackpot released by the one-armed bandit of the casino. In commercial sport, money is a motive, seen in the huge cash prizes won by professional golfers, and the large salaries dictated by professional hockey and football players. Such sordid considerations are theoretically eliminated in amateur sport; in practice, a successful competitor of the Western world may be awarded a scholarship to major in basket-weaving at a football-mad university, or may cherish dreams of retiring with subsequent sale of his smiling face to advertisers of a bank or a corn-oil margarine. In Eastern Europe, equally, many perquisites such as premium housing provide strong material motivation to athletic success.

Nevertheless, forward-looking applied psychologists are agreed that in our present affluent society, money provides an ever-less effective incentive to action. The coach must thus look to other rewards—the various delights of unusual sensory stimulation, satisfaction of curiosity, release of aggression, a developing sense of independence and power, the need for social recognition, and the personal pleasure of successful achievement. Some athletes can find great pleasure in the aesthetic beauty of gymnastics, or the dizzying sensations of a fast turn in skiing. Others are attracted by the novel in what is required of them, and for this reason find a moderately complex routine more stimulating than a drill that is too simple. Many sportsmen have a strong need for others to think well of them, as expressed not only in adulation and attention but in the tangible rewards of travel to exotic places, selection to major teams, and the earning of awards such as medals and trophies. Equally, failure carries a punishing loss of social status for many males. The coach can enhance this particular reward system by expressing his own opinions of performance quite strongly, not only approving the exceptional performance, but also expressing disapproval if he believes effort has been unjustifiably poor. However, punishment must be used with discretion. If excessive and not plainly linked to a poor performance, it can have a very negative effect. The athlete tends to assume, 'If I am going to be punished every time that I try, why bother to make the effort?'—a situation psychologists describe as an avoidance reaction.

Many, if not the majority, of international-level athletes are 'high achievers', people who are rarely satisfied with their efforts. High aspiration levels are partly a product of parental discipline, and partly an assimilation of middle-class social values. However, success also breeds aspiration. The main motivating force for the high achiever is self-fulfilment—he gains satisfaction from seeing his performance improve as he masters technique and realizes his potential. The mature performer of this type often rejoices more in self-improvement than in the defeat of his rivals. The coach can help forward the efforts of the achievement-oriented individual by giving him a 'knowledge of results'—drawing attention to subjective gains in condition ('Didn't it feel easier this time?') and pointing out objective evidence of accomplishments such as improvements in the frequency of training, distances, and times. Feelings about success can be more important to motivation than absolute results. To avoid disappointment, goals proposed by a coach should have at least a 50 per cent chance of realization. Competitors in target-shooting and high-jumping are in the particularly discouraging situation that their deficiencies are continually being brought home to them in a very obvious manner. In other sports, circumstances extenuating a poor performance, such as a hot day or a strong head-wind, can be noted, although deliberate lying to avoid disappointment will in time destroy confidence in the coach. Equally, an excess of ill-merited praise can destroy the effectiveness of this reward.

A further important role of the coach is to remove the various fears that limit both training and competitive performance. Some athletes need much more goading than others. Dr. Counsilman, the respected United States swimming coach, commented that one of his charges, John Kinsella, had to be restrained from attempting more than 14 000 metres per day; in contrast, Mark Spitz needed strong encouragement to undertake a bare 10 000 metres. There is less deliberate holding back if the athlete is confident that the coach has explained all that will be required of him at the start of a given training session.

There may be fears of pain to overcome. The endurance athlete must be willing to encounter once again the unpleasant sensations that follow a maximum work-out, and the contact sportsman must reduce his reactions to minor injuries. There is also the fear of failure and the fear of winning. The latter is perhaps the strongest obstacle to conquer in many competitors. A win is seen as imposing obligations of further unpleasant training, and pressing expectations of success in future competitions.

Peaking of performance. Perhaps the most useful way of expressing the interaction between emotional state and performance is through the concept of arousal, how 'worked-up' a person is. The performance of any task shows an inverted U-shaped relationship to the level of arousal (Fig. 16). A little excitement

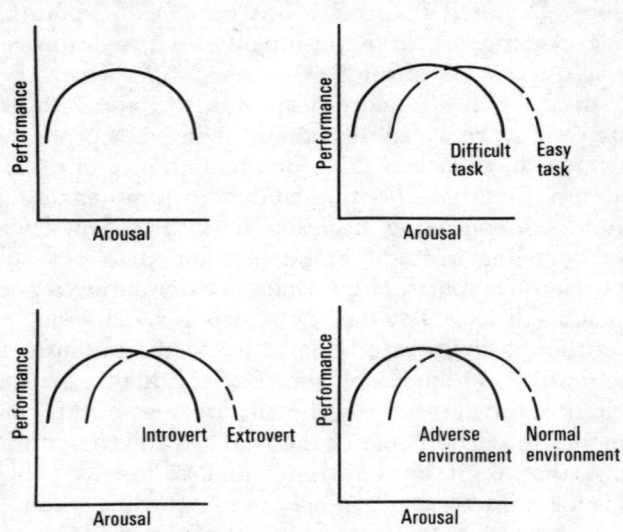

Fig. 16. The influence of arousal (excitement) on the performance of the athlete. Less arousal is tolerated by the introvert than by the extrovert. A difficult task or an adverse environment also diminishes the need for arousal.

helps key a person to top performance, but if stimulation is excessive then effort becomes erratic and performance declines. Individual athletes differ greatly in their need of arousal. The extrovert is usually operating below peak efficiency, and he thus enjoys the stimulation of noise and crowds. The introvert, on the other hand, is already over-aroused, and reacts badly to external stimulation.

The ideal level of arousal depends greatly on the nature of the task to be accomplished. Substantial arousal can be tolerated in repetitive activity with strong physical demands (such as endurance running), or games where release can be found in aggressive body contact (such as American football). Much less arousal is tolerated in skilled tasks such as pistol-shooting and golf putting; in these sports, the optimum level further decreases as the contest progresses, reaching a minimum during the final efforts of a target shooting sequence and on the eighteenth green of a close golf match.

Some athletes reach a peak of arousal early in training, and in others the maximum disturbance may be seen some time after a competition has been won or lost. However, many factors conspire to increase the arousal of the athlete during a key competition—not only the pressures of the event itself, but the noise of the crowd, the heat of the stadium, the strangeness of the foreign environment, a heavy travel schedule, and the stresses of separation from family and friends. Sometimes the watchful eye of a parent or a girl-friend in the grandstand can have an equally unnerving effect. The sum total is usually an over-aroused participant.

The good coach knows the form of the U-shaped curve for each of his charges, and devises measures to restore each of them to optimum arousal at the moment of competition. His notebook may show that in previous contests Jones was aroused to the point of trembling in the changing area, and yet went on to win; in contrast, Smith invariably lost his race when he reached an apparently equivalent level of nervousness. Individual counselling is needed to minister to these idiosyncrasies. Good results cannot be obtained from a shot-gun group pep talk. A brusque, even insulting manner may be adopted towards those who need more arousal; they are also given the physical stimulation of an extended warm-up. In contrast, the nervous majority are treated with gentle, soothing care. A quiet, deliberate, and reassuring manner is cultivated. Euphemisms are found for anxiety, such as excitement, anticipation, and a desire to do well. Care is taken not to discuss the problems presented by powerful opponents, and the athlete is encouraged to do his personal best without worrying excessively about the need for outright victory.

At the same time, practical methods are sought to reduce the tensions created by a strange environment. Familiar food is provided in place of exotic foreign dishes, supplies of books, newspapers, and music from the homeland are made available, and where possible telephone conversations with family and friends should be allowed. The arrangement of a party may help to relieve tensions, and some athletes (including an outspoken Australian girl swimming champion) have suggested that sexual activity on the night before a contest is a prerequisite of success! Others find self-relaxation in hypnosis and bio-feedback; with the latter approach, an athlete listens to his heart beat or muscle tone as broadcast over a loud-speaker until he has mastered methods of reducing his tension at will. The team physician may on occasion supplement such personal efforts by a little psychotherapy, or the prescription of sedatives to counteract sleeplessness. The coach also has a responsibility to separate excessively nervous individuals from other members of a team, so that the whole group does not become imbued with a spirit of anxiety regarding impending defeat.

Habituation. The long-term solution to the over-arousal of a promising athlete is to habituate him to the various stimuli encountered in the competitive environment. Most problems seem largest when viewed for the first time; if met repeatedly, they pale into insignificance, particularly if there has been a successful outcome. This is certainly true of performance before a vast crowd. On the first occasion, it is a terrifying experience, but after a few repetitions the average person discovers the situation is less threatening than he feared, and arousal diminishes accordingly.

Experience is thus a key to success in major competition. The contestant must be thoroughly habituated, not only to the crowded stadium, but also to associated harassments—long journeys, sudden changes of time zones and weather, noisy rooms in a hotel or athletes' village, and perhaps for the first time the pressure of vastly superior competition. Adaptation to such phenomena cannot occur through careful dieting, scrupulous conditioning, and occasional competitions in a small town in Northern Ontario. The budgets of sports associations must be stretched to allow world travel not only for anticipated victors, but also for promising junior members of a team who need international experience.

Overall game plan. Given good teaching of basic perceptual and motor skills, strong motivation to persist with conditioning, and appropriate manipulation of arousal levels, what other measures can be proposed to maximize performance for a crucial competition? Some authors have argued a need to 'taper' training not only from the physiological, but also from the psychological point of view, allowing the athlete a period of recuperation before a major challenge. The usual suggestion is to adopt a more relaxed attitude to preparation during the final one or two weeks. Unfortunately, there is no hard data to show whether this interval is too long, too short, or even necessary.

8
Doping the athlete

Having adopted every known ruse of diet and physiological and psychological preparation in order to excel in a given event, it is perhaps inevitable that some athletes should then be tempted to seek a 'wonder drug' that will give them a competitive edge over other contenders who have been equally diligent in their preparation. When a particularly fine performance is achieved, there is also a strong temptation for the less successful competitors to hint that some form of 'doping' was responsible. A strict control of drug usage is thus vital to the atmosphere of an international contest, protecting the hard-won victory from jealous criticism while at the same time ensuring punishment of dishonest participants.

In this chapter, we shall consider the definition of doping, the nature and dangers of some of the drugs that have been used to alter athletic performance, and the methods currently adopted for the control of doping.

Definition of doping

Doping may be defined as the use of substances or the employment of means in an attempt to augment artificially the performance of an athlete, during either participation or preparation.

This is a rather broader concept of doping than the simple use of drugs—it could encompass other artificial means of trying to change the outcome of a race, for instance a programme of deliberate starvation or dehydration, the transfusion of the athlete's own stored blood, or racing under hypnosis. It would also cover the athlete who used drugs such as the anabolic steroids in an attempt to increase muscle bulk, but who hid this practice from the officials by stopping the drug one or two weeks before competition.

The theoretical definition of doping is quite straightforward, but practical application of such rules is fraught with many difficulties. Often, the dividing line between permissible forms of medical treatment and doping is extremely fine. An athlete may report to the team physician complaining that he has difficulty in sleeping in a strange environment; it seems reasonable enough to prescribe a barbiturate sedative, yet traces of the drug may persist on the following day, with beneficial effects on the performance of an over-excited competitor. A footballer may be given an injection of local anaesthetic to allow him to move his ankle freely after a minor sprain; however, the cocaine derivative used for such treatment may have general effects on the body. An asthmatic swimmer may plunge into a pool with a high chlorine content and develop an attack of wheezing for which ephedrine is prescribed; the asthma is relieved, but as in the case of Rick Demont, the potential gold medallist in the 1500-metre event in Munich, persistent traces of the drug can lead to his disqualification on the day of competition.

There also seems little point in denouncing a drug or procedure that cannot be detected. Many long-distance cyclists drink strong solutions of coffee or cola every few minutes. It is likely that the caffeine modifies performance, but the habit of drinking tea and coffee is so commonplace that it would be difficult to draw up sensible rules prohibiting the practice. Equally, there are no sure ways of proving re-transfusion of stored blood, deliberate starvation, or dehydration. Much must thus be left to the sense of fair-play and sportsmanship of the athlete, coach, and attending physician. The wise athlete is his own policeman. He knows that most of the drugs are of no practical value, and that many have dangerous side-effects. He also realizes that symptoms such as pain and fatigue are warnings that his body has reached the limit of its capacity; attempts to surpass this limit by the use of drugs may cause permanent injury.

Drugs and their dangers

Cocaine. Perhaps influenced by stories of the prodigious feats of the coca-chewing Indians from Peru, Bolivia, and the upper

Amazon, a number of the early long-distance athletes, particularly cyclists, are believed to have taken cocaine in the hopes of postponing fatigue and increasing endurance.

The drug is a powerful stimulant of the brain, and if given as an intravenous injection it can produce an ecstatic sensation of both physical and mental power, with temporary disappearance of feelings of fatigue and hunger. It seems to be one of the few forms of dope that has a positive effect on performance, and at least in the laboratory it can prolong endurance time in bicycle ergometer tests. However, muscle tone is also increased, leading to loss of skill in more complex tasks, and larger doses can give rise to muscle spasm and convulsions.

The body temperature is increased after administration of cocaine, so it could contribute to heat illness; however, a more important reason for avoiding all use of cocaine is that addiction is extremely rapid.

Other stimulants of the brain. Occasional competitors have dosed themselves with other brain stimulants, such as strychnine. Convulsions are produced very readily with this drug, and some physicians have alleged that one of the competitors at the Melbourne Olympics showed spasms characteristic of strychnine poisoning. More recently, urine testing of 139 participants in the World Cycling Championships (Holland, 1967) revealed 2 men who had been taking strychnine. The drug is powerful, and certainly ill-suited for use as amateur medication.

Caffeine is well known as one of the active drugs in coffee and tea. Small doses of the pure compound stimulate the brain, giving a quickening of thought, and a lessening of feelings of fatigue and drowsiness. Larger doses can make the individual over-excited and restless, with wandering of the attention and difficulty in sleeping. The heart becomes more irritable, and may show 'extra beats'; it has also been suggested that caffeine increases the liability of an older person to heart attacks. Some laboratory experiments have shown people to walk as much as 20 to 30 per cent further following caffeine treatment; the drug produces a small increase in the output of the heart and the maximum oxygen transporting power of the body, but the effects on endurance probably arise mainly from changes in the appreciation of effort by the stimulated brain. In the athletic context, there might be some advantage to the man performing boring, repetitive work such as distance cycling, but the increase of excitation would have an adverse effect on most competitors in skilled events (Fig. 16, p. 106). Other potent compounds in tea and coffee are theophylline and theobromine; these also produce some stimulation of the brain, and in the case of theobromine there is commonly an increase in the maximum force of the limb muscles, with loss of co-ordination and recently learnt skills. We have noted the frequent use of tea and coffee solutions by cyclists, and the difficulty in regulating the use of these drugs. Nevertheless, the International Cyclists Union will disqualify anyone convicted of taking pure forms of these compounds as opposed to the more dilute solutions found in normal beverages.

Drugs that depress the brain. Since over-arousal (Fig. 16) limits the performance of most competitors in skilled events, there would seem a theoretical advantage in the use of drugs that depress brain function. A variety of compounds have been used at different times, ranging from dangerously addictive drugs such as morphine and heroin, through a wide range of barbiturates to alcohol. The last is perhaps the commonest choice, and a substantial proportion of competitors in events such as pistol-shooting take moderate amounts of alcohol in an attempt to steady their hands. At the Mexico City Olympics (1968), two of the pistol-shooters were disqualified on this basis.

Amphetamines. The 'speed' addict, or amphetamine user, is an all-too-common phenomenon of modern society, and there seems to have been a parallel growth in the taking of this drug by athletes. The cyclist who died during the Rome Olympics (1960) was known to have used 'Ronicol', a drug increasing blood flow to the limbs; however, he had also taken other medicaments, and it was suspected that both he and two of his companions who had severe heat illness had received large amounts of amphetamine. Other fatalities in which amphetamine derivatives are thought to have played a part include that of Tommy Simpson (Tour de France, 1967) and of a major league soccer player in Greece (1973).

The difficulty in obtaining reliable information on the extent of the problem was highlighted by two almost concurrent questionnaires. In 1957, the American Medical Association circulated a form to coaches, trainers, and athletes, requesting information on the use of amphetamines by competitors; less than 1 per cent of respondents admitted any knowledge that the drug was being used. A rather similar survey was conducted by the American College of Sports Medicine the following year, but this showed 35 per cent of athletes as using amphetamines during competition. When urine testing was introduced in the mid-1960s, the second estimate proved much nearer the truth, at least for the endurance competitors. Tests conducted on Belgian cyclists in 1965 (Table 9) showed 37·5

Table 9. *Percentages of Belgian cyclists with urine samples containing amphetamine, based on data of Dr. Dirix. Note the progressive decline since the institution of urine samples in 1965*

Category of cyclist	1965 (per cent)	1966 (per cent)	1967 (per cent)	1968 (per cent)	1969 (per cent)
Professional	37·5	27·0	0·0	13·0	17·5
Independent	16·5	—	—	—	—
Amateur	23·0	14·5	14·0	7·5	8·5
Junior	{ 7·0	12·5 }	8·0	3·3	5·5
Debutant			3·0	7·7	0·0
Female	—	—	—	0·0	—
Other	—	—	0·0	—	4·3
Average, all categories	25·5	20·0	8·0	8·2	8·1

per cent of professionals and 23·0 per cent of amateurs were taking amphetamines. Among 139 competitors at the World Cycling Championships in Holland (1967), 5 were using amphetamines, and 6 ephedrine (which produces some rather similar effects on the body). In the West, 8 of 57 cyclists at the Pan American Games in Winnipeg (1967) had amphetamine-related compounds in their urine. Since the institution of controls, there has been a substantial decline in this particular form of doping.

Until a few years ago, amphetamine was widely prescribed to treat mild depression and obesity, since it suppresses appetite and at the same time makes a person more cheerful. The arousing effects on the brain were well known to all-night truck drivers, students cramming for examinations, and others who wished to prevent themselves from going to sleep. Most countries now impose rigid controls on the prescription and sale of amphetamines because of their abuse by social addicts.

From the viewpoint of the athlete, the main effects are the elevation of mood, and the constriction of blood vessels in the skin. In theory, the former could allow an endurance athlete to continue running when a more rational assessment of symptoms would tell him to stop. At the same time, constriction of the skin vessels could return blood to the heart, allowing the latter to pump more to the active muscles. Despite these anticipated gains, laboratory trials of amphetamines have obstinately refused to show any advantage to the treated athlete, at least when the experiment was conducted under 'double-blind' protocol, with neither the athlete nor the physician knowing which of the competitors had received amphetamine, and which an inactive substitute.

The deaths associated with amphetamine usage show it to be a very dangerous drug. If the skin blood vessels cannot open up in the normal manner as the user becomes hot, a dangerous heat illness seems inevitable. The cheerful and unrealistic 'high' leads a contestant to ignore the normal warnings of fatigue and pain. Larger doses can cause aggressiveness, delusions, hallucinations, and anti-social behaviour, both on and off the field. Often already aroused by the stresses of competition, the further stimulation of the amphetamine leads to excessive nervousness, loss of skill, and difficulty in sleeping; there is a temptation to calm the nerves by barbiturates or other depressant drugs, leading to a cycle of 'highs' and 'lows' treated by ever larger doses of self-administered drugs. If given intravenously, the amateur often uses a poorly sterilized needle, and blood-borne infections such as hepatitis can lead to the permanent damage of the liver and other vital organs. Occasionally, a mistaken calculation of dosage can produce such a large rise of blood pressure that there is bleeding into the brain or failure of the heart; the normal rhythm of the heart may also be disturbed, and the danger of arrest of the heart during activity is increased.

Despite wide knowledge of these various dangers, a proportion of athletes still use amphetamines, particularly in circumstances where they think they will not be caught. The majority insist that they are using them to alter performance rather than to produce a 'high'. However, it is interesting that many of those implicated continue to use the amphetamine when they are not competing, finding that it also 'helps' them in their daily tasks. Authorities still argue how far a person can become physically dependent upon amphetamine, but psychological addiction is quite rapid.

Anabolic steroids. The anabolic steroids such as Danabol (Dianabol in the United States, methandrostenolone) are compounds rather similar to the male sex hormone testosterone. At puberty, a sudden increase in the secretion of testosterone by the growing boy produces not only the outward characteristics that differentiate him from a girl (such as a deep voice and hair on the face) but also a surge of growth, with increase in the strength of the muscles. The anabolic hormones such as Danabol have a slightly different chemical structure from testosterone, the object of the modification being to enhance the muscle-building effect while minimizing the influence of the drug on sexual characteristics. Normal use is to encourage the redevelopment of musculature in an older person with wasting due to prolonged bed rest, and most manufacturers specify that athletes should not receive this class of compound. In any event, its effectiveness in a normal, healthy young man is doubtful, since his testes are already producing large quantities of the natural hormone. Some laboratory trials have suggested that body weight can be increased by long courses of androgens, particularly if given in association with a high-protein diet; however, at least a part of the weight gain seems to be fluid rather than muscle.

The dangers of the androgens include possible damage to the liver and kidneys, wasting of the testes, and impotence in the male, with acne and the development of secondary male characteristics in the female; in young people, a premature cessation in growth of the long bones is also induced.

Despite these hazards, the androgens are widely used by athletes, particularly those involved in North American football and strength events. Detection is difficult, since no trace of the synthetic hormone can be discovered a week after treatment has stopped. Hear-say reports suggest usage by up to 90 per cent of football players and 70 per cent of strength athletes; it is almost the general consensus among North American athletes that it is impossible to reach the top in weight-lifting events, discus-throwing, javelin, shot-putting, or hammer-throwing without recourse to the anabolic steroids. Individual competitors are understandably more reluctant to disclose their own experiences. One newspaper article quoted Harold Connolly, the Olympic champion hammer-thrower of 1956, as saying that he took Danabol briefly after the 1960 Olympics. The same account reported a conversation with Dave Steen, the Canadian shot-putter, who admitted taking a course of 25 Danabol tablets during the training for his gold-medal performance at the Commonwealth Games in Kingston, Jamaica (1966). Hagerman, the international expert on rowing, obtained other case histories at the World Pentathlon Games (1966) and the Mexico City Olympics (1968) by assuring the athletes concerned that their anonymity would be preserved and that no value judgements would be made. One pentathlon participant admitted using the Winthrop preparation of anabolic steroid, 'Winstrol', for four months, and claimed that he had experienced an increase of both weight and lean tissue, with marked improvement in his swimming and running times. A shot-putter used Danabol sporadically for two years, during which time his weight increased from 225 lb to 280 lb, and he achieved his best throw of 66 feet. A discus thrower likewise went from 220 lb to 268 lb in less than six months, with his throws increasing from around 180 feet to 207 feet. All of the athletes concerned were naturally training hard, and there is no conclusive proof that equal gains in weight and performance would not have occurred if the drug had not been taken.

Other modifications of body weight. Competitors in wrestling and boxing matches will sometimes deliberately go for long periods without fluids, spend time in saunas, and adopt other measures to allow them to compete in a lower weight category than that to which they are entitled by their normal physique. The attempt is plainly unsportsmanlike, since the object of the weight-categorization is to allow a safe contest between well-matched competitors. The effectiveness of the dehydration is also doubtful in terms of competitive advantage, for while a smaller opponent is encountered, the individual's capacity for endurance effort is weakened by the dehydration.

There were reports that before the Munich Olympic Games (1972) some of the very-long-distance runners had deliberately starved themselves, in an attempt to burn away flesh from the upper parts of their bodies, thus reducing the weight to be moved during running. This could be the equivalent of taking a high protein and fat diet at the training table. If there were a switch to carbohydrate feeding two or three days before competition, this might be a very effective method of getting an outstanding result (Fig. 11, p. 87). Nevertheless, it is an unnatural procedure, and should be regarded as a form of doping. Moreover, rigorous starvation can be quite dangerous when conducted outside a hospital—particularly in combination with vigorous exercise—the potassium released from the muscles that are broken down could give rise to a fatal abnormality of heart rhythm.

Blood transfusion. In very prolonged activity, the physiological factor limiting performance seems not the ability of the heart to pump blood to the muscles, but rather the ability of the body to find blood to pump. One would thus anticipate that artificial means of increasing the amount of blood in the body might enhance endurance performance. The majority of laboratory experiments suggest that a small advantage can be gained in this way. It has thus been suggested that athletes could arrange to have one or two bottles of blood taken from an arm vein, store this in the refrigerator while the body regenerated the missing red cells, and then have the material re-infused into the body. There are some risks in transfusion, even when the individual's own blood is used; such risks are justifiable in case of medical necessity, but are certainly not worth taking in order to gain an unfair advantage over one's fellow competitors. There is no proof that any athletes have yet used this manœuvre, but its potential has been discussed in the literature for some years, and one may thus suspect that occasional individuals have experimented with the technique.

Hypnosis. The ultimate limitation in most individuals is psychological rather than physiological. Thus surrender of the will to an outside agency may offer a mechanism of increasing performance. There were reports that athletes in Melbourne (1956) were using this technique, but presumably they had little success, and it is not popular at the present time. Hypnosis is most effective in dealing with unstable individuals, and such people are unlikely to have the perseverance to make the top athletic ranks. Further, as with physical methods of extending performance, there is a danger that a hypnotized competitor may be persuaded to push himself to the point of injury, having lost the normal warning signals of pain and fatigue. Finally, in amateur hands hypnosis can unleash a major psychiatric disturbance in the occasional individual.

For all of these reasons, deep hypnosis is to be avoided. However, our experience with post-coronary patients has been that a medically qualified hypnotherapist can teach the ordinary person techniques of inducing a light trance as an aid to relaxation; such self-hypnosis might help to calm an overanxious athlete, allowing him a good night's sleep and ensuring a more appropriate level of arousal (Fig. 16, p. 106) immediately before competition. If used in this self-administered way, there should be little objection to the practice on either medical or ethical grounds.

The prevention of doping

Methods for the prevention of doping fall into three broad categories—control by governmental or inter-governmental legislation, regulation by athletic associations, and gentle persuasion.

Laws are plainly necessary to control national and international traffic in dangerously addictive drugs such as morphine, heroin, and cocaine, and if physicians, coaches, or athletes violate such laws they will face the risk of severe penalties from the civil authorities. The recent tightening of regulations for the prescription and sale of amphetamines, for example, has undoubtedly contributed to a reduction in the frequency of doping with this particular drug. However, the police of most nations do not have the manpower to enforce rigidly existing legislation governing the possession and abuse of drugs, and they could not conceivably cover every situation where an athlete had in his pocket a small quantity of a drug, appropriate enough for the treatment of a chronic disorder such as asthma, yet unacceptable when self-administered with a view to modifying performance.

Sports associations have adopted the dual approach of drawing up lists of prohibited drugs, and making various types of spot-check to ensure that their rules are observed. At the Olympic Games in Helsinki (1952), unannounced visits were made to sleeping quarters, and personal belongings were searched. In Tokyo (1964), a physician searched cyclists for signs of recent intramuscular or intravenous injections, and found suspicious marks on 13 of 100 contestants; examination of urine specimens from this group failed to show any amphetamines, and further enquiry suggested that most of the injections had been of innocuous and ineffective materials such as methylene blue and camphor oil. The testing of the urine of winners was first formally required at the Mexico City Olympic Games (1968); as a result, several medals were lost, and four athletes were disqualified. In Munich, an even more elaborate system of analysis was established, and six contestants were eliminated from the contest because of positive urine samples. The checks continued at the winter games in Sapporo (1972), and the finding of ephedrine in the urine of a West German hockey player led to the forfeit of the game in which he had been playing. Again in Canada, a member of the national sailing team competing in the Olympics at Kingston was disqualified after taking a popular remedy for a head cold; the sensitive anti-doping controls revealed traces of the prohibited ephedrine in a random check of urine samples.

Some measure of the effectiveness of urine analyses in controlling doping can be made from the experience of the Belgian Cycling League, as analysed by Dr. Dirix (Table 8). Urine checks were begun in 1965. In that year, 37·5 per cent of professionals, 23·0 per cent of amateurs, and 7 per cent of juniors were found to be using amphetamine, an overall frequency of 25·5 per cent positive samples. Apparently, word of the effectiveness of the testing soon spread, and over the next few years there was a steady drop in the percentage of disqualifications. However, it is sad to report that the real crime was considered not doping, but getting caught, and as late as 1969 many positive results were being found among professionals at competitions where a check of the urine had not been anticipated.

Other ways were also being found to outwit the analyst. Occasionally, imposters would report for the medical examination. Competitors with more enterprise than honesty hid bags of 'clean' urine under their armpits, and proceeded to void these bags through realistic simulations of the normal penis. Athletes with a knowledge of chemistry searched through the records of drug companies to find alternative compounds that were either not forbidden or difficult to detect. Some soon discovered that a strong dose of bicarbonate of soda slowed the excretion of amphetamine to a point where it was almost undetectable in the urine. Long arguments also developed in the committee rooms, with appeals and counter-appeals, and it became necessary for the officials to provide an elaborate system of checks to guard the identity of individual samples, to verify the competence of the analytical methods, and to provide duplicate specimens of urine that defending national officials could submit to alternative laboratories for independent analysis. It was vital to ensure that justice was both done, and seen to be done; that innocent athletes were not wrongly disgraced, and that the guilty did not escape disqualification through some minor legalistic quibble.

One very controversial area has been the proving of intent to alter performance. It is very difficult to draw a dividing line between the legitimate medical use of a barbiturate (for sleeplessness) or ephedrine (for asthma) and a deliberate attempt to change the result of an event by use of the same drug. In an attempt to overcome this difficulty, a list of prohibited drugs was distributed to all team physicians before the Munich Games, and in the medical centre at the Olympic site proscribed drugs were marked with a special colour coding. Nevertheless, Rick Demont was given a detectable quantity of ephedrine, apparently inadvertently. The same type of misadventure has occurred at several subsequent international competitions. Factors contributing to continuing misunderstandings may include the tendency of physicians to carry their own drugs rather than use the central pharmacy, and the difficulty in equating a manufacturer's name for a product with its chemical constituents. For example, the Robins compound Dimetapp is widely used (even without prescription) for the treatment of hay fever, and most people know that it contains anti-histamines; but it also contains a close relative of ephedrine, phenylephrine. The same is true of some eye drops used by swimmers as an antidote to irritation from highly chlorinated water. It seems vital that athletes and coaches be cautioned against any self-medication of minor ailments, and that all physicians attending competitions become thoroughly familiar not only with the effects of what they prescribe, but also the chemical constituents of the preparations that are to be used. Government could help in this situation by insisting that pharmaceutical companies label their products with chemical rather than high-sounding trade names.

A second difficulty may come from a lack of specificity in the analytical method. The amphetamines are fairly readily distinguished from the normal constituents of the urine, using an apparatus known as a gas–liquid chromatograph. However, it is much more of a problem to distinguish natural and androgenic steroids. Detection is now becoming possible through what is known as a radio-immune assay. The prohibited material is injected into rabbits, and as a defence mechanism they form antibodies that will precipitate the offending chemical. Serum from the immunized rabbits is treated to make it radioactive, and is then mixed with the suspect urine specimen. If the illegal drug is present, the antibodies will be precipitated as they react with it, the loss of radioactivity from the solution providing a quantitative and very specific method of measuring the material concerned. If positive results are obtained, further checks can be carried out, using both a gas–liquid chromatograph to separate out individual constituents of the urine, and a mass spectrometer to determine the molecular weight of the components thus distinguished; it is rare for natural and synthetic compounds to have the same molecular weight.

The problem with the anabolic steroids is that any effect on muscle mass is long-term in nature, but if the drug is stopped for a week or so it can no longer be detected in the urine. The medical committee of the International Olympic Organization has suggested several ways of circumventing this difficulty. One is to rely on the athlete's inherent dislike of changing his routine; if he realizes he must stop taking the anabolic steroids a week or ten days before every major competition, he may well decide it is preferable to avoid the drugs altogether. A second and very expensive solution would be to make random spot-checks on the urine of competitors at unannounced times during their preparation. A third, and more practical approach is to keep a close and regular check on the weights of top athletes, and make careful examination of any who show a surprising gain.

Regular weight records would provide some control of dehydration in wrestlers and starvation in long-distance runners. In the case of the wrestlers, there have been various attempts to predict what their normal weight should be from other measurements of body dimensions.

No techniques have yet been evolved for the control of blood transfusions. One possibility might be to check on the average age of the red cells in the blood; ageing occurs during storage, and in consequence the oxygen consumption of blood specimens is reduced.

Further advances of technique will certainly enhance the likelihood that offenders will be detected and punished. However, a strong emphasis on the policing of athletic events can add to the excitement of wrong-doing and convince the athlete that there is some advantage to be gained from the use of illegal drugs. In the long run, a more effective approach may be psychological—to appeal to his sense of fair play, stressing that the objective of a sport is not to test the prowess of rival pharmacists, with the athletes serving as dumb exploited guinea-pigs; rather, the intent is to measure the strength and determination of the individuals themselves in a well-matched display of their natural prowess. Pride cannot be taken in a hollow victory; success is only rewarding if earned by honest endeavour. Furthermore, the use of drugs carries its own heavy penalties. Often performance deteriorates rather than improves. Changes of mood and personality can endanger the competitor himself and his fellow enthusiasts. Side effects can range from impotence to death. Surely, such arguments must carry greater weight than the self-important strutting of a minor official wheeling away a cartload of urine samples!

9
The athlete's environment

Variations in the athlete's environment, including contests at high altitudes, exposure to extremes of heat and cold, and underwater competitions are important not only in modifying performance, but also in creating new risks of disability and even of death.

High altitude

An increase of altitude has several practical consequences for the athlete (Table 10). It reduces the density of the air, thus lowering wind-resistance, it reduces the oxygen pressure in the air that is breathed, thus restricting maximum oxygen transport, and it lowers atmospheric temperature. There are also small decreases in the force of gravity, but it would be neces-

Table 10. *Changes in the athlete's environment with altitude*

Altitude (ft)	(m)	Temperature (°C)	Barometric pressure (mm Hg)	Oxygen pressure (mm Hg)	Air density (g per l)	Gravit
0	0	15·0	760	149	1·23	1·00
2 000	610	11·0	707	138	1·15	1·00
4 000	1220	7·1	656	127	1·09	1·00
6 000	1829	3·1	609	118	1·02	1·00
8 000	2438	−0·8	565	108	0·96	1·00
10 000	3048	+4·8	523	100	0·90	1·00
12 000	3658	−8·8	483	91	0·85	1·00
14 000	4267	−12·7	447	84	0·80	1·00

sary to climb to the top of Mount Everest to get a 0·2 per cent advantage from this phenomenon.

Wind-resistance accounts for a substantial fraction of energy expenditures in all events that produce fast movement of man or other objects in air—running, cycling, speed-skating, and throwing, for example. At sea-level, 11 per cent of the energy used in running three miles is expended against wind-resistance; the effect is proportional to the square of the speed, and in cycling it may account for 50 per cent or more of energy usage. Resistance is proportional to the density of the atmosphere; thus, in Mexico City (2240 m) resistance is about 24 per cent lower than at sea-level, giving a potential advantage of (11 × 24) per cent, or 2·6 per cent, to a man running three miles, with even greater benefits to competitors in short distance events.

The reduced oxygen content of the air breathed inevitably hampers oxygen transport. At sea level, oxygen at a pressure of about 149 mm Hg is inhaled and mixed with spent gas already in the air passages, so that the pressure penetrating to the lungs is about 100 mm Hg. The chemical properties of haemoglobin are such (Fig. 17) that this pressure produces about 96 per cent

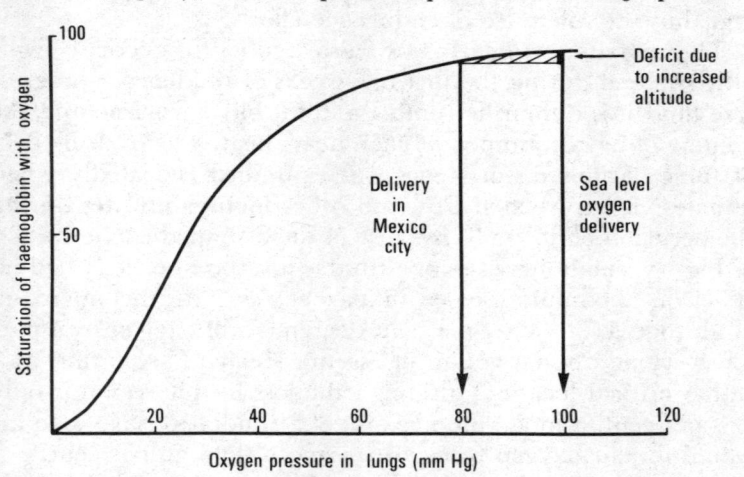

FIG. 17. The oxygen-combining properties of the red cell pigment haemoglobin and the effect of altitude. Note that in Mexico City the arterial blood is less fully saturated with oxygen as a result of the reduced oxygen pressure in the lungs.

complete oxygen saturation of the red cell pigment in the capillary blood vessels of the lungs. Breathing becomes easier as the density of the atmosphere decreases, and in an attempt at compensation for the thinner air respiration is increased both at rest and during effort. Consequently, the oxygen pressure within the lungs drops rather less than that in the outside air. However, the compensation is incomplete, since over-breathing carries its own penalties; an excessive wash-out of carbon dioxide from the lungs leads to intermittent breathing, a drop in blood flow to the brain, and other problems of 'mountain sickness'.

At the altitude of Mexico City, outside air contains oxygen at a pressure of about 112 mm Hg, and the pressure within the lungs is 75–80 mm Hg. It follows from the characteristics of haemoglobin that the oxygen saturation of blood in the pulmonary capillaries is 7–8 per cent less than at sea-level, and since the muscles are unable to extract more oxygen from venous blood, 7–8 per cent less oxygen is transported to the working tissues for every litre of blood that is pumped around the circulatory system. During sub-maximum effort, oxygen transport can be sustained by a proportionate increase of heart rate, but there is inevitably a drop in maximum oxygen intake and thus the tolerance of endurance effort.

The maximum heart rate also tends to decrease with altitude, and during the first few weeks of residence a progressive fluid loss diminishes both the total blood volume and the volume of blood pumped at each heart beat. The overall effect of these various disturbances was examined repeatedly when athletes visited Mexico City and other high camp sites during the period 1966 to 1968. Because of the S-shaped configuration of Fig. 17, small increases of altitude (to 1500 m or less) had no effect on maximum oxygen intake; however, further increases of altitude led to a 3·2 per cent decrement of oxygen transport for every additional 300 m of ascent. Mexico City is thus at a rather critical location; although the loss in this region is only 7–8 per cent, a moderate increase of altitude (to, say, 3000 m) would impair oxygen transport by more than 30 per cent.

Anaerobic capacity and power (Table 5, p. 40) are largely unchanged at moderate altitudes, although there may be some slowing in the repayment of oxygen debts incurred by anaerobic efforts. There is thus no physiological reason to expect any change in isolated sprint performances, although increased recovery intervals are desirable if many repetitions are to be carried out, either in training or in eliminating heats.

If the athlete remains at high altitude, adjustments of body physiology such as reductions in tissue bicarbonate levels, increases in haemoglobin and red cell counts, and restoration of normal fluid levels, lead to progressive improvements in endurance performance over the course of several months (Chapter 6).

The cooling effect of altitude, 2 °C per 300 m, is largely independent of the sea-level temperature. Thus in Mexico the suffocating heat of the border post at Nuevo Laredo is translated to quite pleasant temperatures at the elevation of the Olympic Stadium. In contrast, a cool day in the Derbyshire Dales can become dangerously cold with the added wind and cooling found by a 1000-m hill climb (page 135).

How did actual performances in the Mexico City Olympic contests match predictions based on the combined effects of

Table 11. *Effect of altitude on relationship between world records and winning performances in a given Olympic Contest (based on analysis by Dr. Albert Craig)*

Event	Average for Olympics 1904–64 Performance (percentage of world record)	Athletes beating world record (percentage of successful competitors)	Olympics 1968 (Mexico City) Performance (percentage of world record)	Athletes beating world record (percentage of successful competitors)
Running				
Men	98·7	16	98·2	40
Women	98·8	43	100·6	83
Field Events				
Men	95·5	9	99·1	25
Women	96·2	16	99·2	20
Swimming				
Men	98·5	6	99·2	13
Women	97·9	16	99·2	14
Overall result	97·1	15	99·1	29

Table 12. *The influence of altitude on performance in Olympic throwing events (distances in metres)*

Event	1956 (Melbourne)	1960 (Rome)	1964 (Tokyo)	Ballistic advantage at 2400 m*	1968 (Mexico)	World records 1975
Shot-put	17·6	18·5	19·5	0·058	20·5	21·8 (1973)
Hammer-throw	62·0	65·4	68·0	0·53	73·4	76·6 (1974)
Discus-throw	54·1	56·7	58·9	0·69	64·8	68·4 (1968)
Javelin-throw	77·8	79·6	80·2	1·62	90·1	94·1 (1973)

* Calculations of the ballistic advantage were developed by Dr. Dickinson and his associates of the U.S. Army Ballistic Research Laboratory.

decreased wind-resistance, decreased maximum oxygen intake, and a temperate climate? Previous Olympic winners in running, field events, and swimming had averaged 2·9 per cent poorer scores than world records (Tables 11 and 12). However, in Mexico City, 29 per cent of successful competitors exceeded the best world marks, and the average of all winning scores was only 0·9 per cent below world records. The biggest advance over previous Olympics was in the field events; typically, these had fallen 4–5 per cent below world records, but in Mexico the gap was narrowed to less than 1 per cent. Swimming times in Mexico more than maintained their expected relationship to world records, despite the absence of any significant gain from lower wind-resistance in this sport; the explanation seems that 23 of the 29 races contested were brief (50–200 m) events, covered largely by anaerobic effort. In the running events, records were broken in five of the ten anaerobic events, but with a few notable exceptions (Kip Keino in the 1500-m run, Christopher Hohne in the 50-km walk), there was a progressive deterioration in scores for events lasting longer than one minute; on average, the effect was about 3 per cent for a four-minute contest, and 8 per cent for a one-hour event.

A catalogue of the medical hazards of altitude is quite alarming; potential problems include mountain sickness, oxygen lack in the heart and brain, waterlogging of the lungs (pulmonary oedema), and rupture of the spleen. Most authorities are reluctant to make a categoric definition of safe altitudes for competition. Much depends on the class of event; on the age, state of acclimatization, and general health of the athlete; and on the environmental temperature.

Mountain sickness is an early problem. The recreational athlete rarely encounters symptoms below 3000 m, but some doctors have argued that the heavy training schedule of the international competitor places him at greater risk, so that the unpleasant picture of headache, difficulty in sleeping, irritability, and stomach disturbances are seen in competitions at altitudes as low as around 2000 m. Usually the condition is not too serious, and resolves itself within two or three days. It is sufficient to reduce training temporarily, and to take simple remedies for headache and sleeplessness. Occasionally, the sickness may progress to a more chronic form requiring evacuation of the athlete to sea-level.

Endurance athletes normally push themselves to the point of impending oxygen lack in the heart, brain, and other vital tissues; the risks of a distance event are increased at altitude only if the competitor attempts to sustain the same pace that he would have adopted at sea-level. Oxygen lack in the brain can cause short-lived abnormalities of vision and loss of co-ordination that can increase the risk of physical injury. Oxygen lack in the heart muscle can disturb the normal rhythm of the heart, and in an older competitor it may also increase the chances of a 'heart attack'.

Pulmonary oedema was first given wide attention by its disabling effects on Indian troops rushed to the Himalayas in the border dispute with China. It has been described in recreational athletes at altitudes between 2500 m and 3500 m, vulnerability being increased by cold weather, upper respiratory infections, and sustained exercise. If not treated promptly by the administration of oxygen, the waterlogging of the lungs can be fatal.

Rupture of the spleen at altitude is an occasional hazard in the Negro; it is associated with a sickle-shaped deformity of the red blood cells, and has led to fatal haemorrhage at altitudes as low as 2400 m. It is thus a wise precaution for the team physician to examine the red blood cells of all negroid athletes who will be competing at altitude.

Before the 1968 Olympics, a Toronto journalist interpreted my cautious assessment of these various risks under the banner headline 'Doctor says athletes will die in Mexico City'. Fortunately, the journalist was wrong, both in his interpretation of my writings and in his prediction of the outcome of the Olympic event. One distance runner did develop a partial loss of vision for a brief period, and several other track athletes noted abnormalities of heart rhythm that had not been observed at sea-level; however, there were no heart attacks, no cases of pulmonary oedema, and no ruptured spleens. This does not imply that the problems of altitude can be ignored with impunity, and that other cities at even greater altitude can now press their claim for international competitions. The available evidence supports the 1974 resolution of the Féderation Internationale de Medicine Sportive, urging caution at altitudes greater than 2300 m, and an absolute prohibition of competitions at altitudes above 3000 m.

Heat

Cars over-heated by endurance effort on an expressway are common casualties of the North American summer. However, it is less well known that the moderate heat of central and northern Europe can have an equally disastrous effect on the endurance athlete, particularly if the weather is humid.

The basic problems of the car and the distance runner are similar—heat is accumulating faster than it can be dissipated. Man converts only about 25 per cent of the energy content of food into useful motion (Chapter 4), and the remaining 75 per cent of the calories that are burnt must therefore appear as heat. The total energy cost of a marathon race, for example, is about 4000 Cal, so that the waste heat can be as much as 3000 Cal. On a clear day, this burden may be further augmented by radiant heating from the sun. If none of the heat were lost from the body its temperature would rise by more than 30 °C. Plainly, this would be lethal.

Some heat is lost by the cooling force of the wind and body motion. The effectiveness of convective cooling, as this is called, depends on the difference of temperature between the body and the air, on the wind speed, and on the speed of the athlete. If air temperatures are over 30 °C, little heat can be lost by this route; losses are also less on a calm day, and less for a marathon runner than for a long-distance cyclist.

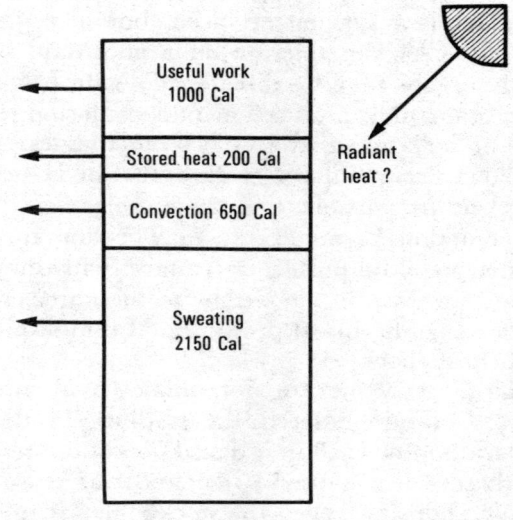

FIG. 18. Typical heat balance during a marathon race.

The main route of heat loss is normally the evaporation of sweat; this depends on humidity and the speed of air movement over the body surface. Any residue of waste heat not accounted for by convection and sweating is temporarily stored through a rise of body temperature. The typical situation of the marathon runner is illustrated in Fig. 18. Convection accounts for a loss of 650 Cal. A further four litres of sweat is produced. Assuming this to be vaporized (rather than rolling uselessly to the ground) it disposes of about 2150 Cal, leaving a residual 200 Cal to be accommodated through a 2 °C rise of body temperature.

Performance of the endurance athlete deteriorates in the heat because blood is pumped to the skin rather than the active muscles; under adverse conditions, as much as a fifth of the total blood flow may be diverted to the skin. There is also a progressive water depletion of the tissues. Even if the competitors are provided with suitable drinks, thirst provides a poor guide to fluid needs, and most athletes have difficulty in sustaining an adequate intake of water. A marathon race can cause a 5 per cent loss of body water, with a corresponding diminution in the volume of blood pumped by the heart per beat. As at high altitude, the normal response of the athlete to these handicaps is a slowing of speed, but if he attempts to sustain the pace he can tolerate on a cool day, blood flow to vital body organs may be threatened. A drop in the blood flow to the brain may produce mental confusion, loss of co-ordination, or collapse, and loss of consciousness (heat collapse). If blood flow to the skin also fails, body temperature rises rapidly and irreversibly, the danger point being a reading of 40 °C: sometimes convulsions may be produced (heat stroke). Other potential problem areas are the kidneys and the adrenal glands; a drop in blood flow to the latter can cause a vicious circle of falling blood pressure and diminishing flow to vital tissues (heat shock).

These alarming events are not unknown in international competition. Dorando entered the stadium in the London Olympic marathon of 1908 in a dazed condition; he turned in the wrong direction, collapsed twice, and was in a semi-coma for two days after the race. In Stockholm (1912), the day selected for the Olympic marathon was again warm and humid, and one of the runners (Lazarro) collapsed at the nineteenth mile, to die in hospital on the following day. Twelve years later, five of the 10 000-metre contestants at the Paris Olympics were admitted to hospital for the treatment of heat stroke. The British Empire Games in Vancouver (1954) were marred by the near death of a British marathon runner, and in the Rome Olympics (1960) three Danish competitors in the 100-kilometre cycle race developed heat stroke, one of the group subsequently dying. In the case of the cyclists, it was suspected that heat elimination had been hampered by doping with drugs that constricted the blood supply to the skin (Chapter 8).

Athletes face even greater problems in the heat of the North American summer, and despite partial acclimatization to the adverse climate, the 'football' season in the Southern United States leads to frequent episodes of heat illness, with three or four deaths in most years. A particular problem of the North American football player is the wearing of nylon clothing and protective equipment that hamper the evaporation of sweat.

If salt intake in the diet is not increased, repeated heavy sweating can lead to a progressive depletion of body stores of sodium ions. Symptoms include chronic fatigue, irritability, and a loss of team spirit; confrontations with the team manager or the referee can sometimes be avoided by the simple expedient of sprinkling a little more salt on salads and vegetables!

Avoidance of heat catastrophes is based on acclimatization to heat, appropriate scheduling of training and competitions, and careful monitoring of fluid and mineral needs by the team physician.

Much of the body's potential for heat acclimatization (Chapter 6) can be realized with a two-week stay in a warm climate; a wise coach will thus relax training schedules until these adjustments have occurred.

In many cities, days are hot, but the evenings are cool. It is thus a simple matter to schedule endurance training and competition during the evening hours. A safety ceiling is usually imposed in terms of the wet bulb globe thermometer reading. A thermometer bulb surrounded by a moistened wick is enclosed in a black-painted globe. This device takes account of the effects of both humidity and radiant heating. Unacclimatized athletes should not exercise for more than thirty minutes at a WBGT of 25 °C, whereas for acclimatized contestants the ceiling is 28 °C. The National Road Running Club in the United States has specified that no contest should take place at air temperatures above 35 °C. Events should also be cancelled if the temperature exceeds 29·4 °C with a relative humidity of over 60 per cent, or 26·7 °C with a relative humidity of over 75 per cent.

Fluid and mineral losses in the sweat should always be made good as soon as possible. Cyril Wyndham, a South African physiologist who has gained an extensive experience of heat disorders from his studies of Bantu gold-miners, brands as 'criminal folly' the international rule that prohibits the marathon competitor from drinking fluid during the first fifteen kilometres of his event.* Most runners dislike drinking while they are competing; nevertheless, given an appropriate choice of fluid and firm advice it is possible to achieve an intake of

* Although Wyndham speaks of 15 km, the Olympic rule until 1976 was 11 km. Medical history was made in Montreal, for under strong pressure from the Canadian Association of Sports Sciences and the American College of Sports Medicine the time of the marathon was set back from 3.30 to 5.30 p.m., contestants were allowed to drink freely, and provision was made to cool the runners by run-through showers. In the event, such precautions proved unnecessary, as the afternoon was both wet and cool.

about 0·2 litres every fifteen minutes. This may not be enough to avoid all dehydration on a very hot day, but it is sufficient to temper the worst effects of water depletion. With regard to mineral needs, sweat contains low concentrations of both sodium and potassium; however, it is undesirable to replace the latter during a run, since potassium is already leaking into the blood stream from the active muscles as their glycogen stores are used up. Following the race, small additional quantities of both sodium and potassium are required, although sufficient amounts are usually obtained from well-seasoned salads and vegetables. Commercial drinks designed for the United States football player contain 5–10 per cent glucose, and quite large concentrations of sodium and potassium. The glucose is intended to provide additional calories during the event, although the contribution made (150–200 Calories per hour) does not seem of much practical value. Apart from the dangers of increasing blood potassium levels, the disadvantage of these strong solutions is that they empty slowly from the stomach, thus restricting the total volume of fluid that can be drunk. A recent position statement from the American College of Sports Medicine has recommended the provision of fluids containing not more than 2·5 per cent glucose and very small amounts of sodium and potassium; differences in response to such dilute solutions and to pure water are far from convincing.

Cold

Cold affects specific groups of sportsmen—the hill-walker who is caught in wind and rain, the cross-channel swimmer, the sailor who is drenched by spray or who capsizes his boat, and winter competitors in skiing, skating, and snow-mobile events. As with heat casualties, problems are not confined to parts of the world with extreme climates. Indeed, difficulties seem more common in countries such as England, perhaps because people are less prepared to meet emergencies with special clothing, reserves of food, and practical experience in the handling of chilled casualties.

The several factors determining the heat balance of the body are similar in the heat and the cold. Convection by a high wind or fast motion of the body is the main basis of heat depletion.

Some heat may also be conducted directly to cold external objects such as the side of a boat or a snow-mobile seat, while in a shaded woodland or on a cool evening heat can radiate from the body to the outside world. Sweating may occur during activity; the trunk of a lightly clothed cross-country skier can be bathed in sweat when the outside temperature is minus 20 °C.

Local chilling of exposed areas such as the nose, cheeks, and ears can cause freezing and death of the affected tissues (frost-bite); the remedy is to cover exposed regions whenever there is a combination of frost and wind or rapid motion.

Small decreases in the general temperature of the body have the opposite effect to a 'warm-up'. The muscles function best when their temperature is increased by about 3 °C over the resting condition; a 1 °C cooling is enough to leave them stiff, with slowing of sprint performances and greater liability to muscle tears. The fingers become numb, and the position sensitive detectors in the muscles and joints function poorly. The competitor thus becomes clumsy, and finds difficulty in carrying out any delicate manœuvres; skilled performance deteriorates, and mistakes may further increase the toll of injuries. The function of the brain begins to fail if the body temperature drops below 35 °C; a hill-walker for example moves more slowly, is unsteady, complains of muscle weakness, and stumbles frequently. Mental symptoms follow—anxiety, irritability, loss of purpose, and confusion. Below about 32 °C, the brain mechanisms regulating body-temperature begin to fail. The skin blood vessels may open up widely, giving a misleading sensation of warmth, and causing the confused victim to remove much or all of his clothing. Collapse occurs within 1–2 hours, and without treatment death is likely.

Dr. Griffith Pugh, medical officer to Sir John Hunt's Everest expedition, has gathered together accounts of 88 incidents involving hill-walkers in Britain; 25 fatalities occurred, and a further 5 cases lost consciousness for varying periods of time. The worst episode involved one of the famous 45-mile 'Four Inns' walks in Derbyshire. The race, held in March 1964, commenced with valley temperatures of 4–7 °C, light wind and drizzle. As the day progressed, the rain became steadily heavier, and valley wind speeds increased to 25 knots. The fittest of the 240 entrants completed the course in an almost normal time, but many of the less well-prepared competitors were unable to walk fast enough to sustain their body temperature. Five exhausted participants were brought down by a rescue team (two in a state of collapse), one further competitor died after being carried down to a hill farm on a stretcher, and two more bodies were discovered some days later.

There have also been occasional disasters in marathon swimming, such as a young man who lost contact with his boat and drowned while attempting to cross the cool waters of Lake Ontario.

Factors disturbing body heat balance and thus contributing to disaster include limitation of body heat production (due to lack of food, lack of fitness, exhaustion by high winds or more powerful competitors, and restriction of movement by physical injury), a combination of high winds and inadequate clothing, loss of insulation (due to wetting of clothing by rain, spray, or sweat), mental confusion (due to cooling of the brain, lack of sugar in the blood, or the use of alcohol to 'protect' against the cold), and an opening up of the skin blood vessels (the misleading sensation of warmth induced by alcohol or marked chilling of the brain).

Some acclimatization to cold can occur with two or three weeks exposure to a cold climate (Chapter 6). Reactions of the heart and the blood pressure to exposure of the hands become less marked, shivering is reduced, and subjective complaints are fewer. However, such physiological adjustments are much less important to performance than the knowledge gained of practical ways of reducing the effects of cold. Warm-up is commenced earlier, possibly while wearing additional clothing. Where possible, the face is turned away from the wind or the direction of motion. Clothing during contests is reduced, to avoid saturation with sweat, and extra garments are donned at the finishing line. More effective clothing is chosen. Insulation depends on the number of layers that are worn, and on the quantity of air trapped in and between the fibres. Natural fibres provide better insulation than synthetic materials. The warm layer of air around the body can readily be displaced by wind, unless an outer wind-proof layer is worn. Drenching with rain or sweat also leads to an almost complete loss of insulation.

Swimmers gain some protection from cold water if they are

THE ATHLETE'S ENVIRONMENT 137

fat; a number of cross-channel swimmers have thus been quite obese relative to athletes in other forms of competition. The smearing of a thick layer of lanoline over the body before entering the water has sometimes been advocated as a further method of reducing heat loss. Swimming itself stirs the water and thus increases the rate of heat loss. The dinghy sailor who falls into cold water is thus advised to remain still in a crouching position unless he is close to the shore; a group of several sailors can further conserve their body heat by gathering in a tight 'huddle' while awaiting rescue.

Underwater

Physical activity underwater carries many hazards during descent, while underwater, and during surfacing. Recreational divers are familiar with most of these problems, particularly if they use Scuba equipment; however, it is rare to encounter difficulties among top athletes competing in diving and swimming events.

The pressure underwater increases by one atmosphere for every 10·4 m of depth. The action of this additional pressure on gas pockets within the body can cause pain and even injury—discomfort in the ear, and even rupture of the ear drum, bleeding into sinuses of the nose, and aching of badly filled teeth. One of the Canadian divers attending the Edinburgh Commonwealth Games (1970) ruptured an ear drum during a dive; in her case, contributing factors included a head cold (making it more difficult for air to penetrate the swollen internal ear passage) and failure to equalize ear-pressures during her descent from cruising altitude in a transatlantic aircraft. Wise precautionary measures would include a dental check well in advance of competition, and if an upper respiratory infection should develop, the use of decongestant drugs, in as far as these are permitted by local rules on 'doping'.

In breath-hold diving, great depths can be reached; the current record is held by Croft, who descended to 73·2 metres and remained underwater for 148 seconds. During such feats, pressure differences can be large enough to cause bleeding into the lungs and into the air-pocket behind any goggles that are worn. Croft used contact lenses and saline filled goggles, and had a sufficient pre-dive lung volume to avoid an injurious 'squeeze' inside the chest cavity.

There is little light underwater, and like the war-time fighter pilots a diver can see much more if he allows himself a period of dark adaptation, wearing red goggles.

The problems of remaining at depth (intoxication by nitrogen, oxygen, or carbon dioxide) are not encountered by the competitive diver, since he is not under water for a sufficient period of time. Nor is he likely to be worried by decompression sickness during ascent. Perhaps the most likely hazard is a sudden loss of consciousness while surfacing from a breath-hold dive. During the period at depth, the oxygen within the lungs is gradually exhausted, but because the gas is compressed the oxygen pressure remains sufficient to sustain consciousness. As the diver ascends, oxygen usage continues, and at the same time the total gas pressure is suddenly diminished—perhaps to the point where the competitor blacks out. One stimulus to ascent is the accumulation of carbon dioxide in the lungs during the breath-hold, and a factor contributing to disaster is an initial wash-out of carbon dioxide from the body by overbreathing, in an attempt to extend the dive.

Structural damage to the lungs by expansion of gas during ascent is possible only if additional air has been inhaled at depth, either from a snorkel tube or from an underwater breathing apparatus.

10
Hazards of sports

Every sport inevitably carries some risk of causing physical injury to a participant; in some instances, there is also exposure to infection or a liability to exacerbate existing disease, and very occasionally violent activity may precipitate death. In this chapter, we shall examine these hazards, discussing how far the greater skill and fitness of the top athlete minimize his chances of misadventure; we shall look also at the roles of the team physician and other officials in the prevention and early care of such problems.

Injuries

Most sports medicine meetings have large segments of time allocated to the discussion of athletic injuries. However, those presenting papers are usually surgeons rather than statisticians, and it is much easier to find information on elaborate operations for the repair of injured knees and ankles than it is to determine how common such injuries are.

The type of statistic that is interesting is the number of days that a given class of athlete can participate in his chosen sport before he will be hurt. Data are available for University-class athletes from the University of Toronto and Harvard University (Table 13). There are some differences between the two series, probably dependent on physical facilities and the seriousness with which individual sports are pursued at the two campuses; in Toronto, a cramped basketball court leads to many ankle sprains, and a keen interest in swimming apparently makes this activity more dangerous than at Harvard. In contrast, the New Englanders' interest in rowing makes this a

Table 13. *Relative safety of different sports, tabulated according to the number of days inter-collegiate play that elapse before an injury is sustained*

Sport	University of Toronto (MacIntosh, Skrien, and Shephard)	Harvard University (Thorndike)
North American football		
—fall	51	42
—spring	—	100
Wrestling	50	—
Soccer	140	116
Field hockey	—	147
Ice hockey	190	—
Cross-country running	—	222
Squash	253	—
Boxing	—	375
Baseball	—	486
Rugger	54	552
Track and field		
—winter	—	568
—spring	—	917
Basketball	107	765
Rowing	7865	3344
Swimming	1399	5844

little more dangerous for them. Contact and team sports are generally more dangerous than the individual events such as track and field, rowing, and swimming. Thus, the nature of the Olympic contests helps to hold down likely injury rates.

With regard to fitness and skill, the University of Toronto data show that inter-collegiate athletes have a seven times greater chance of injury per year than men who are merely enrolled in an intra-mural programme; differences between the two situations include not only the intensity of competition encountered, but also the number of playing sessions per week. In contrast, several studies of skiers have indicated that novices, while skiing fewer vertical feet per day, have more injuries than experts. Presumably, experience makes a larger contribution to safety in highly skilled and non-competitive activity. The ratio of inter-collegiate to intra-mural injury rates in Toronto ranged

Table 14. *Ratio of injury rates in inter-collegiate and intra-mural sports at the University of Toronto (based on data of MacIntosh, Skrien, and Shephard)*

Sport	Number of injuries per 1000 participants per year Inter-collegiate	Intra-mural	$\dfrac{\text{Inter-collegiate}}{\text{Intra-mural}}$
North American football	1027	378	3
Wrestling	1410	69	20
Rugger	862	69	12
Boxing	307	109	3
Gymnastics	295	56	5
Soccer	369	61	6
Ice-hockey	450	53	8
Basketball	742	26	29
Track and field	180	8	23
Fencing	85	10	9
Squash	286	5	57
Swimming	109	10	11
Cross-country running	57	10	6
Water-polo	141	7	20
Volleyball	108	5	22
Curling	12	2	6

from 3:1 to 57:1, more intense competition having a particularly adverse effect on squash, basketball, volleyball, track and field, wrestling, and water-polo injuries (Table 14). We may conclude that in most sports, although the top athlete has the capacity to anticipate problems and the skill to carry out manœuvres that would be impossible for the novice, the demands of severe competition lead to the taking of greater risks, with an overall increase in the chances of injury.

The range of injuries likely in a mixed population of athletes is illustrated in Table 15. At the University level of competition, over 40 per cent of the incidents requiring medical treatment are sprains (partial tears of the ligaments around joints), the regions most commonly affected being the ankle, knee, finger, thumb, and shoulder joints. Strains (injuries to muscle

Table 15. *An analysis of 8020 injuries treated in the men's athletic department of the University of Toronto during the period 1951–68 (based on data of MacIntosh, Skrien, and Shephard)*

Type of injury	Football (3252 cases) (per cent)	Hockey (1064 cases) (per cent)	Basketball (1068 cases) (per cent)	All sports (8020 cases) (per cent)
Sprain } Strain }	44·6	31·6	58·3	40·2 } 4·7
Bruising	26·2	27·2	14·0	23·8
Bone fracture	5·3	9·9	5·2	6·0
Scrapes } Cuts }	6·3	14·2	4·6	1·6 } 5·7
Concussion	3·4	1·0	0·4	1·9
Other injuries (including joint dislocations, infections, and inflammations)	14·2	16·1	17·5	16·1

or tendon produced by muscular contraction) occur frequently in the thigh. Scrapes (abrasions) of the skin usually occur over the lower part of the leg, while cuts are more frequent over the head and face. Concussion is relatively infrequent, but is potentially one of the more serious injuries, with a possibility of permanent brain damage, or continuing and fatal haemorrhage within the skull. Comparing the three major sports represented within the data in terms of the total numbers of injuries seen, North American football as played in Toronto is about nine times as dangerous as basketball and seven times as dangerous as ice-hockey. Unfortunately, most series, our own included, have no good measure of the severity of the injuries sustained. However, from the type of injury seen, one would expect that the footballers would be suffering the most severe injuries (Table 15). Sprains and strains are relatively common in basketball; cuts and scrapes are much more frequent in ice-hockey; and concussion is more common in football.

It is plainly better to prevent injuries than to cure them. The keystones of prevention are the personal condition of the athlete, the wearing of appropriate protective equipment, the devising and enforcement of appropriate rules, and the proper design and maintenance of the competition site.

Domestic accidents are particularly likely when we are fatigued; a fall from a ladder or an accident with the best china inevitably occurs when our sixth sense is depressed at the end of a tiring day. The same seems true of athletic accidents; the safety of the competitor depends greatly on his vigilance and his ability to make quick corrective movements if he feels that he is slipping, spots an opponent on a collision course from the corner of his eye, or realizes he has mistimed a triple somersault. If a contestant is over-tired because of poor physical condition, over-training, or excessive competition, he may fail to notice his problem, or lack the reserves of strength to correct it. The coach must thus ensure that training is not pursued to the point where the next day's practice commences with a feeling of severe fatigue, and particularly in the body-contact sports he has a responsibility to see that an individual or a team are not totally outclassed. In the University of Toronto series, almost 10 per cent of injuries arose as a recurrence of a previous problem—dislocation of a shoulder where the joint capsule was already weakened, or damage to a knee made unstable by previous rupture of cartilages or ligaments. The wounded warrior usually demands to participate, and in professional sport there may be considerable pressure to do so from management and coach; however, the team physician must resist such demands, allowing competition only for those shown to be in satisfactory medical condition at a careful screening examination.

Well-designed and good-quality protective equipment can

Table 16. *The effect of facebar and toothguard on injuries to the face and teeth of footballers* (*based on data of Wisconsin Interscholastic Athletic Association*)

Year	Protection	Injuries to face and teeth per 100 players
1954	No facebar or toothguard	2·26
1955	Facebar introduced	1·83
1959	Facebar mandatory	1·20
1963	Facebar and toothguard mandatory	0·47

do much to reduce the toll of injuries. One well documented example is the addition of one or more face-bars and a toothguard to the football helmet. The face-bar was first suggested by Paul Brown, coach of the 'Cleveland Browns', following a severe nose injury to one of his team. Within four years, the idea had proved its worth to the point that it was made mandatory (Table 16). Addition of a toothguard further reduced the number of injuries and also their severity; Stoddard has commented that in New York State, claims for dental injuries have dropped by 69 per cent since the mouthguard was required, and the cost of the average claim has decreased by 54 per cent. Unfortunately another problem soon confronted footballers, for unscrupulous opponents developed the tactic of seizing the face-bar and jerking the helmet backwards with sufficient force to produce fatal injuries of the spine. Imposition of a fifteen-yard penalty for grasping the face-bar, and the addition of shock-absorbent padding to the rear edge of the helmet seem to have overcome this difficulty.

Protective equipment is equally vital in ice-hockey, where the puck may be travelling at more than 150 km per h, and players waving lethal sticks and wearing razor-sharp skates can collide at impact speeds of 80 km per h. However, the typical professional ice-hockey player scorns to wear a helmet, partly perhaps because it restricts his vision, but more importantly because he fears ridicule.

Many injuries arise from unforeseeable circumstances. However, we have seen above that the pressure of fiercer competition is one factor that causes a steep increase in the number of incidents from intra-mural to inter-collegiate competition (Table 14). The attitude of the players changes from friendly rivalry to a desire for victory at any cost, and all too often this determination is reinforced by the urgings of the coach and spectators; a team-member is repeatedly incited to get on the field and 'kill' the opposition. As with the control of 'doping', the ultimate answer to rough play must be an appeal for good sportsmanship, with a change in the norms of behaviour for both players and crowd at those sports that have become too violent (Chapter 5). It is far more important that the spirit of the rules be obeyed than their letter. Nevertheless, some of the more dangerous infractions of fair conduct can be curbed through suitable changes in the rule-book. We have seen one example of this in the penalty for grasping the helmet of a football player. Another example is the outlawing of the full-nelson hold in wrestling, since this can sometimes break an opponent's neck. Rules are also useful in forcing the adoption of protective equipment by those who are afraid of being considered 'chicken'.

Rules are ineffective unless they are enforced. Competent refereeing is thus a major factor in safety. It is hard to imagine that a determined referee could not reduce the current violence in ice-hockey through the full use of sanctions and penalties in the existing rule-book. Likewise, it has been estimated that in some North American football matches less than a quarter of the fouls that occur are called by the referee. Difficulties are particularly likely in international contests, since the same rules often have different national interpretations. Further, political allegiances are so strong that it may be difficult to find a truly impartial referee. Nevertheless, respect for the decisions that are reached is vital in any type of competition. Attempts to intimidate the referee by complaints from national officials or jeers and taunts from the crowd can lead to timid and hesitant calls, and as a result to a poor and dangerous contest. One can only deplore the current habit of some North American sports commentators in blaming the defeat of their national candidates on poor decisions by the referee or the judges.

With regard to physical facilities, there have been complaints even about Olympic stadia; the track built for the first modern Olympic Games (Athens, 1896), for example, was said to be too sharply curved for the runners. However, most facilities for international competition are of such superlative design that it is rare to find good grounds for criticism. In Montreal, for example it was said that the excellent hydrodynamic design of the swimming pool helped competitors to establish many new records. However, developments in athletic records may present new challenges. Thus, the greater heights attained in pole-vaulting after the introduction of the fibreglass pole led to injuries on descent, and it became necessary to replace the traditional sand or saw-dust pit with an area of foam rubber. Another major technical development was the introduction of artificial turf for team sports. The new surface was attractive to the spectator, withstood all weathers, and was easily cleaned.

However, it had the effect of gripping a player's boot more firmly than the previous grass-and-mud surface, so that knee and ankle injuries increased, and it was necessary to alter the design of the boot cleats to allow for the greater traction.

Arrangements for the early care of the injured should commence well in advance of competition. A preliminary visit to the site by the team physician should serve to establish the nature of local resources and any unusual hazards that may be encounted. Hospitals should be contacted and arrangements for consultations and emergency admissions completed. It may be helpful to organize a medical post in a public building such as a school; here, contestants whose injuries are not severe enough to warrant immediate evacuation to hospital can be examined, treated, and given an opportunity to recover away from the curious gaze of the crowd. Responsibility must be clearly apportioned between medical and paramedical personnel. The attendance of physicians and ambulances should be assured for the more dangerous events. At the other competition sites, care should be assigned to a competent paramedical worker, such as a nurse, St. John's ambulance worker, or the North American trainer; the individual concerned should have good training in first-aid measures together with a specific knowledge of problems likely to occur in the sport that he is supervising. He should be able to decide whether the athlete can remain in a contest, and to recognize the doubtful cases where the opinion of a physician should be obtained. He should also be given clear instructions on the procedure for summoning an ambulance, not always an easy matter when it may be necessary to make the request in a foreign language.

The first priorities in dealing with those who are unconscious and severely injured are to check the breathing and the function of the heart. If respiration has stopped, the mouth must be cleared of debris with a clean handkerchief, the head tilted back, and artificial respiration begun, preferably by the mouth-to-mouth method. If the action of the heart has also ceased, those with appropriate training should also undertake heart massage (in Ontario, this procedure may be carried out only by physicians and certain nurses; however, in other jurisdictions such people as ambulance drivers have learnt to perform heart massage quite effectively). Bleeding should be controlled by firm pressure at the site of haemorrhage. 'Shock' can arise from extensive bleeding, either internal or external, and from injury to sensitive body organs.

Improvement or deterioration in condition can be gauged if the observer starts a regular pulse chart while awaiting an ambulance. However, drinks should not be given, since an early operation will probably be required. If there are signs of a bone fracture, that part of the body should be splinted before the athlete is moved. Where an injury of the spine is suspected, it is particularly important to avoid worsening the injury by moving the back. Transport should be on a rigid board rather than a soft stretcher, and lifting of the body should be carried out only by those well-trained in dealing with back injuries. Drowsiness, confusion, or other disturbances of consciousness may signify an internal injury to the brain. While he is awaiting expert advice, it is again helpful if the observer notes whether such symptoms are increasing or decreasing in severity. Puncture wounds of the sole of the foot should be taken seriously, because of the risks of infection; the contestant should be referred to the physician for opening and cleaning of the wound, with administration of an anti-tetanus 'booster' injection, and possibly a preventive course of antibiotics.

All concerned with the early care of the injured athlete have a serious responsibility to weigh his best interests. The competitor himself may insist that this is his last possible chance to win a gold medal, and argue for a return to the area despite severe injuries. A coach or a team-manager may be equally persuasive in requests for taping, pain-killing drugs, or other palliative measures that will enable a star performer to return to the field. The physician or paramedical worker must strenuously resist such pressures. Without restricting an athlete needlessly, they should never agree to a plan of treatment that could materially worsen an injury or lead to the permanent disability of a competitor.

Disease

Although precautions must be taken for the treatment of major surgical emergencies, the usual problems of the international competitor are minor medical abnormalities. By way of example, the report of the British medical staff on the Mexico City Olympic Games noted only two fractures—a broken nose in a pole-vaulter, and a broken leg in a boxer. However, there were 741 medical attendances by 261 contestants, and 1632 treatments administered by physiotherapists.

The commonest medical problems were infections—head cold in 35 competitors, cough in 9, sore throat in 6, and diarrhoea in 33. The diarrhoea was mild in 18 cases, lasting only one day, with no loss of training; in a further 9 it persisted for two days, and in 6 cases it was more severe, causing a cessation of training for at least two days. Among the 40 other complaints were insomnia, insect bites, sunburn, stubbed toes from the wearing of toeless sandals, and such minor surgical conditions as blisters, bruises, and pulled muscles. Many of the teams visiting Mexico City were disabled by diarrhoea. The Japanese had 49 cases, the Australians 5, and the United States physicians also cited intestinal infections as their most difficult problem.

As in dealing with injuries, the main emphasis of the programme to counteract infection is preventive. Before the team goes anywhere, the team physician discovers what diseases are endemic in the area of competition, and arranges an appropriate schedule of vaccinations and drugs to ward off such major illnesses as typhoid fever, cholera, smallpox, yellow fever, and malaria. All members of the team are educated in the principles of good hygiene. If food cannot be provided from a controlled source, the group is advised to choose only good restaurants with clean glasses and utensils, to take their meat well cooked, to use boiled or bottled water, to avoid cold milk, ice cream and raw fruit and vegetables. Unless windows are screened, insect repellent is used. Laundry and changing facilities are checked for cleanliness. In some areas it may even be necessary to post security guards to exclude prostitutes and thus diminish the risks of venereal disease.

Despite all of these precautions, some infections always crop up. Gastro-intestinal disturbances usually respond well to sulphonamide preparations such as succinyl sulphathiazole. A more difficult decision is presented by the athlete who attends the medical clinic with a feverish cold. The virus responsible for his illness is not susceptible to antibiotics, and normal medical practice would be to avoid their use unless there was clear evidence of secondary bacterial infection that would respond to such therapy; over-prescription of antibiotics is liable to breed micro-organisms of a drug-resistant strain that will have serious subsequent consequences not only for the person treated but for the world at large. On the other hand, development of a secondary infection a few days later could be enough to keep an athlete from competition. There is thus a strong temptation to ignore the normal rules of good medicine, and administer antibiotics at the viral stage of a cold, hoping this will stop any wandering bacteria from gaining a foothold. Such expediency may gain a few medals, but to my mind is not justified. It would be an interesting study to compare the frequency of bacteria insensitive to antibiotics in athletes and in members of the general population treated according to conventional rules.

It is at present unclear whether the athlete is more or less resistant to infection than the average person. Appropriate statistics are difficult to collect, since participation in top competition alters exposure patterns. World travel brings the athlete into contact with a host of unfamiliar micro-organisms that are never encountered by a less mobile sedentary citizen. Heavy sweating (or prolonged wetting of the skin in the case of the swimmer) increases the liability to minor skin ailments such as boils and impetigo, while frequent use of poorly drained changing areas can lead to the rapid spread of fungal infections of the feet and plantar warts. On the other hand, the long hours spent outdoors, the contact with other healthy individuals and frequent medical checks tend to reduce the likelihood of more serious diseases.

Death

We have seen already some of the ways in which a sportsman can die during or immediately following competition—overheating or excessive cooling of the body, waterlogging of the lungs at high altitude, loss of consciousness under water and other forms of drowning, and major injuries including damage to the brain and spine, rupture of internal organs such as the heart, spleen, and liver, and severe haemorrhage from other causes. What we must now consider is whether excessive exercise can be fatal in the absence of injuries or exposure to adverse environmental conditions. Is it possible for a man literally to 'run himself to death'?

Occasional newspaper reports might suggest this to be the case. Examples from the Toronto area include a fifteen-year-old youth who dropped dead on the athletic track at a Port Credit High School, and a twenty-three-year-old University athlete who fell dead after hanging for some minutes from the parallel bars in the gymnasium. In the United States, much publicity was attracted by the death of a footballer, apparently from a heart attack, during a major league game a few years ago.

Fortunately, such events are newsworthy largely because of their rarity, and the assembly of such reports does not prove that sudden and unexpected death during sports competition is any more common than the unexpected death of those who stay at home in an armchair reading the *Sports Illustrated*.

Laboratory experiments with dogs give some support to the idea that excessive exercise can cause death. Greyhounds have been persuaded to run on a treadmill until they died of heart failure. However, it is not possible to make a direct comparison between man and the greyhound; this variety of dog has an almost instinctive desire to run, and because it uses four legs rather than two it lacks the defence mechanism of fainting that brings a long-distance athlete to the ground long before his heart has failed.

A second possible approach is to make a careful post-mortem examination of athletes who die during competition, seeking to determine whether all of those who die have some underlying abnormality of the heart or circulation. Some years ago, Dr. Ernst Jokl searched the world literature and collected a series of 76 cases of sudden death during exertion, the majority of the group being athletes (Table 17). The commonest post-mortem finding was a blockage or narrowing of the coronary vessels supplying the heart muscle. This was noted in 34 instances, and it could have precipitated a heart attack in the individuals concerned. Rupture of the heart or a major blood vessel had occurred 22 times; many of these cases were older people with degeneration of the wall of the aorta or tuberculous disease in the lungs, but in 5 there was a congenital weakness in the blood vessels at the base of the brain.

The third main cause of death was cardiac failure, said to be responsible for 17 cases. In 8 of these, there was chronic disease

Table 17. *Sudden death during physical exercise—the findings at 76 post-mortem examinations (based on data of Dr. Ernst Jokl)*

Finding	Number of cases
Narrowing or blockage of coronary blood vessels supplying the heart	34
Rupture of heart and blood vessels	
Rupture of aorta —11 cases	
Rupture of vessels at base of brain— 5 cases	22
Rupture of heart — 4 cases	
Rupture of lung blood vessels — 2 cases	
Heart failure	
Chronic infection or degeneration of heart muscle — 8 cases	
Acute infection — 5 cases	17
Congenital abnormalities of heart — 4 cases	
Miscellaneous	3

or degeneration of the heart muscle (always a hard item to evaluate at post-mortem), but in 5 there was an acute infection of the heart. It is well known that diseases such as influenza can predispose a person to a sudden arrest of the heart, and it seems a good general rule that athletes should not compete if they have a fever.

Jokl maintained from his literature search that since there was always a reasonable pathological explanation of death in those who were exercising, physical activity did not cause death in a normal heart. Certainly, few would dispute that some congenital abnormalities such as poorly placed coronary arteries, narrowing of the valves guarding the exit from the heart, and weakness of the blood vessels at the base of the brain predispose the individual to catastrophe; narrowed valves can usually be detected by a heart murmur, and periodic abnormalities of heart rhythm may be suspected from a history of occasional fainting attacks, but atypical coronary vessels and weaknesses of the brain vessels may remain 'silent' until death occurs. It is much more difficult to weight the significance of a narrowing in the coronary vessels. Unfortunately, the indiscretions of diet that are common in Western society cause some accumulation of fat in the walls of the coronary vessels in many children and young adults. A diligent post-mortem search can thus almost always bring some small abnormality to light. This can be blamed for death, but it is then necessary to explain why other athletes can participate in sports and stay alive until comparable abnormalities are revealed through death on military service or in a motor accident.

A check on the importance of the coronary findings can be made by gathering together a large group of patients who have already had a heart attack, in order to determine how many were exercising when the incident occurred. Often, the proportion is surprisingly high. Dr. Kavanagh and I found that some form of physical activity was associated with more than a quarter of 233 attacks in patients of working age; there was a corresponding deficit of attacks during normal daily work and sleep. Specific forms of activity that were incriminated included snow-shovelling (9 men) walking (13 men), running (8 men), curling (4 men), tennis (2 men), baseball (1 man), soccer (1 man), basketball (1 man), hockey (1 man), squash (1 man), showering after gymnastics (1 man), dancing (1 man), sexual intercourse (2 men), and various heavy domestic chores (15 men). Interestingly, despite the popularity of summer swimming in the Toronto area, no one reported an attack while in the water. Two features of swimming—the support of body weight by the water, and the distribution of effort over a wide range of body muscles—make this a very safe form of physical activity from the viewpoint of the heart. Other features contributing to the attack seemed to include a recent heavy meal, the addition of emotional excitement such as the defence of a curling championship, and a very prolonged bout of activity without adequate preparation.

It could be argued that the patients' recollection of their illness had become distorted over subsequent months, as they puzzled over the question as to why they should have suffered a heart attack, many recalling what seemed to them an excessive bout of effort at about the appropriate time. A corrective to such statistics is thus to examine the records of long-distance sports events. In Sweden, two annual marathon cross-country ski events have drawn up to 10 000 entrants per year, for each of fifty years. Many of the participants are middle-aged, yet to

HAZARDS OF SPORTS

date there have been only two fatalities, both in 1971. Records from Finland also show only 10 fatalities in more than 12 million man-hours of long-distance country skiing. It is of course possible that many of the coronary-prone are eliminated from winter-sports before the final contest is reached. Nevertheless, such statistics give an indication of the risks of top competition. Deaths are about four times as frequent as in those reading the *Sports Illustrated*.

How does exercise increase the chances of getting a coronary attack? In some instances, it is likely that increased blood flow through the coronary vessels causes bleeding into one of the fatty plaques in the vessel wall, thus blocking the tube completely. In other cases, the increased flow may cause the plaque to break free of the vessel wall, to be carried forward to another point of narrowing, where it lodges and obstructs the passage of blood. More often, the heart attack is caused by a discrepancy between the oxygen needs of the heart muscle and the supply via the narrowed coronary vessels; an increase in blood pressure, and thus the work load of the heart, whether brought about by brief isometric straining or very prolonged endurance work, is the final straw that produces a fatal oxygen lack in the heart muscle. Sudden death is frequently preceded by an abnormality of heart rhythm known as ventricular fibrillation; the heart chambers engage in irregular, writhing contractions that are totally ineffective in pumping blood through the body. The irritability of the heart muscle and its propensity to fibrillate are increased by both oxygen lack and the presence of adrenaline-like compounds in the blood. Extreme effort, emotional excitement, and the illegal use of adrenaline-mimicking drugs such as ephedrine and the amphetamines could thus all increase the risks for the competitive athlete.

Should we conclude from this discussion that exercise is bad for health, and that those who prefer to study a sports magazine from an armchair have made a wise decision? Paradoxically, the answer is no! Vigorous exercise has done no more than reveal a pre-existing propensity for a coronary attack. Even if all deliberate exercise is avoided, sooner or later some physical or emotional demand will be sufficient to precipitate a heart attack. The victim will be in poor physical condition to withstand the emergency, and may well die in the early stages of the illness. Furthermore, he may be on his own, far from assistance, and is unlikely to have the medical and paramedical resources to be found at a major athletic event. Finally, there is increasing evidence that whereas the immediate effect of vigorous exercise may be to precipitate an impending coronary episode, the long-term response is to diminish the chances of such an emergency. For all these reasons, increased activity is to be commended to the armchair sportsman, even if he is at high risk of a heart attack or has already sustained one or more coronary events.

11
The female athlete

As recently as 1940, Professor Terman of Stanford University wrote in *Psychological studies of the biography of genius* that gifted women had little opportunity to develop their intellectual abilities, thus robbing both science and the arts of a large reservoir of potential genius. '... this loss must be debited to motivational causes and to limitations of opportunity rather than to lack of ability.' In the area of intellect, the battle of emancipation has now largely been won, women having almost equal opportunity with men to develop to the limits of their capacity. However, in the physical sphere there is still much social conditioning that encourages a woman to abhor exercise, and it is conceivable that a fair part of the differences in competitive performance between men and women reflects such cultural patterns. In this chapter, we shall try to determine the magnitude of fundamental physiological differences between the sexes, and will evaluate their likely impact on performance. This will inevitably lead us to the discussion of related topics, including sex determination, the femininity of the top competitor, and the effects of the menstrual cycle on physical performance.

Vive la différence

Despite the best efforts of the women's liberation movement, there remain certain indisputable differences of anatomy and physiology between the average man and the average woman. There is also a wide range of physiques within each sex, to the point where the most masculine woman has characteristics that are more male in many respects than those of an effeminate man. For our present purpose, we can compare the average individual of each sex, and can also note the physiological characteristics of top male and female competitors in various sports.

In terms of body-build, women are normally fatter than men. Careful laboratory measurements of skinfold thicknesses can demonstrate small sexual differences from the moment of birth, but the discrepancy becomes much more obvious at puberty, as the female breasts enlarge and the body assumes its more rounded contours. Some 25 per cent of the body-weight in the typical young woman is accounted for by fat, while in a young man the corresponding figure is less than 15 per cent. Athletes of both sexes are thinner than sedentary subjects. Among the women, fat percentages range from 7 per cent up to about 20 per cent, depending on the sport; distance-runners, for example, are often a good deal thinner than the average sedentary male. Most men competitors fall into the range 5–15 per cent fat, but some contact sportsmen carry larger total weights of fat than the average sedentary woman.

There are also sex differences in the amount of lean tissue in the body, the average sedentary woman carrying some 20 kilograms less non-fatty matter than a sedentary man.

Up to the age of ten, boys and girls have a roughly equal oxygen transporting capacity; expressed per unit of body weight, the figure remains remarkably constant at 45–50 ml per kg per min. Values for boys continue to increase at least in proportion to body weight throughout puberty, so that the young adult achieves a figure of about 3·1 l per min, or 48 ml per kg of body weight per min. For girls, however, values start to plateau or decline around the age of twelve, so that the adult value reached is no more than 2·1 l per min, or about 38 ml per kg per min. Part of the sex difference is obviously due to body fat, since this is a dead burden that contributes nothing to oxygen transport; however, most authors are now agreed that there is a residual difference between men and women, even when oxygen intake is expressed per unit of lean tissue. It is less clear whether this residual difference is an inherent 'weakness' of the female, or whether it is a consequence of culturally imposed restrictions of physical activity during the critical growing years of adolescence. Female athletes (Table

Table 18. *Sex differences in oxygen transporting power of top athletes (based on Åstrand's data for Swedish National Champions, expressed in millilitres of oxygen transport per minute per kilogram of body weight)*

Event	Oxygen transport (ml per min per kg) Male	Female	Percentage difference
Cross-country skiing	82	63	30·1
Speed-skating	78	53	47·2
Orienteering	77	59	30·5
Running (400–800 m)	68	56	21·4
Alpine skiing	68	61	11·5
Swimming	67	57	17·5
Fencing	59	43	37·2
Table tennis	58	43	34·9
Normal adult (Toronto)	48	38	26·3

18) generally surpass sedentary men by a substantial margin. In sports demanding maximum endurance (cross-country skiing, speed skating, and orienteering—a form of woodland distance running using a compass) the best male competitors surpass the best females by at least 30 per cent.

Women are again a good deal weaker than men in terms of absolute strength. The Danish physiologist Asmussen has set the strength of the average female at 60 per cent of the male figure, with only about a half of this deficiency being attributable to her shorter stature. Wilmore points out that there are also regional differences; muscles in the upper part of the body are 43–63 per cent weaker in a woman, but in the lower part of the body the discrepancy drops to 27 per cent. For many sports, the crucial factor is the force per unit of body weight; in such terms, the lower part of the body is only 8 per cent weaker than in the male. As with oxygen transport, sex differences in strength first appear at puberty. In the boys, muscle force develops faster than body weight, while in the girls the maximum force either remains constant or declines. The strength spurt of the boys seems related in some way to the male sex hormone testosterone, and it is thus hardly surprising that the girls do not share equally in this development. Wilmore has commented that when men are put through a strength training programme, there is not only an increase in the muscle force that can be developed, but also an increase in the physical bulk of the muscles. Weight training will produce 30 per cent gains in the strength of women already active in athletics, but there is little evidence that new muscle tissue is developed thereby.

Sports records for women

To summarize our physiological comparison: women enter most contests with the handicaps of more fat, less muscle, and a lower oxygen transporting capacity than male competitors. For their further discomfiture, they are on average ten to twelve

Table 19. *Differences in world records for men and women competitors (1975)*

Event	Men	Women	Percentage difference
Speed skating			
500-metre	38·0 s	41·8 s	10·0
1000-metre	77·6 s	86·4 s	11·3
1500-metre	118·7 s	134·0 s	11·3
3000-metre	248·3 s	286·5 s	11·5
5000-metre	429·8 s	541·6 s	26·0
Swimming (free-style)			
100-metre	51·2 s	57·5 s	12·3
200-metre	112·8 s	123·6 s	9·6
400-metre	238·2 s	257·4 s	8·1
1500-metre	932·0 s	1003·0 s	7·6
Track			
100-yards	9·0 s	10·0 s	11·1
220-yards	20·0 s	22·6 s	13·0
440-yards	44·5 s	52·2 s	17·3
880-yards	104·6 s	121·0 s	15·7
1-mile	231·1 s	269·5 s	16·6
Field			
High-jump	2·30 m	1·94 m	18·3
Long-jump	8·90 m	6·84 m	30·1
Javelin-throw	94·1 m	66·1 m	42·4

centimetres shorter than their male counterparts. The effects on sports records are shown in Table 19.

In speed-skating, the body weight is supported, and the crucial factors are the muscle force that can accelerate the body and the oxygen transport that can maintain its speed against the resistance of the wind. Women gain a small advantage from their more rounded contours and the smaller body surface presented to the wind; speed differences are thus only 10–12 per cent except over the 5000-metre course, where the discrepancy rises to 26 per cent.

In swimming, also, the women competitors gain some advantage; the greater fat content of the body increases their buoyancy, so that less work must be done to stay afloat, a factor that increases in importance with the distance to be covered. The greater fat content of the female thigh helps keep the legs more horizontal in the water, and comparisons of the efficiency of swimming generally show that women need to spend less energy to move at a given water speed. Over very long distances, such as cross-channel swims, the added fat of the female also helps to sustain body temperature. The net result of these various factors is a sex differential that decreases from 12 per cent in a 100-metre event to under 8 per cent over a 1500-metre course.

In track-and-field events, the woman is a special case of the small competitor (Table 2, p. 25); she gains some advantage in running, partly offsetting her deficiencies of muscle force and oxygen transport. In the 100-yard dash, the deficiency in speed relative to the male is only 11 per cent, but discrepancies of 16–17 per cent are seen over longer distances.

For the jumping events, the woman has the disadvantage of a low centre of gravity due to both shortness of stature and differences of body form; performance is thus below the male level by 18 per cent in the high-jump, and 30 per cent in the long-jump.

The effects of feminine weakness are brought out most fully in the throwing events, where short stature is compounded by lack of muscle force in the upper part of the body. In the javelin-throw, for example, the discrepancy is over 42 per cent.

Some caution must be exercised when making such comparisons. Records for the women currently seem to be improving faster than those for men, and already many of the performances by female competitors would have ranked as male world records forty or fifty years ago. Only when there are approximately equal numbers of male and female competitors can we be fairly sure that the differences in times or distances are a true measure of physiological differences between the sexes rather than a result of the more limited searching of the female ranks for likely candidates. However, the current roll of women competitors is sufficiently large that it is unlikely that all differences between the two sexes will disappear when the millennium of equal representation is reached.

Sex determination and femininity

Since the best male competitors have an advantage over the females in almost all sports, it is perhaps inevitable that some teams should have added to their numbers 'women' of doubtful sexual credentials. The true sex of several supposed women athletes was questioned at the European Games in Budapest (1966), and a number of competitors withdrew from their events rather than submit to the medical examinations demanded by the organizing committee.

It seems somewhat unfair to require female competitors to strip and parade before a panel of doctors as a prelude to a sporting event, and the testing of sex is now usually made through an examination of cells scraped from the inner lining of the mouth. Cells from a normal female contain 44 ordinary chromosomes, and two of the special X-chromosomes concerned with sexual development; the geneticist thus describes such a person as a 46/XX. In the male, one of the X-chromosomes is replaced by a Y; the genetic designation is thus 46/XY. The basic clue to sexual identity is the darkly staining Barr body, formed by attachment of the second X-chromosome to the inner edge of the cell nuclei; Barr bodies are found in 20–50 per cent of the cells in a female, but are absent in a true male (Fig. 19).

Sex is usually assigned in the first few moments of life, as the mother is told that she has just given birth to a baby boy or girl, as the case may be. Over-enthusiastic young doctors and midwives have been known to make the wrong pronounce-

Fig. 19. Chromosomes from a normal male (left) and a normal female (right), together with normal and abnormal cell nuclei (illustrations reproduced from Mittwoch, 'Sex differences in cells', *Scientific American*, July 1963, by courtesy of the publishers and the photographer, Dr. Anthony Bligh).

The nucleus of a normal male cell with no Barr body.

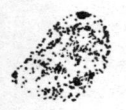

The nucleus of a normal female cell with one Barr body.

The nucleus of an abnormal female cell with two Barr bodies.

ment, even when the sex is quite obvious! On occasion, there is legitimate scope for error, a small or incomplete penis being overlooked, or an enlarged clitoris being taken for a penis. Children having an incompletely developed penis may well be reared as females, and when a normal secretion of the male sex hormones commences at puberty they could gain an unfair competitive advantage over true females. Suspicions are often aroused by deepening of the voice and growth of facial hair, with an absence of breast development and menstruation. The true sex of such individuals is shown quite plainly in cells scraped from the mouth.

Transvestism is a second abnormality that causes occasional

problems in athletics. Certain males, apparently normally equipped, have a strongly female psychological orientation, and choose to both dress and act as women. Sometimes the person concerned believes so strongly that he is female that he goes to great lengths to assume a feminine appearance, even arranging for the amputation of his penis and taking female hormones to induce a swelling of the breasts (trans-sexualism). Again, such individuals would have a competitive advantage, but the true state of affairs can be brought to light through an examination of the genetic make-up of the cells lining the mouth.

In a few instances the testes fail to develop fully, or the other body tissues fail to respond to what seems a normal secretion of the male sex hormones. The contours of the body, the development of the breasts, and the appearance of the external genitalia all strongly suggest that the individual is a female, yet the cells from the mouth show the male 46/XY format. Since there is no effective secretion of androgens in such cases, they have no competitive advantage over normal women, and there is no theoretical reason why they should not be allowed to enter female contests if they choose to do so.

Mouth scraping is a very simple, painless, and rapid method of sexual screening. In most instances it is accurate. However, top-level athletics is the study of the unusual, and we should thus note several rare conditions where it can be misleading. Occasionally, a woman may develop a tumour of an adrenal gland. Genetic analysis shows a standard 46/XX appearance, but a massive secretion of androgenic hormones from the tumour leads to masculinization of appearance, with substantial gains of muscular strength. The Y-chromosome can also become fragmented, so that at conception an X-bearing egg-cell is fertilized by a sperm that carries not only an X-chromosome, but also a small portion of Y; a genetic constitution of $46/XX^y$ then leads to a very mixed pattern of development. Some cells inactivate the X-chromosome, responding to testicular hormones with a male pattern of development. Others inactivate the X^y-chromosome, allowing the development of female attributes under the influence of ovarian hormones. This type of situation could explain the true hermaphrodite, that rare individual who has both male and female sex organs. Other oddities include cases with one chromosome missing (45/XO) or with one chromosome in excess of the normal complement (47/XXX, 47/XXY). In the first case, we have a female who lacks Barr bodies. The second type is also female, but has two Barr bodies per cell, while the third has intermediary sex characteristics and one Barr body per cell. All of these conditions are very rare, and other aberrations of development typically keep the individuals concerned from participation in top competitions.

Is it fair to conclude from the foregoing discussion that irrespective of genetic make-up, women who participate in athletic contests have more masculine attributes than those who sustain the traditional feminine abhorrence of the physical? Much inevitably depends on the class of competition. In some areas such as gymnastics and figure-skating, the chauvinistic virtues of a good figure and delicate, dainty movements are likely to earn points, particularly if the judges are male (Fig. 20). The swimmer with well-developed breasts and rounded thighs equally has a practical advantage over a girl with less body fat. But if one is to equate masculinity with such items as height, strength, and endurance, then it seems inevitable that in many sports women on the masculine side of average will move into the top competitive ranks. At the same time, unless there has been 'doping' with androgenic steroids, there is no particular reason why the women concerned should have a bass voice and an ugly face complete with beard and moustache. Casual inspection of the photographs of Olympic victors suggests that the range of conventionally interpreted beauty is much as in the general population. Indeed, it is arguable that a good posture, firm muscles, and an absence of surplus fat give the Olympic winner a grace not found among the common herd.

Many women fear not merely that athletic participation will brand them as being masculine in type, but also that the strenuous training programme needed for success will push their appearance further in the direction of masculinity. Even among University physical-education classes, I have heard girls deplore jogging on the grounds that their boy friends will object to the resultant thickening of their shapely calves. The studies of Wilmore and his associates suggest that these fears of excessive muscle-building are groundless. Women gain strength

Fig. 20. The Canadian gymnast, Teresa McDonnell (illustration reproduced from *Record*, by courtesy of the Canadian Olympic Association).

without vast increases of muscle bulk, unless they have been 'doped' with compounds such as Danabol. It is even possible that by jogging in the right places they may succeed in drawing to the attention of an unobservant male those details of the calf that are causing the girl's concern.

Performance and the menstrual cycle

Tradition has regarded the female period as a disability, best treated by inactivity, particularly during the early phases of heavy menstrual flow. Interestingly, when a team of female athletes spend a long period in a common dormitory, some grouping of the times of menstruation seems to occur. However, in normal circumstances, at least one woman in seven is liable to be menstruating on any given day, and it is thus an impossible task to arrange athletic competitions in such a way as to avoid the periods. If the individual suffers greatly from cramps and nausea, it may be possible for her to re-schedule the time of menstruation by an appropriate use of birth-control pills. However, current assessments suggest that the effect of the menstrual cycle upon performance is remarkably small.

Tension rises before the onset of menstruation. This is akin to an increase of arousal, and can lead to some gains of performance in events calling for extremes of muscular force (such as shot-putting), with a deterioration of more complex skills. During menstruation, some mechanical problems can arise, particularly if standard sanitary napkins are worn. However, internal tampons now allow most types of activity to be pursued with little limitation. Even swimming is quite practicable. Although about a third of all girls have disease-causing bacteria in their vaginas during menstruation, there is no evidence that these leak into the water in sufficient quantities to cause any deterioration in the cleanliness of a swimming pool.

Among 66 sportswomen participating in the Tokyo Olympic Games (1964), 41 per cent reported some disturbance of menstrual flow during either training or competition; however, only 17 per cent noted any loss of performance. The least confident were the swimmers, about a third of this group avoiding training during menstruation. Further questioning of the 1964 and 1968 United States Olympic teams established that women had won gold medals and established new world records at all phases of their menstrual cycles.

Pregnancy is no obstacle to victory. One Olympic bronze medallist in Helsinki (1952) was pregnant at the time of competition, and some champion athletes continue to compete until a few days prior to delivery. Most studies suggest that labour either occurs normally or is facilitated by the greater strength and endurance of the athlete; in a series of 729 Hungarian contestants, Caesarean section in subsequent pregnancies was 50 per cent less common than in the general population.

Many mothers are also to be found on the athletic field. Noack found 16 national champions and two silver medallists competing in the 1948 Olympics who had each borne one or more children.

Other medical considerations

Male endurance athletes have some tendency to anaemia, and the regular loss of iron in menstrual bleeding makes the female competitor even more vulnerable to this problem. Those using intra-uterine contraceptive devices such as the 'loop' have particularly heavy periods, and a corresponding increase in their iron needs.

Anatomical differences in the female lead to some variations in injury experience relative to the male. In skiing, it has been suggested that lesser muscular strength and weaker bones enhances the likelihood of injury. In water-skiing, a fall while the legs are widely spaced can force water into the vagina with sufficient force to rupture it. The breasts provide an additional very vulnerable area; protective brassieres have been designed, but do not seem likely to be widely used by the modern female.

12
The adolescent athlete

There has been much pressure in recent years to subject young teenagers to the full rigours of both training and participation in international sport. The pressure has been generated by beliefs that training is more effective in the young than in older recruits, and that winners also are to be found within the ranks of the very young competitors. We will look at the truth of both of these propositions, and will consider the wisdom of intense competition from the viewpoints of physical and psychological injury and the total development of the child.

Training in adolescence

Coaches from Eastern Europe advocate a very early start to training, and many declare categorically that if serious preparation is delayed beyond the age of fifteen a competitor is unlikely to reach the top of his particular class. Animal experiments give some support to this idea. Training is most effective during the period when growth is occurring, and it becomes progressively harder to improve working capacity as an animal ages. The number of fat cells in the body is determined soon after birth, and thereafter the amount of fat in the body can be varied only by starving or over-filling existing fat cells. Similarly, exercise of a young animal can cause the growth of new muscle fibres, but in later life increases of muscle force depend on an increase in the size and a modification in the chemical constituents of existing fibres.

In man, the number of both fat and muscle cells seems to be fixed after the first year of life, so that there is little possibility of starting training early enough to change the number of cells within the body. Many studies of children have shown a disappointing response to endurance-type training, the observed gains being smaller than in an adult given an equivalent programme. However, this is partly a reflection of the greater habitual activity of the child. For training to be effective, the demands made on the body must exceed those encountered in normal play and recreation.

There is no good evidence that child athletes exceed the fitness of their contemporaries by a wider margin than one would expect for adults. Cunningham found that male swimmers aged 10–16 had an average maximum oxygen intake of 57 ml per min per kg. Although this is not far below the figure encountered in many world-class adults, it is also less than 20 per cent better than in the average Ontario boy of the same age. Irma Åstrand reported data on thirty of the best adolescent girl swimmers from Sweden. Their maximum oxygen intake averaged 54 ml per min per kg, with a reading of 60 ml per min per kg for the best competitor; they thus had an advantage of more than 40 per cent over Toronto school-girls of the same age: partly an expression of the culturally accepted inactivity of the Canadian teenage girl. Some five years after the Swedish girls had stopped swimming, the laboratory measurements were repeated. Maximum oxygen intake had now dropped to the level of the sedentary Torontonians, and the only possible permanent gains from the rigorous programme of twenty-six hours of training per week were some increase of the heart and lung volumes; even these apparent rewards may really have been inherited advantages that caused the girls to enter the swimming programme in the first instance.

We may thus conclude that an early start to training may help a candidate find better ways of using his physiological resources, but there are no strong grounds for supposing that the power of the heart or muscles will be augmented more than in a person who starts his preparation two or three years later.

The optimum age of competition

The optimum age of competition depends very much on the opposing influences of cumulative skills and experience versus waning physiological powers. A detailed analysis of the ages of

Table 20. *Average age of male and female competitors in selected sports (based on data of Karvonen for the Helsinki Olympic Games)*

Event	Average age Men	Average age Women	Age of winner Men	Age of winner Women
100-metre free-style swimming	21	19	22	17
200-metre breast stroke	22	20	22	25
400-metre free-style swimming	21	20	19	19
100-metre track	24	21	21	21
200-metre track	24	22	25	21
High-jump	24	21	21	30
Long-jump	24	23	24	23
Gymnastics	26	23	31	31
Spring-board diving	26	21	21	22
Javelin	25	24	24	30
Discus	28	29	22	23
Shot-put	26	25	20	21
Foil	30	32	24	26
Average	24·7	23·1	22·8	23·8

participants in the Helsinki Olympic Games was made by Karvonen and his associates (Table 20). In terms of average age, the women were almost two years younger than the men; however, much of this difference seems due to a lesser persistence on the part of unsuccessful female competitors, and the average age of the winners was one year greater than for the men. Seventeen boys aged 17 years or younger participated in 19 events, 12 of these being various types of swimming competition. Similarly, eight girls aged 15 or less participated in 9 events, 7 of which were swimming contests. These figures thus support the view that a high level of proficiency in swimming can be reached at quite an early age. On the other hand, older competitors usually fared better even in the swimming events. Seven of the seventeen boys and five of the eight girls were eliminated in early heats. The best achievements of the 15-year-old girls were fifth places in the 100-metre backstroke and springboard diving events. The 17-year-old boys included a silver medallist in the 100-metre backstroke, a silver medallist in wrestling, and silver and gold medallists in shooting.

More recently, young teenagers have continued to set new records in swimming contests. In 1966, a 15-year-old Vancouver girl, Elaine Tanner, became a national heroine by winning four gold and three silver medals at the Commonwealth Games. A relay team of 12-year-old boys from Tunbridge Wells succeeded in swimming the Channel in 1968. Five years later, a 16-year-old United States girl, Lynne Cox, set a new record of 9 hours 36 minutes for the cross-channel swim, while in 1974 another 16-year-old, Cindy Nicholas, covered the 32 miles across Lake Ontario in 15 hours 15 minutes. The year 1975 brought further successes: 13-year-old Nancy Garrapick setting a world record for the 200-metre backstroke event, to have it surpassed six weeks later by a 15-year-old girl from East Germany.

Physical dangers of activity in adolescence

At one time, it was widely held that children 'outgrew their strength' in the years before puberty, so that over-vigorous physical activity at this stage could 'strain the heart'. Calculations were adduced which purported to show that the great artery leading from the heart, the aorta, did not grow fast enough to transport the blood pumped from the cardiac chamber in really strenuous effort. Examinations of athletes who had competed as children showed 'enlarged' hearts, and careful listening with a stethoscope often disclosed ominous murmurs.

Some caution in prescribing exercise for children may have been appropriate at a time when rheumatic heart disease was a common ailment. Today, however, it is well recognized that fears for the heart of the child athlete are groundless. The calculations of inadequate growth in the aorta are now known to be erroneous. The 'enlarged' hearts of the endurance competitors are seen to be a result of athletic selection rather than cardiac strain, and a greater understanding of the physical properties of flowing blood has demonstrated that soft murmurs can arise in a perfectly normal circulation during vigorous exercise.

Injury to developing and incompletely calcified bones is of more concern. The ends of a child's bones are attached to the shafts by softer areas of cartilage where growth is occurring, and these regions are vulnerable to damage by either over-vigorous traction from muscles or external violence. Repeated jerking of the tendon can lead to a chronic inflammation of the growth zone. 'Little-leaguers elbow' is perhaps the most notorious of this class of injury, although excessive running or jumping can cause problems at the knee, and repeated throwing can cause a similar inflammation at the shoulder. The 12-year-old baseball pitcher throws the ball at upwards of 100 kilometres per hour, each of his efforts applying a terrific jerk to the inner side of the elbow. Dr. Adams, a Californian orthopaedic surgeon, took X-ray photographs of the elbow region of 162 baseball players; 80 were pitchers, and all had varying degrees of inflammation of the arm-bone at the elbow. In contrast, the X-rays were normal in all but a small proportion of the boys who played in other positions. Remedies proposed have included a ban on the throwing of 'curved' balls by boys under the age of fourteen and a general restriction on the number of innings permitted each week.

Occasionally, a single more violent strain, such as in a bad landing from a jump, may cause the part of the bone to which a tendon is attached to separate completely from the remainder of the shaft. Direct injuries to the bones occur rather more commonly in children than in adults, partly because the bones are incompletely calcified, and partly because there is less overlying protection from muscle and fat. Fortunately, rupture of the softer adolescent bone is often incomplete (greenstick fracture'), and healing proceeds more rapidly than in an adult. The main source of difficulty is that in about 13 per cent of cases the fracture runs through the growth area. There is then a chance (10–20 per cent) that the bone will stop growing prematurely or will develop in misshapen form.

Prevention of bone injuries in the child follows the same general principles enunciated for the adult. There must be good medical supervision both before and during competition, proper long-term conditioning and adequate immediate warm-up, careful coaching with avoidance of hazardous manœuvres, full use of protective equipment, safe physical facilities, and good officiating with a thorough enforcement of the rules. Particularly in contact sports, it is difficult to ensure a fair matching of competitors before puberty. One early-maturing twelve-year-old may already be 6 feet tall with a massive frame; his opponent may be a late-maturing and slight boy of 4 feet 6 inches. The ideal arrangement would be to arrange contests in terms of biological age rather than calendar age or scholastic attainment. However, simple and unequivocal methods of determining biological age have yet to be worked out, and in their absence inequalities of competition are a strong argument against taking contests too seriously.

Psychological effects of intense competition

Very young children seldom like playing a game unless it is likely that they will win. One expression of maturity is the ability to handle both victory and defeat appropriately. It is a relatively easy matter to learn to live with defeat in a game of snakes and ladders, but it is rather a different question when the pride of a nation hangs upon one's performance. Some psychologists have thus argued that the stress of major competition can endanger the emotional stability of young children. Unfortunately, there are few reliable tools for measuring emotional stress. Studies of little-league baseball players have shown a proportion of the boys too excited to eat normally after games, and in some instances the disturbance persisted for sufficient time to cause loss of sleep. However, a questionnaire circulated to 1300 doctors whose sons were involved in little-league baseball showed 97 per cent convinced that the contests were not adversely affecting the emotional health of their sons. Our own studies of the minor-league hockey players in Quebec have shown surprisingly normal behaviour during the final competitions, with teachers rating classroom manners as above average both before and after the contest.

Physical activity and development

There have been very few longitudinal studies to follow what effect participation in vigorous sporting activity has upon the course of growth and development. A small group of boys were followed for 32 months in Sweden. Over this time, the body-weight of the vigorously active subjects increased 45 per cent, compared with 28 per cent in the inactive controls. Changes were slightly greater for the active and slightly smaller for the inactive than would have been predicted from respective changes in height. Lung volumes increased by 54 per cent and 34 per cent, and heart volumes by 49 per cent and 36 per cent; in both cases the active boys showed larger gains than would have been predicted from their height, while the control boys showed changes of the expected order. Maximum oxygen intakes increased by 60 per cent and 38 per cent respectively, both active and inactive students showing larger gains than would have been anticipated from the height increment. It is plain that the main effects of the vigorous exercise were upon height and weight, and the apparent gains in lung and heart volumes could be due to no more than an acceleration of the pubertal 'growth spurt' in the active boys. To answer the question of the effects of activity on ultimate size, it would be necessary to continue the study for another five years, until both active and inactive boys reached maturity. To date, no research laboratory has had the patience to complete such an investigation.

13
The ageing athlete

From time immemorial, man has searched the elixir of youth, the magic potion that would restore spent vigour, or at least slow the relentless hand of time. Studies of athletes soon showed that hard physical training produced changes diametrically opposed to those associated with ageing. The capacity of the heart and lungs to transport oxygen was increased, flabby fat was replaced by firm flesh, joints became more supple, and bones stronger. It thus seemed logical to explore the possibility that an athlete might age more slowly and live longer than an ordinary sedentary individual.

The immediate effects of sports upon health (Chapter 10) do not give much encouragement to such a view. The risk of injury is enhanced, any influence on the course of disease is slight, and sudden death is rather more likely than when resting in an armchair. Despite these adverse findings, this chapter will look further at the health of the older athlete, comparing his rate of ageing and longevity with that of the general population.

Health of the ageing athlete

When examining reports on the health of older 'athletes', it is first necessary to enquire whether the sportsman is still participating actively in his chosen event. As far as the Olympic Games is concerned, there are few competitors over the age of forty, except in shooting, riding, fencing, marathon, and long-distance-walking contests. In most cases the individual is discouraged by his declining performance and withdraws from competition, but even if he persists the age handicap leads to early elimination in national heats. An attempt has now been made to overcome this difficulty through the organization of age-stratified 'Masters' contests; however, in general these attract recent athletes rather than those who were top competitors in their younger days. While the novitiate sportsman finds the competition of middle age a stimulus to his training programme, it is hard for a former champion to contemplate worsening times, and possibly defeat by people that he could have beaten easily a few years earlier. This point was demonstrated clearly in a study of Michigan State University graduates carried out by Montoye and his associates (Fig. 21).

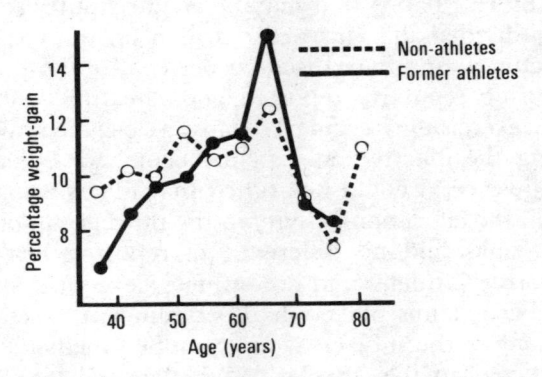

FIG. 21. Weight gain after the age of forty: a comparison between former athletes and non-athletes (based on data of Dr. Henry Montoye).

At the age of 30, more of the ex-athletes were participating in sports than the non-athletes; however, the activity of the former athletes decreased progressively, and in the fifties and the sixties a smaller proportion were engaging in regular sports than their non-athletic colleagues.

The team sportsman in particular finds difficulty in throwing off his habit of hearty eating, and after retirement becomes more obese than his non-athletic colleagues. Meylan questioned 108 former Harvard oarsmen; on average, they were almost 20 kg heavier than their non-sporting contemporaries, much of this difference representing weight gained since leaving college. Montoye plotted the percentage weight-gain against age (Fig. 21). The non-athletes gained about 10 per cent over their college weight by the time they were forty years old, but showed little additional increment between forty and seventy. In contrast, the former athletes went from 6 per cent to 15 per cent weight-gain over this period, with a steep weight-loss in the small group who were over seventy years of age.

Once the discipline of training was relaxed, the ex-athletes also began to indulge themselves with tobacco and alcohol. Some 69 per cent of former athletes smoked, compared with 60 per cent of non-athletes; again, 78 per cent of ex-athletes drank varying amounts of alcohol, as compared with 67 per cent of non-athletes. When assessing the health of the former sportsman, we must thus consider not only the period of intense activity, but also any bad habits that may be acquired after retirement.

Meylan divided the Harvard oarsmen on the basis of their current activity, and found that 60 per cent of those who were still exercising regularly reported good health. Among those who were exercising irregularly, only 51 per cent were well, and among the inactive only 25 per cent had a clean bill of health. However, it could be argued that illness was the cause rather than the effect of inactivity in the third group of subjects. Montoye could find no difference of reported health status between former athletes and non-athletes, except that the men who had been tennis players had a significant excess of complaints. None of the subjects were examined medically, so that the report was unable to clarify whether the tennis players really were more sick, or whether a more neurotic segment of the student population had chosen to play tennis during their days at University.

Both Meylan and Montoye asked their subjects whether they would take up athletics again if they were able to repeat their life at college. Meylan found 103 of the former Harvard oarsmen out of the 108 giving an unqualified 'yes'. The verdict of the alumnae of Michigan State University was also decisive, 85 per cent of former athletes and 76 per cent of non-athletes expressing a desire for participation, with only 5 per cent and 8 per cent of the two samples opposed.

The heart of the athlete

The idea that regular exercise can reduce the chances of having a heart attack in middle age comes mainly from comparisons of populations with contrasting levels of occupational activity. The groups studied have included London bus-drivers and conductors, postmen and postal clerks, and field and office workers in the Jewish Kibbutzim. In all cases, the active groups have had about half as many heart attacks as their inactive counterparts.

Could athletes anticipate similar protection as a result of sport? The evidence from the occupational comparisons is certainly suggestive that regular endurance activity diminishes the risk of a coronary attack, particularly a fatal attack. However, scientists are not completely convinced that the benefit is due to exercise. There is also the question of initial selection; it may be the fat, lazy, and coronary-prone man who chooses to be a bus-driver in the first instance, while the lean and healthy individual prefers the more active task of collecting fares. However, there are many plausible mechanisms whereby regular daily activity could have a beneficial effect upon the heart. Let us name but a few. Exercise could open up the blood vessels supplying the heart, making them less liable to obstruction, and where a partial blockage has developed, vigorous effort could encourage the development of new alternative pathways for the blood. Regular training could also lessen the physical stresses of daily life through an increase in the reserves of strength and power and a diminution in the dead-weight of fat. The burning of excess fat could in itself diminish the likelihood of a blockage of the coronary vessels by fatty plaques, while the decrease in clotting tendency of the blood associated with exercise would also help to keep the coronary arteries open. Lastly, physical exercise could have a cathartic function (Chapter 5), helping to relieve emotional stress.

It is less certain that the athlete gains all of these hypothetical benefits. Take, for example, emotional stress. Many find top competitions cause intense psychological stress. However, the sportsman might expect many of the other advantages of regular effort, particularly if his event calls for sustained endurance work. Unfortunately, the benefits are retained only for as long as the physical activity is continued. The bus-conductor continues climbing the stairs on his double-deck vehicle until he is 65, apparently gaining useful protection against coronary attacks. On the other hand, the athlete who retires to a life of overeating, over-drinking, and heavy smoking at 35 or 40 cannot expect to see much difference in his risk of a heart attack relative to the most sedentary of businessmen. In some respects, the athlete is even at a disadvantage. We saw that as a consequence of either selection or training, he has a large heart. This means that oxygen must travel further to supply individual muscle fibres, unless he develops and maintains an above-average network of coronary blood vessels by regular physical activity.

During life, the only reliable way of examining the extent of the coronary blood vessels is to take X-rays after the injection of an opaque dye into the heart. This method is quite useful when deciding the suitability of heart-attack patients for surgery, but is plainly too drastic to use on healthy athletes. One indirect alternative is to look at the configuration of the electrocardiogram during vigorous standardized exercise. If the heart muscle is becoming short of oxygen, one particular part of the tracing, the so-called ST segment, shows a marked de-

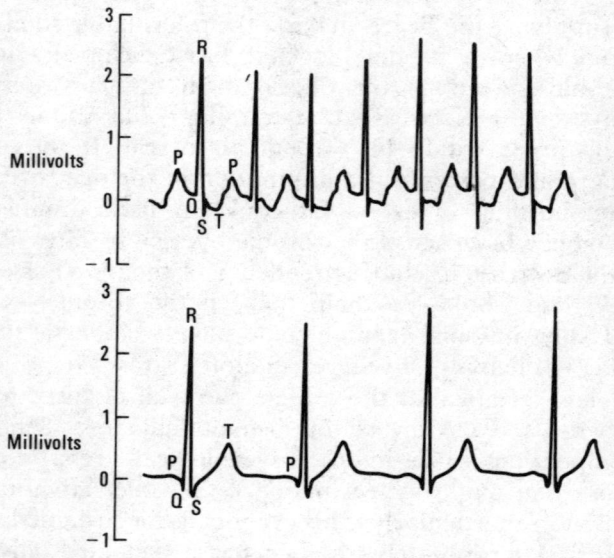

FIG. 22. The development of ST segmental depression in the chest electrocardiogram. The upper panel shows a normal electrocardiogram of a subject at rest. The lower panel shows the same subject during vigorous exercise, and because the heart muscle is short of oxygen there is a downward displacement of the record between the S and T points.

pression (Fig. 22). There is at present disagreement concerning the normality of electrocardiograms among former athletes; one German study reported a high incidence of ST abnormalities, but two reports from Scandinavia suggested that the frequency was the same or less than in the general population. In a few instances, it has been possible to examine the athlete's heart at an eventual post-mortem: one particularly interesting report concerned Clarence de Mar, the famous distance runner of the early 1930s. He had a very large heart, but this was apparently more than compensated by the development of very wide coronary arteries.

Rate of ageing of athletes

There have been two reports, one from Cologne and the other from Seattle, that the normal, age-related deterioration of maximum oxygen intake occurs more slowly in the athlete than in the general population. However, critical examination of the data shows that these conclusions rest upon the unusual behaviour of the control populations rather than on any inherent advantage in the experience of the athletes. Losses (all given in millilitres per kilogram body weight per minute) reported for the continuing athletes were, respectively, 0·7 and 0·6 per year, compared with 0·5 per year in the general population of Toronto. Further studies of champion runners and physical education alumnae have confirmed that the loss in very active people is about 0·6 per year, if anything slightly greater than that experienced by sedentary groups. On the other hand, because the athlete has such a high maximum oxygen intake as a young man, at the age of 65 he may still retain a larger oxygen transporting power than a sedentary person of 25.

A second common accompaniment of age is an increase in the percentage of body fat, with an accumulation of lipids in the blood stream. Saltin looked at a group of orienteers. At the age of 25, their average weight was 70 kg. By the age of 45, many were no longer participating in the sport; their weight had increased by 5 kg, although the continuing orienteers still weighed 70 kg. Ten years later, the penalty of the inactive group had increased to 12 kg, and at 65 they were still 7 kg heavier than the continuing orienteers. Both active and inactive groups had rather high blood-cholesterol readings at the age of 65, but the fat levels in the blood of the continuing orienteers were only 60 per cent of those in the retired sportsmen.

Although many reports have suggested that athletes retain their large hearts into old age, it is interesting that in Saltin's study the heart volume of the inactive orienteers had dropped to 11 ml per kg of body-weight at the age of 45, compared with a figure of 15 ml per kg in those who had remained active.

Data on the deterioration of muscle force and lung volumes are restricted to physical-education alumnae. In these groups, the rate of loss of function with ageing was at least as great as in the general population.

We may thus conclude that continuing activity will control middle-age spread, but will do little else to arrest the normal course of ageing. Nevertheless, the high initial standing of the athlete leaves him in better shape than his contemporaries in middle age and later life.

Longevity of athletes

If athletic participation had a beneficial effect on either health or the rate of ageing, we should expect to find athletes living longer than non-athletes. Some early studies apparently supported this view. Dr. Morgan, himself a university oarsman, examined the age at death of 294 men who had rowed in the Oxford and Cambridge boat race between 1829 and 1869. The rowers lived 2 years longer than the 'average' Englishman, as deduced from the insurance statistics of the day. Meylan had very similar findings in the United States. Men who had rowed at Harvard lived 2·9 years longer than the general insured population. A high proportion of his sample of oarsmen met violent deaths, and if allowance was made for this factor, the remainder of his sample lived as much as 5·1 years longer than predicted from insurance tables. Nor was the benefit peculiar to rowing. Anderson obtained data on 808 Yale men who had participated in crew, football, track, or baseball teams between 1855 and 1905; for all of these classes of sport, death-rate was only about half that of the general population. Again, 9 of the 58 deaths among the athletes were violent in nature, 2 being due to suicide.

THE AGEING ATHLETE

The fallacy of making comparisons with insurance statistics was first pointed out by Greenway and Hiscock. They commented that this approach made no allowance for the privileged life of the nineteenth-century University graduate. They analysed statistics for Yale graduates, both former athletes and non-athletes. The year was 1926, and University privilege was waning. Nevertheless, the non-athletes had only 83 per cent of the mortality predicted from tables. In contrast, the former athletes had 93 per cent of the expected mortality, this excess of deaths being due entirely to violence. Greenway and Hiscock suggested that the athlete was naturally both energetic and courageous, and tended to expose himself to danger both in war and in peace. Certainly, fatal war injuries were 50 per cent more common in the ex-athletes than in their sedentary counterparts.

A few years later, Dublin carried out a much more exhaustive study, comparing 4976 former athletes from eight eastern United States universities with both general students and scholastic honour winners. At the age of 22, life expectancy was 45·6 years in the athletes, 45·7 years in the general student body, and 47·7 years in the honours students, all comparing favourably with the life insurance prediction of 44·3 years. By the age of 62, life expectancy had diminished to 14·1 years in the former athletes, 14·5 years in the general student group, 15·6 years in the honours students, and 13·1 years in the insurance tables.

The most recent analysis of Cambridge University athletes points to rather similar conclusions. Rook compared 834 sportsmen who had played against Oxford University with a random sample of 379 non-athletic students and a group of 382 intellectuals, all of whom had attained high academic honours. The average age at death in the athletes was 68·0 years, with insignificant differences between track-and-field, cricket, rowing, and rugby sub-groups. The randomly selected students had a very similar life expectancy (average age of death 67·4 years), and as in Dublin's study the intellectuals lived longer (average 69·4 years).

The one investigation that has apparently showed an advantage to the athletes is a comparison between participants in the marathon cross-country ski races of Finland, and sedentary

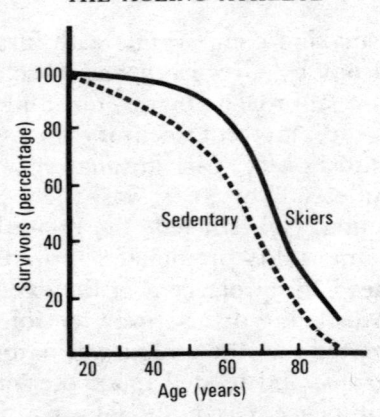

FIG. 23. Percentage survivors in the Finnish population at various ages. Note that those who continue to participate in long-distance cross-country skiing events live considerably longer than do sedentary members of the community (based on data of Karvonen).

people from the same region (Fig. 23). The cross-country ski enthusiasts live about seven years longer than the sedentary group. It is possible that cross-country skiing is more effective in extending life than other sports because it is continued into middle and old age; the participant thus is less likely to suffer the loss of virtue seen in many middle-aged former University athletes who become overweight and inactive. However, it must also be remembered that cross-country skiing is such a vigorous sport that it inevitably has a selecting effect upon the composition of both the experimental and the control samples. Those who are too sick to ski transfer themselves from the athletes to the sedentary group, and by their sickness they depress the average life expectancy of the latter population. Although the Finnish data is interesting, much more analysis will be required before we can safely conclude that sustained athletics will extend a man's life.

14
The handicapped athlete

According to Dr. Gershon Huberman, the word 'handicap' developed from an ancient game of chance known as 'hand-in-cap'. A player would challenge his opponent for some possession, matching the stake with an appropriate article from his own belongings. If the umpire decided that one of the articles wagered was inferior to the other, he would order that a compensating sum of money be placed in a cap, thus ensuring both the quality and the equality of the contest. Later, the term also became applied to people, as judges awarded handicaps that would compensate for physical or mental limitations, permitting a fair and well-matched competition.

The proportion of the population that are handicapped is quite large. Some problems date from birth—deformed babies such as the thalidomide victims, the deaf, the blind, and the dumb, and those with mental deficiencies. Other disabilities are first incurred by young adults—paralysis by poliomyelitis, and spinal injuries sustained in war, in industry, and in motor-vehicle accidents. In Britain, a register is kept of some 650 000 individuals who are 'substantially handicapped' in obtaining or holding employment on account of injury, disease, or congenital deformity. Much smaller disabilities make a contest unequal for the sportsman; moderate deafness, for example, can keep a rower from hearing the instructions of his coach, bellowed from a megaphone on the tow-path. Australian workers have estimated that 9 per cent of their population have chronic disorders sufficient to cause some restriction of sports activities, and that in 5 per cent the limitation is severe.

It is plainly wrong that sport should be denied to this segment of the community. The life of the handicapped individual is restricted relative to that of a healthy person, with a proportionate increase in the need for the pleasure, interest, relaxation, and relief from monotony. Sports participation can help. Further, it is wrong to assume that one disability such as an amputation grants immunity from other forms of ill-health such as heart attacks, high blood pressure, and obesity. The handicapped have the same need of physical fitness as the general population; indeed, since walking and other daily activities are harder for them than for normal people, it is arguable that they need an enhanced level of fitness.

The idea of wheelchair sports seems to have originated during World War II, as a need was seen for exercise and recreation for severely injured servicemen. It was greatly developed and placed on an international footing through the efforts of Sir Ludwig Guttman, founder of the National Unit for Paraplegics at Stoke Mandeville, on the northern outskirts of London. Daily contact with the paraplegics showed Sir Ludwig the frequency with which a paralysed person developed an inferiority complex, becoming anxious, lacking in self-confidence, self-pitying, and anti-social. Sport was seen as playing a psychotherapeutic role, bringing a man to terms with his defect, restoring contact with the normal world, providing the companionship and encouragement of other disabled persons, and restoring self-respect and self-discipline.

The first formal games were held in England in 1948. By 1952, the organization had become the International Stoke Mandeville Games. It was soon affiliated with more than fifty national organizations, and held contests in the same countries as the Olympic Games; events were held in Rome (1960), Tokyo (1964), Tel Aviv (1968), Heidelberg (1972), and Toronto (1976). The disabled group did not meet in Mexico City in 1968, since it was decided that the altitude would present an unjustified stress to some of the competitors. A Commonwealth Paraplegic Games was begun in Perth (1962), and this has continued in the same country as the Commonwealth Games for normal individuals (Kingston, 1966; Edinburgh, 1970; and Dunedin, 1974). Other events are held in parallel with the Pan American Games. Unfortunately, there are three international associations currently concerned —the International Stoke Mandeville Games Committee, the International Sports Organization for the Disabled, and the International Sports Organization for the Deaf. A merging of these somewhat rival associations would undoubtedly give the disabled a stronger voice on the national and international scenes.

The principles of sport for the disabled are to classify patients in such a way that competitors are equally handicapped, and to modify the rules of a given contest to accommodate the disability. Wheel-chair paraplegics are currently separated into six categories, depending on the level to which muscular function is preserved. The importance of the sense organs in the skin is brought out by this classification. Spinal injuries destroy both muscle function and sensation, but poliomyelitis affects only the muscles; polio victims with an equivalent paralysis thus often out-perform those with traumatic injuries to the spine. The management of a wheel-chair is an important aspect of readaptation to normal life, and thus early games placed a strong emphasis on the 100-metre wheel-chair dash, and the wheel-chair slalom. International competitions now include also 400- and 1500-metre events, with javelin, discus, and shot-putting contests, archery, fencing (Fig. 24), basketball, and table-tennis.

Basketball is perhaps the most spectacular event, and in Tel Aviv it attracted more than 6000 spectators. Mastery of the chair and the ball while retaining an appropriate orientation to one's team-mates and opponents presents a stern challenge to muscular co-ordination and endurance, and brings out the residual ability of the paralysed person to the full. The game also provides an interesting example of the way in which normal rules are modified. The chair is considered as an extension of the player, and a collision with another chair thus becomes a personal foul.

The introduction of wheel-chair sports has had a marked effect on wheel-chair design. The heavy wooden armchair with cumbersome iron-rimmed wheels, still found in a few older hospitals, has now been replaced by ultra-lightweight high-speed chairs, very manœuvrable, and usually collapsible to allow road or air transportation to competition sites. Performance characteristics still differ substantially between models, and some top athletes use their own special designs. There is

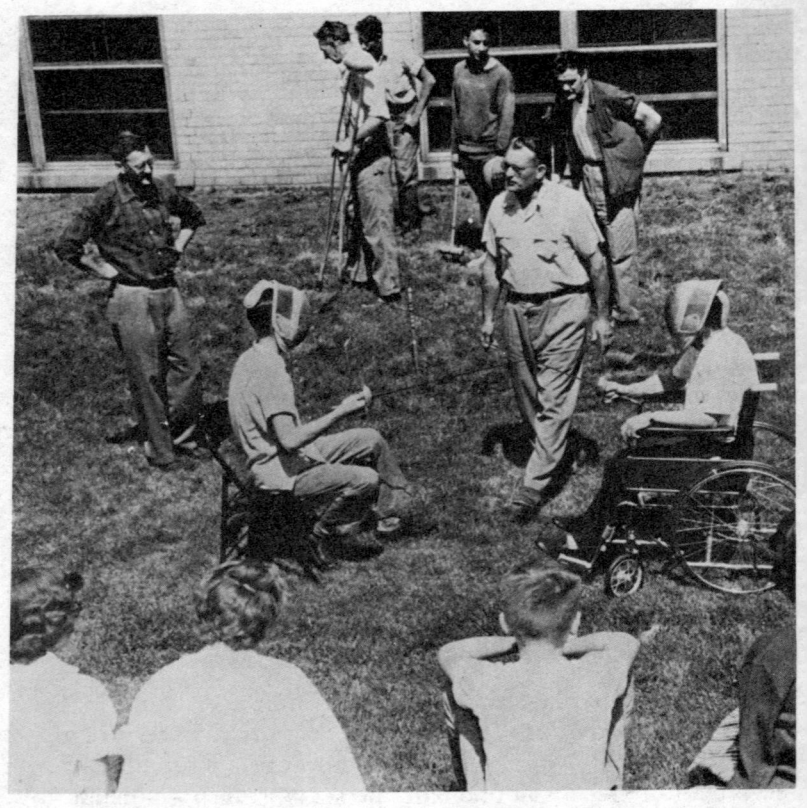

FIG. 24. A fencing contest for the physically handicapped, with suitably modified rules (illustration reproduced from Ernst Jokl, *The clinical physiology of physical fitness and rehabilitation* (1958), by courtesy of the author and the publisher, C. C. Thomas, Springfield, Illinois).

thus agitation for a standard specification that will provide greater equality in competition. Already there is international agreement that in order to minimize the risk of injury to the legs, foot-rests should be at a uniform height of 10 cm, with the seat no more than 51 cm above the ground.

Modifications of stadium design are necessary to accommodate the handicapped, both as spectators and as sportsmen. Desirable features include reserved parking areas near to entrances, the replacement of stairs by ramps and elevators, and the installation of lavatories and bathrooms with doors at least 1 m wide. For the wheel-chair races, lane-widths must be increased to 1·5–2·0 per competitor. Swimming events require a pool with a ramp allowing the athletes to enter the water at seat height.

There have been very few physiological studies of handicapped athletes. Observation suggests that wheel-chair basketball may be the most demanding of the sports for the disabled. Certainly those who excel at this also earn top points for their class in swimming, and in track-and-field events.

A report from the Wingate Institute in Israel (Table 21)

Table 21. *A comparison between normal active and sedentary men, and active and sedentary paraplegic men (based on data of Zwiren and Bar-Or)*

	Normal Sedentary	Normal Active	Paraplegic Sedentary	Paraplegic Active
Height (cm)	171	181	173	169
Body weight (kg)	69	79	73	60
Fat (per cent)	18·3	12·5	21·9	17·4
Lean tissue (kg)	58	67	56	51
Grip strength (kg)	48	58	55	51
Lung capacity (l)	5·0	6·0	4·3	5·0
Maximum oxygen transporting power (ml per min per kg)	26	38	20	35

compared eleven international competitors from the Spewack basketball team with nine other cases of polio or traumatic paraplegia who were not taking part in any physical training. It was not possible to carry out standard bicycle ergometer or treadmill measurements of maximum oxygen intake. Instead, a bicycle was mounted at a convenient height for the pedals to be turned by the hands. This arrangement yielded normal values for both athletes and sedentary subjects that were about 70 per cent of the oxygen transporting power measured during leg work. As in the normal population, participation of the wheel-chair group in athletics was associated with low body-fat and high oxygen transport relative to inactive men. There was also a suggestion that lung volumes were larger in athletes than in non-athletes. Questioning of the men engaged in this experiment suggested that before injury the two groups of wheel-chair subjects were of roughly equal fitness. A cross-sectional comparison of this sort cannot prove conclusively that athletics improves the physical condition of the wheel-chair victim, but it certainly suggests quite strongly that such a change is produced.

After nearly thirty years of Paraplegic Games, those charged with the care of wheel-chair patients still debate the relative merits of participation versus competition in sports. Some argue that the psychological trauma of the disability itself is such that it is unfair to expose a paraplegic to the possibility of further defeat. A practical expression of this reasoning was seen at the 1963 International Games in Linz, where the sportsmen all performed a pentathlon-type event, competing only against a stop-watch and a tape-measure. Exponents of more normal competition argue that paraplegia does not change man's basic nature—the wheel-chair athlete has the same desire to move faster and to throw more strongly as any other sportsman. Furthermore, a reintegration of the disabled person with society is an important dividend of the public contest; it affects not only the athletes themselves, but also the spectators, as the latter gain a fresh insight into both the problems and the indomitable spirit of the paraplegics.

15
The athlete and society

In this final chapter, we consider what contribution the fit athlete has made to society, and see how far the objectives set by the Baron de Coubertin have been realized. We shall discuss professionalism, spectatorism, sport as an emancipating force, and sport in the promotion of international understanding.

Professionalism

National sporting associations have shared the Baron's desire to guard the amateur status of the top athlete. Perhaps originally a matter of maintaining class barriers, the emphasis of concern has shifted more recently to exploitation of the participants and a deterioration in the quality of competition.

In the 1830s, the Henley Regatta Committee saw fit to reject as amateur oarsmen all those who had been employed as mechanics, artisans, or labourers, irrespective of their attitude towards rowing for money. In contrast, it saw nothing amiss when gentlemen of the Oxford and Leander crews rowed for £200 a side. At this period, the word amateur was used interchangeably with gentleman, a habit that has persisted on the cricket field.

Closely linked to this definition of an amateur was the middle-class notion of sportsmanship. The public school background of the wealthy young man imbued such a strong sense of fair play that a referee was hardly needed to avoid 'ungentlemanly' conduct. There were fears that not all of the working class subscribed to the same code. Thus, if contests were open to all ranks of society, there would be episodes of cheating, poaching of players from other clubs, bribery, and vicious competition.

Despite the efforts of the Marquis of Queensberry (1866), there is evidence that professional boxing suffered from many of these evils, and with the outlawing of the sport in the United States it even fell under the influence of organized gangsters. Occasionally, there was a fatal outcome to a brutal match, as in the death of Luther McCarty at Calgary in 1913.

However, the more general association of professionalism with lack of sportsmanship and corruption seems unwarranted. In recent years, the professional sportsman has played the game no better and no worse than his amateur counterpart.

Definition of the professional in terms of financial reward rather than breeding has been a gradual change. In 1878, W. G. Grace was reputed to have received quite large sums of money without injuring his status as a gentleman, but by 1902 the Canadian Amateur Athletic Union rules excluded all who had competed for a stake, bet, monies private or public, or gate receipts. Further, it ostracized those who competed with professionals for a prize, those who taught or assisted in the pursuit of any athletic exercise as a means of livelihood, those who received direct or indirect bonuses for loss of working time, those who entered competition under an assumed name, and those who had been guilty of selling or pledging their prizes.

Nevertheless, it proved difficult to enforce such exacting standards. At the 'Olympic' marathon held in Athens in 1906, the Canadian winner (Bill Sherring) received not only 'a grand statue, standing as high as myself' (*Toronto Globe and Mail*, 1906), but also 300 other gifts from all parts of Greece. His companion Linden was second in the 1500-metre race, but he also received a hero's welcome on his return to Toronto, the mayor presenting him with a purse of $180 and a gold watch.

Exploitation. Idealists were concerned to prevent exploitation of boys as professional sportsmen. They argued that sponsors would deprive players of needed education, only to reject them when their days of profitability were ended.

The reality of such fears is illustrated by the story of Tom Longboat, an Onondaga Indian. He entered the Boston marathon of 1907 with experience in only two previous races, yet clipped more than five and a half minutes off the existing record. Despite persistent rumours about his amateur status, he was admitted to the Olympic Games, only to drop out of the marathon with what was described as 'sunstroke'. The manager of the Canadian team thought otherwise and stated 'his sudden collapse and the symptoms shown seem to me to indicate that some form of stimulant was used.' Shortly after this incident, Longboat openly turned professional. In 1910, he was reputed to have earned $17 000, and a supporters committee raised enough money in nickels and quarters to build him a comfortable bungalow near the Brantford reserve of his tribe. By 1920, his running times were deteriorating, and he was to be seen nightly at the Edmonton exhibition, running 'against the clock'. Five years later he had committed the cardinal sin of pawning his cups and medals, and was working as a street cleaner in Toronto.

More recently, there has been concern about the contractual freedom of the professional player to move from one sponsor to another. In 1946, the two American baseball leagues successfully black-listed players who had arranged to join a newly formed Mexican league. Hockey players, also, have complained that they have been denied the right to negotiate 'market-place' compensation for their services. In both sports, the players have argued that management acted as a restrictive trust. However, there was difficulty in applying anti-trust laws, since the United States supreme court (1922) ruled that while the players moved from one state to another, the game did not. There was thus no inter-state commerce for a federal court to regulate! This judgement was finally revised in 1952, since soaring television revenues provided new evidence of inter-state trade.

Occasional stars are still dazzled by immediate incomes, failing to realize that their days of appeal to a fickle public are limited. However, an increasing number of professional athletes are well-educated university graduates with firm plans for a second career, and at current salaries there seems little basis for complaints of exploitation.

Quality of competition. Supporters of the amateur competitor have argued that sport should be a spontaneous celebration, and that the demands of professional sport rob it of this spirit. A light-hearted approach adds to the zest of recreational sport, but is hardly compatible with top competition, either amateur or professional.

A more powerful argument against the professional player is that he offers unfair competition, making contests impractical for the amateur contender. The speed with which the amateur can be eliminated is illustrated by the history of the English Football Association. In 1878/9, the total gate money received by the Aston Villa club in Birmingham was £43. By 1882/3 it had risen to £567, and despite promulgation of rule 16 forbidding payments to players other than expenses and 'any wages actually lost', this was the last year in which an amateur team reached the finals.

Canadian football suffered a similar fate. Whereas the University of Toronto team were able to win the Grey Cup in 1909, 1910, and 1911, from this time forward city teams began to outclass the Universities. By the end of World War II, clubs were faced with a hard choice. They could continue as amateurs, facing the twin problems of declining gates and mounting losses, or follow the lead of city teams in recruiting and paying players. The battle was finally resolved in 1966, the Canadian Rugby Union turning the Grey Cup over to the Canadian Football League and renaming itself the Canadian Amateur Football Association.

Contests between those who earnestly keep the rules and others who do not are plainly dispiriting. In recent years, we have seen Canadian amateur hockey players refuse to compete against Russian teams, on the grounds that the latter were disguised professionals. National pride was restored only when a series was negotiated between Canadian professional hockey players and the Russian team, with victory again going to the Canadian side.

The complexity of current International Olympic regulations suggests that the battle against professionalism is going badly. It is likely we will continue to see some true amateurs at Olympic contests for a number of years—men such as the Canadian paddlers who scrape together a few hundred dollars of their hard-earned wages to build their own canoes and kayaks. But such gallant competitors seem destined to form an ever smaller minority at world events, and their pleasure will come largely from competing against others like themselves rather than from surpassing performances by state-supported and scholarly athletes who can train on a full-time basis. The demands of modern training make full-time sportsmen almost inevitable. Roger Bannister, for example, quickly saw that while training for a four-minute mile was just possible as a medical student, it was incompatible with the developing career of a qualified physician.

Men such as Baron de Coubertin might well deplore current developments. However, uniform modest state support would restore fair competition and enhance the achievement of outstanding performances. Nor is there good evidence that such support would lead to a deterioration of sportsmanship or a lessening of enthusiasm on the part of the participants.

Spectatorism

Baron de Coubertin conceived the Olympic movement as a stimulus to personal participation in physical activity. He also spoke of the need to reduce the number of spectators at the major events. However, one of the striking paradoxes of the twentieth century has been that outstanding Olympic performances have created an almost universal interest in watching sport, while participation has dropped to an all-time low.

Many of the modern spectator sports were a product of the industrial revolution, the factory punch-clock giving a clear line of demarcation between working and leisure hours. A second contributory factor was the development of mass transportation. Early Canadians tended to travel by boat, and some of their first commercial spectacles were displays of rowing. The railways also had a financial interest in the promotion of spectator sport. The Toronto rower, Ned Hanlan, received a commission of $3900 from a consortium of railroad companies that stood to profit from his appearance at four regattas. The Canadian Pacific Company, with a line winding through suburban Montreal, also offered free passes to managers and half fares to players interested in competing against the Montreal baseball team.

By 1880, Toronto had at least five public stadia. In Britain, growth was equally rapid. The first challenge cup of the Football Association, held at Kennington Oval in 1872, attracted a mere 2000 spectators. For the comparable event in 1901, a crowd of 110 800 thronged to the Crystal Palace.

Sport as theatre. When William MacGregor founded the English Football League in 1888, his avowed aim was to offer entertainment of the type provided by the theatre. His idea was enlarged by Maheu, who saw spectator sports as the 'true theatre of our day', purging the emotions in the same way as had been postulated for Greek drama (Chapter 5).

Observations made on football and baseball crowds hardly support Maheu's idea. After watching a tense game, sentence completion tests commonly indicate an increase rather than a decrease in aggressive emotions. Often, the spectator becomes so involved in the game that a defeat becomes personal, and there is a need to vent frustration through verbal aggression against the players or the referee. Frequently, railway carriages, stations, and shops have become the targets of attacks and vandalism.

Interaction with the players. Many major clubs value the spectator not only as an immediate source of revenue, but also as an important ingredient in victory. Steps are thus taken to organize the sales of flags, confetti, musical instruments, and other means of mass communication.

The reactions of the competitor depend very much upon his initial level of arousal (Fig. 16, p. 106). If he is already keyed-up, the tumult of the arena may worsen the performance of skilled manœuvres. On the other hand, in dull but demanding tasks such as distance-cycling, the cheers of the spectators can liberate latent energy and spur the flagging performer to renewed effort.

A further variable is the attitude of the spectators. Da Silva tells of a soccer player who was transferred to an ailing club in a last attempt to avoid relegation. After one or two poor matches, the crowd began to taunt the unfortunate player by chanting the transfer fee whenever he came near the ball. He rapidly became a nervous wreck! Frank discussion of the problem with the leaders of the supporters' club brought a sympathetic response, and replacement of jeers by cheers worked a speedy rehabilitation of the player.

Since World War II, English professional sport has been hard hit by television. Club survival has depended largely on the efforts of local officials in organizing football pools and whist drives. The combined attendances at soccer and rugby-league matches dropped from 86 million in 1949/50 to 28 million in 1960/61, and the following season the historic Accrington Stanley team was forced into liquidation.

American professional sport has not suffered a comparable eclipse. Indeed, expenditures on spectator sports and attendances at major league games have increased steadily over the comparable period (Fig. 25). One reason has been a substantial investment in modern stadia on the part of American entrepreneurs. Both players and spectators have been seduced by the comfort of enclosed, all-weather facilities, air-conditioned and

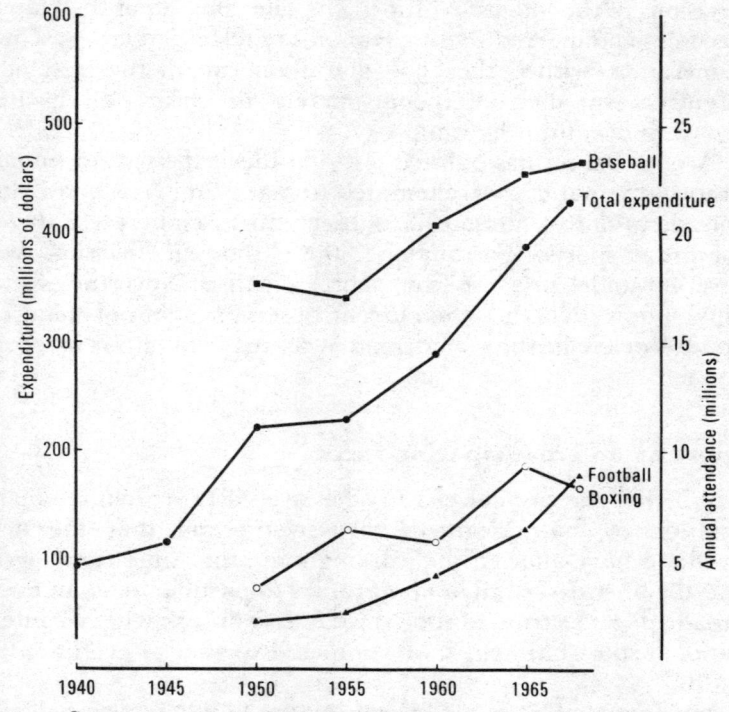

FIG. 25. Spectator sports in the United States. Data for individual sports show the annual attendance; the long line shows the total annual expenditure of the U.S. population on spectator sports.

attractive in appearance. A second important consideration has been the imposition of radio and television 'black-outs' in the city of play.

In the Olympic context, the spectators contribute much to the sense of festival. However, they also have many negative effects. Physical facilities for the games must be much larger than the host city needs, or indeed can afford to maintain. The ancillary investment in hotels, expressways, and subways places a heavy burden on the economy, possibly creating resources that are in excess of normal demand. World-wide television of the events has a tremendous potential for the promotion of international understanding, but all too often this potential is dissipated through nationally biased commentaries that criticize the performance of foreign athletes and even the decisions of the judges. At times, the safe conduct of the Games becomes endangered by the demands of television crews. Thus, cameramen wished the 1976 marathon run in the heat of a Montreal summer afternoon, merely to ensure an excited crowd and natural lighting.

Arnold Beisser has pointed out that this is the second time in history that nations were tempted to make time, resources, and considerations of human life subservient to elaborately staged spectator sports. Fortunately, the Montreal decision was reversed under pressure from sports scientists. Nevertheless, we may enquire whether the current obsession does not herald a decline of civilization as dramatic as that which occurred in Rome!

Sport as an emancipating force

Given that the present century has seen a far-reaching emancipation of many segments of society, and that the new freedoms have allowed the working man, the American Negro, and the liberated woman opportunity to participate in an ever-broadening spectrum of sports, we must now ask whether international sport has helped or hampered this social evolution.

Social mobility. The rags-to-riches myth, so much a part of the American dream, is particularly prominent in the world of sport. Various plausible mechanisms have been suggested whereby the young athlete could take a sudden surge up the social ladder. Participation in athletics might improve self-image and thus earn the scholastic grades that would ensure success in the business world. Athletic prowess might earn a University scholarship, thus opening the door to one of the professions. Membership in a middle-class sports club might foster attitudes and behaviour patterns valued in a large corporation. A wealthy alumnus might take a fancy to a young player, offering him a cosy position in his company after graduation. Failing all else, he might dazzle a wealthy heiress by his performance on the football field.

Formal studies of such hypotheses have been few. Luschen looked at 1880 youths attending sports clubs in Germany. Some 14 per cent were judged to be moving up the social scale, while only 7 per cent were moving downwards. These observations certainly suggest that the ambitious are to be found in sports organizations, but it does not necessarily prove that sport is the cause of either the ambition or the upward social movement.

Within the United States, substantial class differences remain within and between sports. In 1960, only 6·7 per cent of athletes were drawn from the lowest fifth of United States society (family income less than $2790 per year). Some 18·4 per cent of individual athletes, but only 8·4 per cent of team athletes came from the top fifth of society; 32·9 per cent of the parents of individual sportsmen, but only 10·1 per cent of the parents of team sportsmen were classed as professional or technical personnel.

Loy (Table 22) calculated scores defining the occupational status of both athletes and their fathers. Boys proficient in wrestling, boxing, and football often had fathers who had not completed high-school and held low-status 'blue-collar' jobs. In contrast, the boys active in swimming, tennis and golf generally had fathers who had completed high-school and had 'white-collar' jobs. The initial jobs of the sons were almost all of higher status than those of their parents, although rather uniform for the different classes of sportsman. Thus the wrestlers and the boxers moved further up the social scale than did the cricketers and the swimmers.

Further evidence that either sport or the associated scholar-

Table 22. *Occupational mobility and sport participation (based on data of Dr. John Loy for Inter-collegiate Athletics in Los Angeles)*

Event	Father	Son (first job)	Son (present job)	Fathers failing to complete high-school	Fathers in blue-collar work
Wrestling	43	70	77	50·0	48·1
Boxing	47	—	—	—	—
American football	48	63	74	51·6	34·6
Baseball	49	64	75	50·0	36·5
Soccer	51	74	79	22·9	26·3
Rifle-shooting	51	—	—	—	—
Rugby football	52	—	—	—	—
Handball	53	—	—	—	—
Track and field	53	67	77	43·5	30·5
Team manager	55	—	—	—	—
Volleyball	55	—	—	—	—
Basketball	57	69	77	37·4	16·4
Gymnastics	58	67	80	38·2	26·3
Fencing	60	—	—	—	—
Rowing	62	69	78	23·9	10·4
Ice hockey	62	—	—	—	—
Cricket	63	—	—	—	—
Swimming	64	67	78	27·2	13·3
Tennis	64	70	75	25·9	13·3
Golf	74	—	—	—	—

ship benefit the athlete can be inferred from the fact that more athletes than non-athletes from working-class families complete their four years of University study, the difference being particularly marked if comparisons are restricted to homes where there is little parental encouragement of higher education.

In general, we may conclude that a person who becomes involved in sport has an above-average chance of moving up the social ladder, but it is less clear whether the driving force is the individual's ambition, sport, or the associated psychological and material rewards. Some authors have even suggested that the maximum effects are seen if a student is an athlete at high school, but abandons his sport on reaching University.

The Negro. The Negro has seen in sports a means of gaining social acceptance denied to him through other means. A black contestant won an American boxing championship as early as 1805, and by 1890 they had become champions in almost every weight category. Nevertheless, it was not always politic to be black and win. When Jack Johnson gained the heavyweight title in 1910, it was reported that within an hour a black man had been lynched in Charleston, another had been dragged from a Harlem streetcar and beaten to death, and a third was sheltering in a doctor's kitchen while the physician held off the neighbours at gun-point.

Despite such incidents, boxing led the way for a breakdown of the colour bar in sports, and champions such as Joe Louis have expressed a firm belief that their sport was helping the fight for equal rights in other segments of society.

In the first decade of the present century, blacks also began playing on formerly all-white football teams, particularly in the north-eastern corner of the United States, and some were able to use this recognition as a stepping-stone to social and career advancement. W. H. Lewis, captain of the Amherst team, went on to Harvard, and in 1892/3 was named to the all-America team. He qualified as a lawyer, and in a brilliant career rose to become Assistant Attorney General in the administration of President Taft.

Nevertheless, some discrimination persists. Sociologists have calculated that black football players are still assigned the less-favoured playing positions, where there is less opportunity for interaction with other members of the team. Incidents such as the demonstration by militant United States Negroes in Mexico City have shattered the harmony of the Olympic Contests, and there remain regions of the world where sport has not succeeded in breaking the ugly barriers of racial discrimination. However, more progress has been made towards racial peace on the sports field than in most other areas of society.

Women's liberation. Sport is also credited with doing much to equalize opportunity for women. The safety bicycle, in particular, is said to have accomplished more in ten years than had been realized through several decades of polemic.

Dress was a major obstacle to liberation of the Victorian woman. Feathered hats, high-button necks, crinoline skirts with hoops and stays, and high-laced boots looked elegant in a drawing room, but hardly facilitated a full life. Because of such problems, tennis was played from a standing position, and basketball was modified to a three-court game, with no woman allowed to run from her third of the court. In advocating lacrosse for the Canadian girl of 1867, George Beers suggested widening the goal mouth from six to fourteen feet to accommodate billowing skirts. Even swim-suits needed vast quantities of cloth. One ladies' magazine suggested as an appropriate costume a sailor blouse, skirt, and trousers, the whole requiring some nine yards of material.

Attempts were made to modify the safety bicycle so that it could be operated in a ladylike manner, but skirts showed an obstinate tendency to catch in sprockets and chains. The answer was plainly dress reform. Some ladies merely took the scissors to their skirts, or adopted the daring expedient of the split skirt. Others chose the Bloomer dress. Stern Victorian matrons arose in horror at such undignified displays of the female person, but their campaigns were singularly ineffective. By the turn of the century, a substantial proportion of the League of American Wheelmen were in fact women, and restrictive conventions of dress were becoming a thing of the past.

The formal request of a woman to enter the 1896 Olympic marathon was refused, but an 'Olympic Games for Women' was held in Paris in 1922. Male observers were sufficiently impressed to recommend that women be admitted to the Amsterdam Games (1928) on an experimental basis. Many still found it hard to accept women competitors. One reporter described the 800-metre race in these terms: 'Below us on the cinder path were eleven wretched women, five of whom dropped out before the finish, while five collapsed after reaching the tape. I was informed that the remaining starter fainted in the dressing room shortly afterwards.' The 100-metre race was closely disputed by an American (Elizabeth Robinson) and a Canadian (Fanny Rosenfeld). The Canadian coach disputed the judges' ruling, but Dr. Lamb, manager of the Canadian team, refused to support his appeal. Dr. Lamb seemed to regard the whole incident as one more example of female temperament, and in his capacity as President of the Amateur

Athletic Union of Canada he shortly afterwards voted against the further participation of women in Olympic competitions.

Fortunately, Dr. Lamb was over-ruled, and subsequent Games have seen ever increasing numbers of women entrants. However, women have remained excluded from pole-vaulting and ski-jumping, and only in 1972 were they admitted to Amateur Athletic Union marathons and Olympic cross-country skiing.

The modern woman still has victories to win. A sports journal for women that opened with a flourish in 1970 collapsed after but two disastrous issues. Girls from countries such as India still find themselves fettered by conventions of dress. Perhaps most importantly, participation in Olympic events is still only a small fraction of the male figure, and one must conclude that many young ladies still fear that intense athletic competition will impair their femininity.

Nationalism and internationalism

The promotion of international understanding is a major theme of politicians who open world competitions. However, in practice athletic endeavour has often served as a vehicle for nationalism rather than internationalism.

Olympic nationalism was first seen in the early 1920s. Newly independent nations such as Finland and Norway began to achieve striking successes. Men like Paavo Nurmi (who won the 10 000-metre event in 1920, the 1500- and 5000-metre events in 1924, and the 10 000-metre race again in 1928) became both national heroes and powerful symbols for the integration of their state. At this stage in athletic history, it was relatively easy for interested governments to foster victories, since the total pool of contestants was quite small, and selection and training were both practised in a very haphazard manner.

The 1930s witnessed the dominance of the totalitarian powers—Italy, Germany, and Japan. All three began to lay great stress on sport, both to prepare the populace for 'national defence' and also as a means of gaining international recognition. At the Berlin Games (1936), the Axis powers (with only two-thirds of the population of the English-speaking world) won 50 per cent more medals, Nazi Germany heading the list of competitors.

Marked successes by the communist nations began when Russia first entered the Games (1952). Karl Marx himself had declared that total education involved a combination of technical, intellectual, and physical instruction, with sport playing an important role in the development of the new Soviet man. The communist party both fostered and controlled sport, seeing it as an important tool in the political and cultural training of the masses.

Recent application of the doctrine can be seen in the subjugated territories of Eastern Europe. In Estonia, the number of sports officials, mostly unpaid umpires, increased from 5122 to 28 686 between 1955 and 1965. Over the same period, communal sports instructors increased from 2791 to 24 672. All schools were given quotas to fill in preparing children for various sports, and by 1965 74 per cent of pupils were participating in the activities of the sports collectives.

The successes of the Soviet Bloc have generally been won at the expense of the older-established social democracies of western and northern Europe, countries that were learning to emphasize international rather than national culture. A recent trend has been the appearance of some of the newer nations of Africa. They also have begun to collect what some regard as more than their fair share of medals, and there have been mutterings that the attainments of the few highly selected competitors from these countries are representative of neither the standard of physical condition nor the general quality of life in Central Africa. Nevertheless, the main feature of the last two decades has been the continued rivalry of the Soviet Union and the United States, both seeing in the Olympic Games one more instrument to be used in the power struggle between the two ideologies.

At the personal level, young competitors undoubtedly gain from international travel and the opportunity to mingle freely with those from other lands. It is also better for rival ideologies to compete in the stadium than on the battlefield. Nevertheless, the immediate future holds little prospect that the Games will achieve the full potential for international co-operation and understanding promised in the speeches of the opening ceremonies.

Suggestions for further reading

Fifteen or twenty years ago, it might well have been possible to compress most worthwhile knowledge of the fit athlete into a volume the size and scope of this one. Today, this is manifestly no longer feasible. The reading list given below offers a few suggestions for further general and specific exploration of what is rapidly becoming one of the most fascinating areas of human enquiry.

Physiology of the athlete

HERBERT DEVRIES (1974). *Physiology of exercise for physical education and athletes* (2nd edn). William C. Brown, Dubuque, Iowa.

This is perhaps the best of the simpler texts used by physical education undergraduates in North America.

ROY J. SHEPHARD (1972). *Alive, man! The physiology of physical activity.* C. C. Thomas, Springfield, Illinois.

A more advanced text of some 600 pages, this volume ranges quite broadly over topics of exercise physiology, sports medicine, and responses to a changing environment. Despite the breadth of the material explored, critics have suggested that the book is quite readable for the person with some background in biology.

ROY J. SHEPHARD (1977). *Endurance fitness* (2nd edn). University of Toronto Press.

Exercise physiology is here discussed mainly from the viewpoint of the ordinary person who wishes to improve his level of physical fitness.

P. O. ASTRAND AND K. RODAHL (1970). *Textbook of work physiology.* McGraw-Hill, New York.

Many graduate students use this book. Detailed references are given with each chapter; the only criticisms are a heavy reliance on information from Scandinavia, and occasional passages where the literary style lacks clarity.

J. KEUL, E. DOLL, AND D. KEPPLER (1972). *Energy metabolism of human muscle.* University Park Press, Baltimore, Maryland.

The current trend is to move from the study of the whole man to examine mechanisms at the cellular level. This is perhaps the best book on exercise biochemistry yet written; it has been translated elegantly from the original German by Dr. James Skinner.

J. KEUL (1973). *Limiting factors of physical performance.* Thieme, Stuttgart.

Papers from a symposium discussing the relative importance of physiological and biochemical determinants of human performance are brought together under the editorship of Dr. Keul.

R. J. SHEPHARD. *Human physiological work capacity: IBP synthesis volume 4.* Cambridge University Press, London. (In press).

This volume will include chapters on the inheritance of athletic success and the effects of extreme environments. Other specialized books on environment include:

ROY GODDARD (1967). *The effects of altitude on physical performance.* Athletic Institute, Chicago.

R. MARGARIA (1967). *Exercise at altitude.* Excerpta Medica Foundation, Dordrecht.

E. F. ADOLF (1947). *Physiology of man in the desert.* Interscience, New York.

C. S. LEITHEAD AND A. R. LIND (1964). *Heat stress and heat disorders.* Cassell, London.

BRUCE DILL (ed.) (1964). *Handbook of physiology*, Section 4. *Adaptation to the environment.* Williams & Wilkins, Baltimore.

Psychology of the athlete

B. OGILVIE AND T. TUTKO (1966). *Problem athletes and how to handle them.* Tafnews, Los Altos, California.

A descriptive analysis is given of various personality types and their reactions to specific situations. The material in this book is very readable and contains much applied common sense, although it perhaps lacks in scientific documentation.

BRIAN CRATTY (1968). *Psychology and physical activity.* Prentice-Hall, Englewood Cliffs, New Jersey.

Dr. Cratty's book represents a rival school of sports psychology with more extensive use of statistical techniques such as principal component analysis.

WILLIAM MORGAN (1970). *Contemporary readings in sport psychology.*
C. C. Thomas, Springfield, Illinois.

This is an interesting collection of classical papers in sports psychology.

History and sociology

P. C. MCINTOSH (1963). *Sport in society.* International Publications Service, New York.

This small book provides an eminently readable account of how sport developed from the classical era through to the early 1960s.

CARL DIEM INSTITUTE (1966). *The Olympic idea.* Carl Diem Institute, Cologne.

The writings, letters, and speeches of Baron de Coubertin are here translated into English.

DEUTSCHES MUSEUM (1972). *100 Jahre deutsche Ausgrabung in Olympia.* Prestel-Verlag, Munich.

Photographs of German excavations at Olympia are collected in this book.

E. JOKL AND P. JOKL (1968). *The physiological basis of athletic records.* C. C. Thomas, Springfield, Illinois.

The authors discuss the progressive development of athletic records in a broad philosophical perspective.

Sports medicine

A. RYAN AND F. ALLMAN (1974). *Sports medicine.* Academic Press, New York.

This textbook is based on a post-graduate course offered at the University of Wisconsin. There is much useful material on injuries and disease, although a profusion of authors leads to some repetition of information.

J. WILLIAMS AND P. SPERRYN (1976). *Sports medicine* (2nd edn). Edward Arnold, London.

Dr. Williams writes from his considerable experience as secretary of the Féderation Internationale de Médecine Sportive.

A. THORNDIKE (1942). *Athletic injuries. Prevention, diagnosis and Treatment.* Lea & Febiger, Philadelphia.

This book reviews the detailed injury experience of the Harvard teams.

E. JOKL AND J. T. MCCLELLAN (1971). *Exercise and cardiac death.* University Park Press, Baltimore, Maryland.

Reports of sudden death during physical activity are collected in this monograph.

M. WILLIAMS (1974). *Drugs and athletic performance.* C. C. Thomas, Springfield, Illinois.

An up-to-date account is given of problems of 'doping' and its prevention. More general modification of performance by such methods as hypnosis is discussed in:

W. MORGAN (1972). *Ergogenic aids.* Academic Press, New York.

Miscellaneous topics

J. M. TANNER (1964). *The physique of the Olympic athlete.* George Allen & Unwin, London.

This classical study of the physique of athletes is based on measurements made at the Rome Olympics.

M. L. HOWELL AND W. R. MUMFORD (1966). *Fitness training methods.* Canadian Association of Health, Physical Education and Recreation, Ottawa.

A. M. TAYLOR (1974). *The scientific aspects of sports training.* C. C. Thomas, Springfield, Illinois.

Details of specific training techniques for individual sports are given in this monograph sponsored by the Canadian Association of Sports Sciences.

L. RARICK (1973). *Physical activity, human growth and development.* Academic Press, New York.

Problems of the child athlete—physiological, psychological, and surgical—are discussed in this book.

Some problems of the handicapped athlete are discussed in:

J. YEO (ed.) (1974). *Recreation for the handicapped.* Australian Council for Rehabilitation of the Disabled, Melbourne.

The reader who wishes to go yet further should consult primary sources such as:

Medicine and Science in Sports
Journal of Sports Medicine and Physical Fitness
British Journal of Sports Medicine
Canadian Journal of Applied Sports Science
Research Quarterly
Physician and Sports Medicine

Index

acceleration 26, 39
acclimatization 132-3, 136
achievement orientation 51, 104; *see also* attitudes; self-image
acidity 92; *see also* bicarbonate
activity, physical 68, 72, 168, 175; repetitive 107; underwater 137-8
addiction 84, 112, 113, 114; *see also* doping; drugs
adenosine triphosphate 40, 42, 81, 82, 91-2
adolescents 28, 41, 65-6, 77-8, 167-73; *see also* growth; height; maturation
adrenal tumours 162
age 45-6, 168-70, 174-82; biological 172; *see also* adolescents; children; maturation
agility 41, 45; *see also* flexibility
aggression 55-8, 115, 144, 194; *see also* rough play
air, density 124; resistance 26, 28, 39, 43, 124-5, 159; *see also* body contours
alcohol 84-5, 113, 136, 176, 178
altitude 2, 39, 69, 71, 72-3, 124-30; training 74-5
amateurs 8, 14, 27, 189-93
ambulance services 146
American College of Sports Medicine 22, 23, 114, 133, 134
American Medical Association 114
amino acids, essential 88
amphetamines 113-16, 120, 153
anabolic steroids 33, 110, 116-17, 122-3, 163, 164

anaemia 86, 166
anaerobic capacity 126; *see also* adenosine triphosphate; oxygen, debt
anaerobic training 91-3
annual training plan 97
antibiotics 149
anxiety 44, 48, 49, 50, 51-2, 98, 105, 107, 108, 113, 135, 184; soothing of 107; *see also* arousal; emotional stress
architecture 15, 145, 186-7, 195-6
arousal 59, 106, 194
asthma 111, 120, 121
attitudes 48-53
automatic movement 44

balance 41
ball watching 100, 103
Bannister, Sir Roger 24, 52, 53, 59, 193
barbiturates 115
Barr bodies 160-3
baseball 14, 32, 37, 38, 100, 141-2, 152, 171, 172, 180, 191, 193, 195, 198
basketball 31, 32, 36, 37, 38, 100, 101, 139, 140-2, 152, 185, 198, 200
bed rest 76, 90, 116
Bergmann-Allen laws 70
bicarbonate, sodium 72-3, 74, 75, 92, 121
bio-feedback 108
birth control pills 165
bleeding 146
blisters 148

blood, grouping 63; pressure, falling 132, high 115, 184; sugar, 45; vessel, rupture 150–1; volume 74–5, 90, 92, 118, 131
body, build 2, 25–7, 31–5, 77, 156, 172; checking 57; contours 39, 43, 159; *see also* fat; height; lean tissue
bone, architecture 93; development 41, 116, 171
boredom 59, 95, 100, 101
boxing 6, 32, 33, 38, 83, 140–1, 195, 197–8, 199
brain blood flow 126; *see also* oxygen lack, cerebral
breathing 126
breathlessness 40
breeding 30, 35, 66–7
Brightwell, R. 30
British Association of Sports Medicine 22
bruises 142, 148

caffeine 112–13
calcium 86, 93
calories 81, 83; *see also* energy
Canadian Association of Sports Sciences 23, 133
capillary development 93
captain 45, 61
carbohydrate 88
carbon dioxide lack 126
cardiac massage 146
cartilage 93
centre of gravity 26
children 28, 41, 77–8, 156, 157, 167–73, 202; dangers to 170–2
cholesterol 84, 180
chromosomes 160
cigarette smoking 176, 178
circuit training 96
class distinctions 11, 15, 18, 27, 34, 58, 189–201
clothing 28, 29, 33, 39, 132, 134, 136, 199–200; nylon 132; removal of 135
coaching 21, 24, 28, 45, 46, 49–50, 61, 79–80, 103, 104, 105, 107, 142, 144, 147, 171, 202

cocaine 111–12
cold 37, 69, 71, 73–4, 75, 127, 134–7, 159
collapse 132, 135, 191, 200
common cold 137, 148
Commonwealth Paraplegic Games 184
competition, intercollegiate 141, 144
competitions, level of 108, 141, 172, 192; quality of 191–3; regional 78–9
competitors, number of 16–17, 27
concussion 142
confusion 131, 132, 134, 135, 136, 138, 147
conscientiousness 51
contact sports 53, 54, 66, 94, 96, 105, 107
controlled movements 43–4
convulsions 102, 132
coronary enlargement 179; narrowing 150, 153, 177
Cox, L. 170
cramps, menstrual 165
creatine phosphate 40, 42, 81, 82, 91–2
cricket 14, 36, 99, 100, 181, 197, 198
crowd interactions 52, 69, 106, 107, 108, 144, 145, 194–5; *see also* anxiety; arousal; emotional stress
cuts 142
cycling 11, 28, 36, 38, 39, 42, 43, 54, 82, 83, 94, 111, 112, 113, 114, 120, 125, 130, 132, 200

danabol 116; *see also* anabolic steroids
deafness 183
death 73, 132, 135, 149–54, 190
de Coubertin, Baron Pierre 1, 12–18, 23, 193
dehydration 33, 110, 111, 117–18, 123, 134
Demont, Rick 111, 121
depressants 113
development and physical activity 172–3; *see also* maturation

diet 35, 50, 69, 70, 81-9; *see also* meals; nutrition
dinghy sailing 33, 36, 38, 41, 45, 53, 60, 134, 137
discomfort 2; *see also* pain
discus 8, 24, 25-7, 36, 117, 128, 168, 185
disease 147-9; prevention of 148
disqualification 120
diving 52, 103, 137-8, 168-70
dominance 58
doping 110-23, 132
dress 7; *see also* clothing
drills 102
downproofing 137
drowsiness 147; *see also* confusion
drugs 69, 110-23, 132, 191; decongestant 137; prohibited 120

education 9, 10, 14, 172, 197, 202; in principles of hygiene 148; *see also* intelligence; scholarships, athletic
efficiency 39, 42-3, 77, 130, 159
electrocardiogram 178
emancipation 196-201
emotional stress 44, 48, 49, 98, 108, 152, 172, 177; *see also* anxiety; arousal
endurance 36-7, 42, 93, 112, 115, 119; training 90-1
energy, intake 81, 83; release 85; stores 39-40
environment 30, 34, 64-5, 69-75, 107, 124-37
enzymes 73, 91
ephedrine 120, 153
equipment 28; protective 143-4, 171
Eskimos 63, 70-1
Ester, Sylvia 29
evaporation 130-1; *see also* sweating
evening racing 133
evolutionary pressures 71
excitement 172; *see also* arousal
exertion, perceived 53-55
exhaustion 36, 40, 53, 73, 96, 98, 101; *see also* fatigue
exploitation 190-1

explosive power 35, 36
extra beats (cardiac extrasystoles) 112, 115, 129
extroversion 52, 60, 106
eyes 41, 99

facilities, physical 19, 145, 171; *see also* architecture
failure 60, 104, 105, 188
family relationships 66-7, 107
fat 40, 81, 82, 84, 88, 91, 137, 156, 159, 175, 179-80, 184, 187; cells 167; fatty acids, essential 88
fatigue 53, 92, 99, 100, 101, 112, 132, 142; mental 45
fear 52, 105
Fédération Internationale de Médicine Sportive 22, 130
female, *see* women in sport
fencing 32, 38, 41, 141, 157, 174, 185-6, 198
festival 15-16, 196
fibrillation, ventricular 153; *see also* heart, attacks
figure skating 36, 41, 44, 53, 163
fitness 136, 143, 171, 184; *see also* participation
flexibility 41, 93, 135; *see also* agility
flotation 159
fluids 74, 75, 82, 84, 86-7, 89, 98, 116, 131, 133
food 108, 136, 148; *see also* meals, nutrition
football 5, 6, 9, 11, 32, 104; Association 36, 37, 38, 39, 41, 140-1, 192, 193-4, 195, 198; North American 33, 37, 38, 53, 54, 57, 60, 84, 107, 116, 132, 140-2, 144, 145, 150, 180, 195, 197-8, 199; Rugby 37, 38, 53, 96, 140-1, 181, 198
force 26
forgetting, control of 103
fractures 86, 142, 147, 148, 171
frostbite 72, 135
frustration 56
fungal infections 149

game plan 97
Garrapick, Nancy 170
gas-liquid chromatography 122
genetic packages 63; *see also* chromosomes
glucose 82, 89, 134
glycogen 40, 81, 82, 87–9, 92, 98
golf 54, 104, 107, 197–8
grab start 39
gravity 124
Greece 6–8
Greene, Nancy 30
group interactions 44–5, 53, 61, 132; *see also* crowd interactions
growth 167
guilt 57
gymnasium 8, 10, 17, 21, 94
gymnastics 26, 31, 36, 38, 41, 44, 52, 103, 141, 150, 152, 163, 164, 168, 198

habituation 55, 108
haemoglobin 72–3, 125–6
handicap 183
handicapped athlete 183–8
health, general 176; mental 58–61
heat 2, 7, 33, 42, 69, 70, 75, 112, 113, 115, 130–4, 196; conduction 131; shock 132; *see also* death
headache 129
heart, attacks 75, 76, 113, 115, 118, 129, 150, 152, 153, 177, 184; *see also* fibrillation, ventricular; enlargement 170, 178, 180; failure 150–1; murmurs 170; rate 90, 95, 126; volume 90, 170, 178, 180; wall, thickening 91
heavy weights 33
height 25–7, 34–5, 46, 70, 158, 172–3; *see also* short competitors; secular trend in 34–5, 70
hepatitis 115
heroin 113
hill-walking 134–7
hockey, field 11, 32, 38, 140–1; ice 37, 38, 42, 58, 104, 140–2, 144, 152, 172, 191, 192, 198

Hohne, Christopher 128
holiday for athletes 97
homesickness 74, 107
hostility 57, 58; *see also* aggression
humidity 133; *see also* heat
hygiene 22, 148
hyperventilation 138; *see also* breathlessness
hypnosis 108, 119

impetigo 149
impotence 116
Indians 32
influenza 151
inheritance 1, 41, 42, 51, 62–80, 99; maternal 67
injuries 76, 85, 90, 94, 98, 105, 119, 129, 135, 139–47; prevention of 142–5, 171–2; recurrent 143; severity of 142; spinal 144, 185
insulation 72, 136
insurance statistics 180–1
intelligence 7–8, 58–60, 181
International Biological Programme 63, 72
International Olympic Committee 16, 18, 19, 21, 23
International Stoke Mandeville Games 184
internationalism 201–2
interval training 95–6
iron needs 86, 166
irritability 132, 135
isolated communities 62–3
isometric strength 35, 36, 158

Japanese 31, 33, 35, 70
javelin 8, 25, 36, 117, 128, 159, 168, 185
Jeux de Québec 21
jogging 95
jumping 8, 24–6, 36, 38, 105, 168, 171

kayak paddling 33, 38, 44, 46–8, 94, 192
Keino, Kip 69, 128
Kinsella, John 105

lactic acid 40, 73, 92
lanoline 137
laws, anti-doping 119-20
lean tissue 92, 156, 187
learning 43, 56, 94, 99, 100-3
little-leaguer's elbow 171
liver damage 116
Longboat, Tom 190-1
longevity of athletes 180-2
lung function 91, 180, 187

marathon runners 32, 38, 73, 82, 96, 130, 133, 174, 190-1, 201
marriage between athletes 30, 66-7; patterns of 35
masculinity 53, 163; masculinization 116, 162
mass 26
mass spectrometry 122
massed practice 100-1
Masters' contests 175
maturation 28, 77, 172
meals 88, 108, 152, 175, 178
medical treatment 111, 121
memory 103
menstrual cycle 165-6
minerals 83, 86-7, 133; see also calcium, potassium, sodium
mood elevation 115; see also drugs
money 103-4; see also prizes, professionalism
morphine 113
mothers as athletes 166
motivation 70, 102, 103-6; see also rewards
mountain sickness 74, 126, 128-9
mouth scrapings 160, 162
muscle 41-2
muscle, biopsy 41-2; bulk 93, 163; see also lean tissue; cells 167; pulls 148; tone 112
muscular Christianity 14
mutations 69
myoglobin 92

napkins, sanitary 165
national income 27

nationalism 21, 60, 145, 196, 201-2; see also political considerations
natural selection 70
nausea 165
'need' tension 102
Negroes 21, 32, 33, 34, 71, 129, 198-9, 202
nervousness 100, 107; see also anxiety; arousal; emotional stress
Nicholas, Cindy 170
Nigerians 71
Nurmi, Paavo 201
nutrition 70, 81-9, 94, 108, 175; see also diet; food; meals

occupational status 197
Olympia 6-7
Olympic, archives 17; competition 4, 12-30, 200; diplomas 16; oath 15; ode 7
Olympic Games 16, 18, 200; role of Government in 18-21
orienteering 38, 157, 179-80
over-breathing 71
over-learning 103
over-training 98
Owens, Jesse 20
oxygen, debt 73, 91-2, 126; see also anaerobic capacity; extraction 91, 126; lack, cerebral 129, 138, cardiac 153, 178; pressure 124, detectors 71; transporting power 36-7, 40, 72, 76, 90, 112, 124, 126, 156, 179, 187

pace 75, 77
Packer, D. 30
pain 40, 53-5, 92, 105
paraplegia 184-8
parental characteristics 77
participation, mass 20, 193; national 27
Pax Olympica 7, 15, 16
personality 48-53
pharmaceuticals, labelling of 122
physiological performance, prediction of 44, 46-8, 50
playing position 199

pole vault 24, 28, 145
poliomyelitis 185
political considerations 4, 20–1, 27, 201–2
position receptors 41, 99
post-mortems on athletes 150–1
posture 41, 42
potassium ions 128, 134
practice, mental 103; speed 101
pregnancy 166
prizes 14, 104, 189–90; see also rewards
professionalism 4, 8, 14, 28, 45–6, 104, 114, 189–93
protein 81, 82, 83, 84, 88, 116, 118
psychiatric disturbance 119
psychological, data 50; effects in children 172; orientation 162; preparation of athletes 98–109
psychosomatic problems 60
psychotherapy 108, 184; see also hypnosis
pulmonary oedema 129
pulse chart after injury 147
punishment 103; see also rewards

racial characteristics 32
radiant heat 131, 133, 135
radio-immune assay 122
reaction time 38–9, 55, 94, 102
records, athletic 24–30, 159–60; world 127, 158
red cells 72–3, 75, 118; ageing of 123
refereeing 58, 145, 172; see also rough play; rules
regulatory training 93
repetitions 96
respiratory infections 86, 137, 148–9
rest 98
results, knowledge of 105
rewards 52–3, 58, 98, 103–4; see also prizes, punishment
rhythmic movement 36
rough play 33, 57, 58, 144, 189; see also refereeing; rules
rowing 11, 32–3, 36, 37, 38, 94, 95, 139, 141–2, 175–6, 180–1, 193, 198; simulators 95

rules 58, 144–5, 172, 185, 192, 200; see also refereeing; rough play
running 7, 8, 11, 24–6, 32, 35, 37, 38, 42, 45, 52, 54, 60, 94, 107, 125, 127, 132, 133, 141–2, 152, 156, 157, 168, 200

salt 132; see also sodium, potassium
saunas 117–18
scholarships, athletic 34, 104, 193, 197
scrapes 142
screening athletes 79
seasonal problems 94
sedatives 108, 111
selection 27, 34, 51, 59, 67–8, 70–1, 77–80, 160, 177, 182, 201; natural 70
self control 57
self fulfilment 105
self-image 59, 60, 104, 184, 197
sensory input 99; augmentation of 55; reduction of 55; stimulation of 104
sex, activity 108, 116–17, 152; characteristics 161; determination 160–5; differences 155–8
shaving 29, 39
Sherpas 71
shivering 73, 136
shock 146
short competitors 31–2, 159
shot putting 25–7, 117, 128, 168, 185
showering 152
sickle-cell disorder 129
sinuses, nasal 137
skating 38, 41, 125, 134, 157, 158–9; see also figure skating
ski-ing, cross country 37, 38, 42, 67–8, 152–3, 157, 181–2, 201; downhill 30, 38, 42, 134, 157, 166
ski-jumping 24, 28, 29
skill 42–6, 70, 78, 113; transfer of 101; skilled movements, perception of 99–100
skin blood flow 73, 91, 131, 132, 135
sleeplessness 108, 115, 119, 121, 128, 148, 172

INDEX

social mobility 196–8
social recognition 104
sociology 4, 11, 189–201
sodium ions 132, 134; *see also* minerals; salt
sore throat 148
spatial orientation 102
spectatorism 15, 20, 193–6
speed 37–40, 45, 102
Spitz, Mark 105
spleen, rupture of 129
sportsmanship 111, 123, 144, 189
sports, medicine 3, 21–24; physician 22, 24; science 23, 24
sprains 142
sprinters 32, 35, 38, 42, 93, 127
squeeze, lungs 137–8
ST segment (electrocardiogram) 178–9
stabilometer 41
starting signal 38–9
starvation 71, 83, 110, 111, 118, 123, 136
state supported athletes 192
steaks 82
steroids, *see* anabolic steroids
stimulants 111–13
stimulation 55; faradic 94
stomach, distension 134; disturbance 128, 148; strains 142, 148; strength 35–6, 93, 96, 97, 113, 116–17, 157, 180, 187
stretching exercises 41
stride 25, 43
strychnine 112
success 60
sweating 71, 73, 85, 86, 91, 130–1, 132, 136, 149
swimming 24, 29, 37, 38, 42, 43, 54, 74, 75, 77, 97, 108, 122, 127, 128, 134, 136, 137–8, 139–41, 145, 152, 157, 158–9, 163, 165, 168, 169–70, 187, 197–8, 200

Tanner, Elaine 170
task difficulty 100
team sportsmen 52, 61, 132
technique 28

television 195–6
temperature, air 124, 133; body 73
tennis 6, 9, 11, 38, 54, 93, 95, 99, 100, 152, 176, 197–8, 200
tension, menstrual 165
tetanus 147
theobromine 113
theophylline 113
time, judgement of 55, 100
tough-mindedness 51
track and field 11, 32, 127, 140–1, 158, 159, 168, 180–1, 198
training 3, 28, 48, 51, 53, 65–6, 68, 73, 74–5, 76–7, 89–98, 158, 167–8, 172–3, 201; camps 74, 75, 79; diminishing returns 98; frequency of 95; intensity of 95; isometric 93, 94, 96, 158; regulatory 93; rhythmic 93; specificity of 89, 94, 98; structural 93; tapering 109
transfusion 110, 111, 118, 123
trans-sexualism 162
transvestism 161–2
travel 107, 108, 149, 202
trustfulness 52
twins 42, 64–6

uphill running 43
urine tests 112, 114, 121–2, 123

vagina, infection of 165; rupture of 166
variability 64
vegetarians 84
visual, disturbances 129; field 144
vitamins 83, 85–6
vomiting 88

walking 38, 97, 134, 152, 174
warm-up 135, 136, 171
water 134, 148; *see also* fluids; pressure 137; resistance 26, 29, 39, 43, 159
weakness 92; *see also* fatigue
weight, decrease 117–18; *see also* dehydration, starvation; increase 117, 123, 158, 175; *see also* lean tissue
weight lifting 24, 31, 36, 38, 53, 117
weight supported sports 37

weight training 93, 96
wheelchair sports 184–7
windproofing 136
women in sport 7, 30, 154–65, 199–201
'worked up' 106; *see also* arousal
World Congress of Sports Medicine 23
wounds, healing of 85
wrestling 6, 9, 33, 36, 38, 42, 53, 54, 57, 83, 89, 117–18, 123, 140–1, 144, 197–8

GV706.8 .S53
athlete /

MERCY COLLEGE LIBRARIES